Rhetoric before and
beyond the Greeks

Rhetoric before and beyond the Greeks

Edited by

Carol S. Lipson
Roberta A. Binkley

State University of New York Press

Published by
State University of New York Press, Albany

For information, address State University of New York Press,
90 State Street, Suite 700, Albany, N.Y. 12207

Production by Diane Ganeles
Marketing by Anne M. Valentine

Library of Congress Cataloging-in-Publication Data

Rhetoric before and beyond the Greeks / Carol S. Lipson and Roberta A. Binkley, editors.
    p. cm.
    Includes bibliographical references and index.
    ISBN 0-7914-60099-1 (alk. paper) — ISBN 0-7914-6100-9 (PB : alk. paper)
    1. Rhetoric—History.   I. Lipson, Carol S., 1944–   II. Brinkley, Roberta A., 1941–

PN187. R45 2004
808'.009—dc22   2003055621

10 9 8 7 6 5 4 3 2 1

Contents

Introduction

Why This Collection?

The historical tradition of classical rhetoric has been the focus of intense study in a number of academic disciplines, including the field of rhetoric and composition. Broadly, rhetorical teaching in the western world has canonized Aristotelian/Platonic rhetoric as Rhetoric, with its sanctioned principles, goals, and conventions. But recent scholarship increasingly recognizes the need to extend the historical understanding of rhetoric in a variety of ways. A number of scholars give attention to the value of the broader Sophistic rhetorical tradition as opposed to the Aristotelian (Jarratt, Neel, Poulakos, Vitanza), while others focus on the Isocratean tradition (Welch, Whitburn). Increasing numbers of scholars argue for the need to search for rhetorical traditions that don't appear in the standard texts. For instance, Patricia Bizzell and Rich Enos argue that our research must "include alternative modes used by women" (Bizzell 16; Enos "Archaeology," 65), and feminists such as Lisa Ede, Cheryl Glenn, Susan Jarratt, Andrea Lunsford, Jackie Jones Royster, Jan Swearingen, and Molly Wertheimer advocate a search for new ways to un-cover the rhetorics of women, since such rhetorics are not represented in the standard rhetorical evidence and thus the available history. Such issues were raised by a panel at the 1997 Conference on College Composition and Com-munication on the Politics of Historiography, entitled Octalog II, which fol-lowed by approximately ten years a prior such panel—Octalog I. Responding to the second Octalog panel in 1997, printed in *Rhetoric Review,* Thomas Miller pointed out that in the ten years since the first panel's discussion of his-toriography of rhetoric, the convention program had far fewer presentations on classical rhetoric. Miller presented an interpretation of this phenomenon: "we have become more broadly engaged with the rhetorical practices of groups who have been excluded by the dominant intellectual tradition" (Octa-log II, 42). Miller clearly favored such attention and even argued four years previously in *Learning from the Histories of Rhetoric,* that, "the rhetorical tra-dition is a fiction that has just about outlasted its usefulness" (26). Roxanne

1

Mountford expressed a similar need for rhetorical study to expand its focus: "We must look for rhetoric where it has not been found—in many cultural locations" (Octalog II, 33). While Miller points attention to the need to examine rhetorical traditions of women and people of color, Mountford includes other types of cultural locations, such as other academic fields and disciplines.

We endorse Miller's observation that the fields of rhetoric and composition have increasingly become interested in alternate rhetorics, different from those in the Aristotelian tradition. In the later twentieth century, the dominance of an Aristotelian and Athenian-based approach to rhetoric has come into question. Feminists have particularly objected to the agonistic focus of Aristotelian rhetoric, as have those interested in creating space for a range of alternate ways of being. For example, the Winter 1992 issue of *Rhetoric Society Quarterly* was devoted to feminist perspectives on the history of rhetoric, as was the Winter 2002 issue of *Rhetoric Society Quarterly*. A collection published in 2001 by Laura Grey Rosendale and Sibylle Gruber entitled *Alternative Rhetorics* discusses rhetorics often overlooked or marginalized in contemporary western culture and raises questions about rhetorics of race, ethnicity, gender, and class. If classical Athenian rhetorical principles continue to be reified as *the* rhetorical principles, then those whose grounding involves differing approaches remain seriously disadvantaged.

Despite the increased interest in alternate rhetorics, little attention to date has been given to one type of needed addition to the history of rhetoric: examination of nonwestern rhetorics and particularly of ancient nonwestern rhetorics prior to and contemporary with the development of classical rhetoric. In an essay published in 2002, Susan Jarratt points out that studies of "ancient . . . non-Western rhetorics—including Egyptian, Chinese, and Japanese practices—broaden the field" (75–76). George Kennedy's 1998 *Comparative Rhetoric* pioneers in this arena and is often used in the many courses being created at undergraduate and graduate levels on comparative, alternative, or multicultural rhetorics. But there is need for much more work, particularly for studies that approach the analysis of ancient cultural rhetorics from perspectives that do not seem to reify classical rhetoric as the culmination in the development of ancient rhetorical systems. The current collection is intended to begin to fill such a gap in the study of early rhetorical history and specifically to extend the examination of ancient rhetoric outside of the dominant western tradition.

Most histories of ancient rhetoric, with the prominent exception of Kennedy's, begin with the discussion of Greek classical rhetoric as Ancient Rhetoric. Of course there's some sense to such a practice, since the term *rhetorike* originated with the Greeks.[1] But this practice also has consequences. For one thing, it tends to normalize as rhetoric the rhetorical system of one particular western culture. Also, this practice might suggest that Aristotle's system represents the others preceding it, and that other early cultures followed the same approaches that Aristotle described, analyzed, and began to theorize. Alternately, this practice might suggest that other early cultures developed only primitive approaches to communication, not worthy of study, lacking interest or importance. These early cultures existed so long ago, and their rhetorics have generally disappeared by now, while classical rhetoric has prevailed in the western world for 2,500 years. On the other hand, some of these early cultures themselves thrived for 2,500 years or longer prior to the Greeks. It's difficult to believe that these cultures could have sustained their longevity and power without well-honed understandings of how to communicate for significant social functions and of how to convince and persuade, or without conceptions and practices of language use that supported the purposes and activities of these cultures. If we begin the discussion of rhetorical history with the Greeks, we lose much of our ability to see the early rhetorics, and especially to *see* the early history of rhetoric as culturally situated and embedded.

This collection, then, attempts to recover understanding of the language practices of early cultures—focusing on Mesopotamia, Egypt, China, and ancient Israel. Even in Greece itself, other rhetorics thrived, and one of these—the rhetoric of Rhodes—is here examined. Historical accuracy demands attention to the gaps in early rhetorical history, but our aim extends beyond illuminating the gaps and shadings within the current understanding of the history of rhetoric. We are firmly convinced that history matters to contemporary life. We are committed to developing a better understanding of how different rhetorical approaches functioned and were situated within very different cultures, because we believe that such knowledge can help illuminate how a range of rhetorics can and do function within our culture. And we believe that better understanding of how rhetorical historiography has led to marginalization of major ancient rhetorics other than Athenian Greek rhetoric can help illuminate similar marginalizing effects in other modern and contemporary scholarship.

Scholarly work on the language use in early cultures is carried out in a variety of fields. This volume presents research by prominent scholars in fields as diverse as Assyriology, biblical studies, Egyptology, and rhetorical studies. Thus, we bring together work by authors of varied scholarly backgrounds, work not readily available to nonspecialists in those areas. Four of the authors represent a range of such areas of specialty (Religious Studies, Egyptology, and Assyriology), while nine authors are specialists in fields of rhetoric and composition. While the editors have shaped the collection to respond to issues of current importance in the field of rhetoric and composition, this collection clearly speaks to the interests of a much broader audience, including scholars in anthropology, cultural history, ancient history, ancient literature, women's studies, religion, biblical studies, and the humanities more generally. Each of the authors applies knowledge and analytical systems that can enrich and challenge work in related fields. The cross-disciplinarity affords the opportunity to share understandings developed in different fields about the various rhetorical systems as they developed in and influenced particular ancient cultures; in addition, the cross-disciplinarity of the collection offers insight into how the different fields address the methodological issues involved in studying cultural rhetorics in this early period, with the concomitant limitations on available artifacts and texts, as well as on contextual information that can address understanding of expedience and particular rhetorical goals involved in specific texts.

The majority of the essays view rhetorics as situated in particular cultural settings and look to ways that particular genres, conventions, and practices functioned within their particular cultures. Significantly, one essay, by James Watts, challenges the suggestion of a cultural situatedness for rhetorical conventions, identifying and examining a set of conventions that appear similarly in very different cultures. Jan Swearingen places her project as part of a scholarly movement that is working to "bring together the traditions of the Near East, Greece, Israel, and Egypt." She suggests that similar roles existed for women across these different cultures in the early period—as singers of songs. However, her essay goes on to point to the ways that particular elements in the developing Athenian culture led to changes in these roles allotted to women, who came to fall outside of the new canonical rhetoric focused on prose.

It is not our intention to supplant or denigrate the canonical rhetorical texts, such as those in the classical tradition, nor even the rich narrative of rhetorical history. Rather we hope to extend historical understanding by spotlighting other traditions in other cultures—other ways of being, seeing, and making knowledge. Between 5000 and 1200 B.C.E., six areas of the world produced new forms of culture broadly defined as civilizations, that is, societies with a clear hierarchical state organization (Adams, 4). These areas include the Middle East, Egypt, the Indus Valley, China, Mesoamerica, and the two Andean civilizations. Of the last two listed, civilization appears to have developed almost simultaneously, but only one, the Mesoamerican-Mayan culture, developed a script, which appeared in the 3rd century A.D. In this book, we deal with only three of the six civilizations: the Middle East, Egypt, and China. Our selectivity in no way reflects an opinion or judgment of the contributions of these six civilizations, but simply results from the exigencies of space and the dominant interests of current rhetorical scholarship. We hope with this volume to encourage broader attention to early cultural rhetorics, including explorations of ancient rhetorics from the Indus Valley, Mesoamerica, and the Andean civilizations. While we are looking to the rhetorics of ancient cultures in their own right, we recognize the possibility that some of these rhetorics might well have influenced Greek rhetoric in ways that remain subtly obscure. The influence of these cultures has only begun to be recognized in our euro-centered discipline of rhetoric and in the humanities as well. However, investigation of such influence is beyond the project of this book.

Methodological Issues in Studying Ancient Rhetorics

The recovery and analysis of ancient rhetorics is by its nature a historical enterprise, and thus work on ancient rhetorics lies at the intersection of contemporary debates about rhetoric, history, and historiography. In large part, these debates have surrounded feminist work in recovering women's rhetorics (Gale, Glenn, Biesecker, Campbell). Some of the contested issues have arisen in situations where scholars find themselves without texts, or with small numbers of texts, as is common if one wishes to study groups such as ancient women, whose rhetoric is not preserved in the artifacts. How to recover such rhetorics in a rigorous scholarly way is an issue that a number of the essays in this volume address in practice. The authors in this collection instantiate a variety of approaches to such a situation, as all seek to enhance knowledge of rhetorics that are not well known and that differ substantially from western classical rhetoric.

Undoubtedly, work in ancient rhetorics, and especially in alternative ancient rhetorics, crosses disciplinary boundaries. For fields that study the rhetorics of the ancient Near East, for instance, rhetorical scholarship depends on research in fields such as Assyriology, Mesopotamian studies, Egyptology, biblical studies, and Near Eastern studies in general. As valuable as the research in these fields is to the rhetorical study of the respective fields, the crossing of disciplinary boundaries often forces reexamination of assumptions and practices that underlie the scholarship in the fields consulted, and reflexively in one's own field as well.

The work of Jan Assmann, a prominent Egyptian scholar, whose work is itself considered interdisciplinary, offers a useful site for framing a discussion of some of these issues. In a 1996 study of ancient Egyptian history, translated in 2002, Assmann describes the major three approaches to historical study of ancient cultures. Acknowledging that history is a cultural form, a product of culture (p. x) that changes in different cultural settings, Assmann categorizes the three alternative approaches as follows: traces, messages, and memories (6). He associates the category of traces with the archaeological search for artifacts that serve as remnants of the culture. The second approach, which he terms messages, involves epigraphic and iconographic studies of inscriptions, images, and a variety of types of other texts;

this approach aims to determine the ways that the culture represented events in such messages, as well as the ways these representations might differ from the testimony of the archaeological traces (10). The third category, memories, involves looking at the culture's myths and traditions to ascertain the ways the culture represented its history in its collective memory—the way the culture passed on the representations of historical events over time. Assmann presents the first category—archaeological in nature—as the most scientific, with the greatest certitude and the least degree of construction; indeed he terms these traces, which bring facts to light, "nonconstructed." Those in rhetoric and composition might well dispute Assmann's positivist depiction of the virtual lack of construction involved in the organization and presentation of archaeological artifacts, yet Dimitri and Christine Favard Meeks point out that such a view of the facticity of the artifacts, and of historical discussion of such artifacts, prevails in Egyptian studies (and we would add, in Near Eastern studies as well until recently). The Meeks point out, for instance, that ancient Egypt left large numbers of written records and texts that have not been inventoried or published, and certainly not translated (3–5). The same is true for Mesopotamia. Thus the values within the responsible fields have operated to filter "the basic facts," by choosing what are the most important texts to develop editions of, and in developing methods for doing so. In both cultures, the systems by which the elite perpetuated themselves in scribal schools that were virtually restricted to male students yielded a set of artifacts that cannot give us a representative picture of rhetoric as deployed across the culture, since some groups are not represented. Assmann suggests that historical study involves dialogue among the three approaches, with findings from investigation of texts and from study of memories being held up against the facts–the traces—from archaeology. Traditional historiography demands such backing through documentation or facts. Yet in areas where the artifacts are not available to scholars, for a variety of reasons, alternate approaches must be utilized. Such is often the case in rhetorical study of ancient cultures.

The contributors to this volume are engaged in a specific type of historical study, one heavily oriented toward Assmann's second category: texts. Our project is to develop an understanding of the rhetorical conventions operative in each of the cultures studied, and the ways these might have changed over time with changes in cultural conditions. For some of the fields involved, such as rhetoric and composition, the project likely extends beyond describing the conventions involved to developing a sense of the underlying rhetorical theories. These scholars are interested in understanding why particular rhetorics developed in particular cultural settings—why certain genres and conventions arose, what enabled their growth, and what they themselves enabled in their cultural settings. Scholars do not have artifacts in which the ancient cultures studied in this volume presented systematic theoretical analyses of their own rhetorical systems. On the other hand, we do have maxims or other wisdom texts that offer advice that is rhetorical in nature, addressing how to speak in specific situations, when to speak, when to be silent, etc. Some cultures, such as the Mesopotamian, provide examples of debates, diatribes, disputations, and monologues. These are often practical and situational in nature and perhaps can be seen as forming the equivalent of Assmann's third category—memories—for they present the ways that the culture viewed its rhetorical understandings through its collective memory. In ancient Egypt, for example, such wisdom or instruction texts were often fictionalized, presented as coming from a father to a son, and often as arising from a very ancient and famous figure. Many were written in Middle Egyptian, and their very language was no longer in use by the New or Late Kingdom, when they continued to be recited and copied, memorized and revered. These advice texts became memories, traditions that represented the revered way of the golden age of the culture—an age the culture desired to resurrect. But these texts do not necessarily, then, reflect the rhetorics in actual use in the culture at the time a manuscript was copied.

Clearly, then, in addition to the historical and historiographical complications, doing such work in recovering histories and theories of ancient rhetorics inevitably raises a range of methodological issues that are rhetorical in nature. To understand the rhetorical systems of a culture distant in time and space from ours, scholars must develop an understanding of the culture and its textual practices. To acquire such rhetorical understanding, one must have texts or artifacts to study along with a sense of the purposes of the texts or objects, their audiences, and contexts. Yet for many ancient cultures, the availability of textual or other artifacts is somewhat random, and often problematic. There are limits on what we can claim from the texts or objects, if we don't know how representative they are or precisely what were their exigencies or their range of goals. In undertaking such scholarship, the rhetorical scholar is often in the odd position of studying ancient rhetorics in situations that seem arhetorical, without the possibility of close knowledge of the contexts and uses of particular texts. And some of the practices of translators in dealing with copies of texts created in specific periods compound the problem by making it very difficult for scholars to actually see the precise text as fashioned for its audience in that period. That is, much of the work in the fields on which such scholarship depends has been based on sets of values and practices that can skew the objects under analysis, or skew our perspectives. The Egyptian translations into English provide a concrete, instructive example of some of the types of issues that arise.

The Example of Egyptology

The texts of ancient Egypt only began to be translated approximately 150 years ago, and for about half a century, the main attention was devoted to determining the vocabulary and grammar before substantial progress could be made in rendering full complex texts into modern languages. To carry out such translations, the fledgling field of Egyptology adopted paradigms and methods from classical studies—a much more developed field at the time. But those practices and values directed the practices of translation in ways that did not provide a good fit with the artifacts of the Egyptian culture. And the dependence on a classical studies framework encouraged an emphasis on those aspects of the Egyptian artifacts that most closely resembled the western values, at times misrepresenting Egyptian practices. Egyptian religion, for instance, was presented as monotheistic, in close alignment with western religions (Meeks, 2).

In the process of translation into English under these conditions, Egyptian texts faced some modification and skewing. While scholars found that different papyri or tablets often contained different versions of the same text, as had been the case with Greek and Roman texts as well, they adopted the classical valuation of the original, uncorrupted text, seeing variations as corruptions. However, there were too few manuscripts of any one Egyptian text to apply the main methodologies from classical studies, such as the stemmatic method, for determining the original version. In one resulting approach to translation, if the oldest manuscript is the fullest, it is translated, presented, and referred to as *the* text. In another approach, scholars create a composite text for translation, picking favored parts from the different versions and presenting them in translation as *the* text (Foster, xix). And finally, if versions of a text exist that do not overlap, with no parts in common, scholars combine these and translate them, presenting the combination as *the* text (Lichtheim, "Merikare").

In the first approach, we are presented with a translation of a version of the text that did in fact exist, though it is only one version. In the other two approaches, we are given a translation of a text that might never actually have existed in the form we are given. As a result of such translation practices, we lack the ability to study the scribal practices involved in copying and modifying texts, since modification was considered as corruption in the antecedent discipline of classical studies. The Egyptian scribal practices clearly allowed room for a significant amount of variation—for bringing a text up to date, and for making it fit current circumstances. Copying a text did not mean rendering it word for word, line by line. Egyptian scholars had for long attempted to explain away the differences as due to mis-hearing from oral dictation, errors of student copyists, or to scribal misreading in copying. However, careful study of the changes has found such explanations inadequate to account for the extent of the changes (Burkard, Williams).

For instance, for the popular wisdom text known as *The Instructions of Ptah Hotep*, the authoritative French edition presents the three major manuscripts in hieroglyphic and French versions. These manuscripts span the middle to late kingdoms in Egyptian history. The editor, Zaba, finds a total of 647 different lines, of which 333 occur in the oldest and longest version. A close study of Zaba's edition reveals that close to one-half of the 647 lines appear in common in the three versions, while one-fourth appear in only one or the other version. The other fourth appear in two, but not three of the versions. Thus fully one-fourth of the 647 lines of text are unique, and notably, these are not regularly to be found in the longest version. The variation is substantial, and it is clear that the practice of introducing changes must have been deliberate and part of the normal process in making new copies. Yet the values of modern textual practices lead to English translations that mask the ancient Egyptian practices and values.

Ironically, a sizable body of scholarship has arisen in classical studies in the last fifteen to twenty years that examines and reveals the extensive practice of variation in the early Greek texts (Robb, Thomas, Worthington). However, the point remains valid that the study of alternate ancient rhetorics puts pressure on the assumptions and practices that we—and the scholarship we turn to—bring to such study.

Should We Call it Rhetoric?

One such pressure point arises in the use of the term rhetoric, since the term was developed by Plato and refined by Aristotle, and carries with it a body of definitions, practices, and values. To apply this term to cultures with very different values and practices raises both ethical and methodological issues. A good deal of discussion of this issue has taken place in response to the challenge to the tradition of classical rhetoric made by scholars who look to Sophistic rhetoric as an alternative (Poulakos, Neel, Jarratt). Edward Schiappa has argued that the term rhetoric implies a set of "specific theories and doctrines. . ." ("History and Neo-Sophistic Criticism," 312), and that rhetoric did not exist before the period of Plato. Poulakos, on the other hand, counters that the existence or absence of the term rhetoric does not necessarily correlate with the existence or absence of the concept ("Interpreting," 222-3). His backward glance extends to the Greek Sophists. In our view, Aristotle's definition focuses on persuasion, and the paradigmatic text in his rhetorical system is the argument. Yet in some of the cultures studied in this volume, we do not find overt argument in general within written texts; and the cultures' maxims also project a distaste for direct argument in general cultural life, though argument is seen in specific, well-defined locations. Such is the case for ancient Egypt. If we use the term rhetoric and its associated analytical system to examine a set of texts from a culture whose approaches and values differ markedly from those of Aristotle, are we in fact violating the term, as Arabella Lyon suggests in this volume? Are we doing a disservice to Aristotle's body of work by extending his terminology in this way to refer to systematic approaches that differ so markedly from those of classical rhetoric? Aristotle's use encompasses a body of systematic analysis and categorizing of types of texts, common situations, and suitable approaches. Is it appropriate to apply the term to language use that is not systematized but embodied? In one sense, we pay tribute to the power of the terminology by applying it to these cultures. In another sense, though, we need to be careful that we not do an injustice to Aristotle's system through such application. And we must also be careful that we do not condemn Aristotle, as developer of classical rhetoric, and the Greeks in general, for not creating an analytical system entirely appropriate for cultures they did not mean to address. And we must be extremely cautious that we not allow the lens of rhetoric to blind us or to bias us in our examination of the ancient cultures and their texts.

To avoid this problem, a variety of alternate lenses or terms might be used in place of rhetoric, each with its own disciplinary framework. These terms include discourse systems, communication norms, or principles for language use, among others. In fact, a wide range of definitions of rhetoric encompass such terms.[2] The more recent definitions of rhetoric have usefully acknowledged the implications of rhetoric in relations of power, an aspect that is not captured in some of the other available terminological lenses, but that is crucial to the study of ancient texts.[3] Power issues determine whose rhetorics are available in writing, whose rhetorics are available only as mediated by scribes, whose rhetorics are translated and made available for study, and whose rhetorics are considered as rhetoric. In the end, none of the alternate lenses and terms has the breadth and richness of the term rhetoric, which implies invention and approaches to developing text along with guidelines for organizing and delivering text. The classical rhetorical system has built within it an understanding that *ethos* and *pathos* are central factors in the success of a text (along with *logos*), and that *ethos* and *pathos* must be appropriately suited for the particular audience. It's not much of a stretch to look at rhetoric as contextualized culturally, with practices and values and norms differing in different cultural settings. Indeed, in the field of rhetoric and composition, the term alternative rhetorics is being used to describe rhetorical approaches in particular cultures that differ from the dominant paradigm. That use has been institutionalized. It ties such work to the community of scholars who are interested in histories of rhetoric and to rhetorical issues. Despite some of the problems, we situate ourselves in the field of rhetorical studies.

In doing rhetorical study of such ancient cultures very different from the Athenian culture and from our own, we are faced with two main possible avenues of approach. One approach involves application of classical rhetorical concepts to the ancient texts we study. George Kennedy's book on comparative rhetoric demonstrates such an approach, in which he points to those elements in the texts he examines that fit with the conceptual system of classical rhetoric. An alternative approach is exemplified by Claude Calame, in his studies of texts from ancient Greece. This approach is basically anthropological, involving as much of a scholarly immersion as is possible in the ancient culture being studied, and an effort to let the resulting understanding of the culture guide the analysis. Here the scholar attempts to let the culture itself provide the analytical framework and terms. Xing Lu, in her study of the rhetoric of ancient China, calls this approach a hermeneutic method. Of course, these are two extremes. We can never entirely leave our own cultural system and its analytical categories, and we can never fully experience the ancient cultures we study and their systems of thinking. But the two approaches do designate different starting points and two different ways of addressing their objects of study. Both approaches are evident in this volume.

Structure and Contents of This Collection

Mesopotamia

Archeologists acknowledge that among the oldest written texts are those that come from Uruk toward the end of the fourth millennium B.C.E.. Written symbols were impressed on clay tablets and then baked to preserve an enduring record. The invention of writing may have spread rapidly to Egypt. Yet each culture developed its own forms to phoneticize script from pictographs. In Mesopotamia by the very early third millennium, a growing class of scribes had already begun a long literary tradition. Throughout the third millennium, Sumerian, a language of unknown antecedents, was spoken. Although gradually replaced by Akkadian, Sumerian continued as the written language through the second millennium, and the Sumero-Akkadian system of cuneiform persisted for the next three thousand years. Thus a continuous cuneiform literary tradition existed throughout this area based upon an elite class of scribes who transmitted the traditional rhetorical practices of their culture in systematically arranged archives and scribal schools. This tradition has been much studied.

Most of the texts from ancient Mesopotamia were not discovered until the mid- to late nineteenth century. Thus the predominant focus in Mesopotamian textual study has involved compiling grammars, assembling dictionaries, and issuing editions of texts for analysis. One effect of the extensive and continuous existence of the scribal schools in Mesopotamian culture is that numerous copies exist of works the culture considered important. Thus any textual edition must take into account numerous tablets, with all the discrepancies. The nature of cuneiform itself leads to differences in scholarly readings, since the multivalent quality of cuneiform characters inevitably puts editors in a position of having to make decisions as to which of the many possible readings for a cuneiform applies in a specific instance. As a result, much of the scholarly attention has involved settling on and fixing the text. Additionally, we note that decisions as to which texts constitute important knowledge for the discipline of Assyriology have inevitably influenced decisions as to which texts merit publication and translation. Many extant texts have thus received little or no attention. To date, the predominant type of rhetorical studies of Mesopotamian texts has involved rhetorical criticism and stylistic analysis. Since an article in this volume by William Hallo offers a careful summary of the focus and content of such rhetorical studies, we will not do so here.

The three essays in this section address different aspects of the rhetoric of this long textual tradition. The first essay comes from the field of Assyriology and is written by a recently retired distinguished scholar, while the next two are written by rhetoricians, one with a coauthor in religious studies. The first essay, William W. Hallo's "The Birth of Rhetoric," points to ways that rhetoric, and the humanities, can be traced to Sumerian precedents. Professor Hallo analyzes some of the problems inherent in a rhetorical approach to cuneiform literature through a survey of the available Sumerian and Akkadian literature and the nature of cuneiform evidence. Additionally, he surveys the use of rhetorical approaches to cuneiform literature by scholars in Assyriology and biblical literature. Hallo suggests some new directions that a rhetorical approach might take, such as examination of the diatribes (involving men or women who outdo each other in inventive invective) and disputations (formal debates). The essay then focuses on the Gilgamesh Epic, looking at the use of proems and perorations and other rhetorical devices in this epic and in other Sumerian and Akkadian literature.

The essay by Roberta Binkley focuses on issues that arise in doing a rhetorical study of an ancient figure such as Enheduanna, the ancient poet, priestess, and princess (ca. 2300 B.C.E.). Binkley looks at some of the methodological conflicts involved in working across disciplinary boundaries to study the rhetoric of a noncanonical, pre-Greek figure. She points to Eurocentric assumptions embedded within the discipline-centered methodologies of rhetoric and Assyriology, assumptions that influence the interpretation of written texts and also conceptions of the Other—the Other of an alien culture, gender, and spiritual tradition. Studying the ancient figure of Enheduanna foregrounds often unconscious assumptions, simultaneously problematizing and enlarging the conceptions and definitions of who we are and how we situate ourselves in relation to our conception of the Other that is the object of our study.

In the final essay in this section, Paul Hoskisson and Grant Boswell offer a rhetorical examination of one genre of Mesopotamian rhetoric—the Assyrian annals. Since such records have received little attention from the perspective of rhetoric, Hoskisson and Boswell closely analyze one set of annals, those that end Sennacherib's third campaign. The final campaign of this text, against the Kingdom of Judah, occurred in 701 B.C.E., at the height of Assyrian power. This annal was the last to be carved in stone and to be displayed in the palace. In the third campaign, Sennacherib encountered the most resistance; this was the most difficult of his military campaigns. King Judah was not captured or killed, though his country was devastated. He did agree to pay tribute to Sennacherib. Thus rhetorically, the annal ends with the worst case, and even that constitutes a victory. Hoskisson and Boswell argue that the arrangement seems rhetorically strategic, as do other associated phenomena: the constant revision, the repetition of wording from popular literature, and the lack of an ending. They view the annals genre as performative, embodying the continuing process of a king fulfilling his duty, demonstrating that he deserves the kingship. They suggest that the annals present an argument for the king's legitimacy; an ending to the annal would represent an ending to the kingship.

Egyptian Rhetoric

The use of writing is generally understood to have arisen in ancient Egypt in 3000 B.C.E., though recent research supports a beginning date of 3300 or 3200 B.C.E., one or two hundred years prior to the development of writing in Mesopotamia. This new dating is based upon a recent archaeological discovery by Gunter Dreyer, Director of the German Institute of Archaeology in Cairo, but remains under debate by Egyptologists (The Write Stuff). In any case, the ancient Egyptian culture is termed the first in which writing became central to the life of the culture (Martin). Though writing was restricted to the elite, all levels of society encountered the demands of writing through tax accounts, letters, legal petitions and decrees, and funerary objects.

In rhetoric and composition venues, half a dozen studies have appeared to date that address ancient Egyptian rhetoric; all are article or chapter length (Fox, Harpine, Kennedy, Lesko, Lipson). The first to appear was a major contribution by biblical scholar Michael Fox, in the first volume of *Rhetorica* (1983). This study looked to the popular genre of text called instructions to locate the Egyptian conception of rhetoric, delineating and discussing five major canons of ancient Egyptian rhetoric: (a) the value of silence in communication, (b) the art of knowing when to speak, (c) the art of restraint and self-control, (d) the canon of fluency, and (e) the canon of truthfulness. An article by Egyptologist Barbara Lesko on ancient Egyptian women's rhetoric appeared in a collection entitled *Listening to Their Voices,* edited by Molly Wertheimer. Within Egyptology itself, much of the work on rhetoric has involved literary analysis of tropes and figures, though in recent years, two scholars have begun to address the rhetoric of women—Barbara Lesko, cited above, and Deborah Sweeney, an aspect of whose work we are fortunate to include here.

Two essays in this volume explore facets of ancient Egyptian rhetoric. Carol Lipson, in an essay entitled "Ancient Egyptian Rhetoric: It All Comes Down to *Maat,*" looks at the ways the culture's central concept of *Maat* undergirds the conventions of a variety of major genres, as well as forming the subject of some of the major genres. This essay argues that the texts and genres not only reflect and reinforce the culture's concept of *Maat,* but also address *Maat.* That is, Lipson proposes that *Maat* serves as superaddressee for the public texts of the culture, and for many of the private texts.

In an essay entitled " Law, Rhetoric, and Gender in Ramesside Egypt," archaeologist Deborah Sweeney studies ancient Egyptians' everyday utterances—texts that present and describe legal practices and proceedings. Since changes occurred in language use over the three thousand years of ancient Egyptian culture, Sweeney looks at one particular period known as the Ramesside era, from approximately 1300 to 1070 B.C.E.. She observes the legal practice of the time through documents that record legal cases, found in official archives and in private collections. These texts offer summaries of the proceedings, not exact wording. Women rarely served on the court, but did participate as witnesses, the accused, or accusers. With no professional lawyers in this culture, individuals presented their own cases on the whole. The summary texts are not written by women, but they do (re)present the speech of women in legal arenas within the ancient Egyptian culture. This essay thus looks closely at the evidence during this period to determine the rights and roles of women in legal situations and particularly to determine their rhetorical approaches. For both sexes, Sweeney finds little forensic oratory. She finds the speech patterns of males and females do not differ much, though she points out that the meaning of this resemblance is not clear, and the similarity itself might be an artifact of scribal representation of female speech.

Chinese Rhetoric

The earliest extant writing in ancient China dates back to approximately 1500 B.C.E.. Chinese writing was not based on phonetic symbols, but on signs representing words or concepts. The Shang dynasty developed the earliest known Chinese writing system, which was etched onto turtle shells or animal bones and used for ritualistic purposes. In approximately 500 B.C.E., the script was simplified and widely used in the Han dynasty for bureaucratic and state purposes.

Scholarship on ancient Chinese rhetoric has explicitly addressed crucial questions about doing rhetorical study of cultures very distant from Athenian Greek culture. Robert Oliver in 1971 pointed out that rhetoric did not exist as a separate area of study in ancient China, distinct from other areas such as politics (10), and George Kennedy's recent book similarly suggests that the French Jesuits spurred development of rhetoric as a field of study in China (144). Both Oliver and Kennedy examine ancient Chinese texts to form conclusions about the culture's theoretical principles of rhetoric as well as its textual conventions and practices. Both use terms from Greek rhetoric to describe these theories and practices, and both seem to approach the culture as uniform over large periods and in different locations. Xing Lu, in 1998, protests such a tendency to describe Chinese theories and practices in western terms, pointing out that the attempt to show equivalence masks the differences and tends to favor the western terms and approaches. She advocates a hermeneutic method, which allows the ancient Chinese texts to speak for themselves without imposing assumptions or terminological equations on them. Lu examines ancient Chinese writing, identifying key Chinese terms that together comprise a conceptual framework for Chinese rhetorical theory. She goes on to compare this theory to Greek rhetorical theory.

Scholars of ancient Chinese rhetoric meet with similar hurdles as do researchers of ancient Egyptian texts. Mark Ed Lewis points out that different parts of the Shang Shi texts, for instance, were compiled at different periods for different groups. Yet the Shang Shi tends to be handled as a fixed, authoritative text, not as a rhetorical text responsive to particular exigencies. Edward Said has also pointed to what he terms orientalist tendencies that consider Chinese practices and theories as fixed, unchanging over time and place, ignoring the complexity, diversity, and responsiveness to particular underlying conditions—political, historical, or circumstantial.[4]

The three essays in this volume on ancient Chinese rhetoric are written by scholars either fluent in Chinese or conversant with the language. The caution conveyed in a powerful article by Yameng Liu in *Rhetoric Review* about the distortions and errors that can result from dependence on translations makes this fact all the more valuable. In "The Use of Eloquence: The Confucian Perspective," George Q. Xu addresses the oft-repeated statement that Chinese rhetoric, as represented in the Confucian *Analects,* abhorred eloquence, advocating and preferring silence. Xu explains the Chinese terms and concepts—particularly *li* and *ren*—looking at the historical and political conditions in Confucius' time and in the period of the followers (370–230 B.C.E.), in order to contextualize the disaffection with glib tongues as endangering kingdoms and good government. Xu puts forward a scale involving moral valuation of speech, consistent with the doctrines of Confucius and his two most powerful followers, Mencius and Xunzi. Silence is at the top of the scale, associated with *tian,* or heaven. Glib talk (*ning*) is at the bottom. Addressing the irony of Confucians, as masterful speakers and writers, using rhetoric to make their presentations persuasive—presentations that denounce eloquence—Xu looks to the ways that Confucius and his followers accomplish this move rhetorically and to the political goals and results. He also points to the ways that Confucian tenets against eloquence have subsequently been promoted by rulers of China to further their own ideologies and to stifle dissent. Xu concludes that the Confucian negative attitude toward eloquence has "deeply penetrated into the collective consciousness of the Chinese people," and has become internalized while also being reinforced from above.

In her essay entitled "Confucian Silence and Remonstration: A Basis for Deliberation?," Arabella Lyon also looks to the Confucian preference for silence. She acknowledges the possible distortion involved in applying the term rhetoric, and in applying rhetorical concepts and terms to study ancient Chinese language practices and attitudes. Lyon points out that to do so risks "doing violence" both to Aristotle's rhetoric and to the ancient Chinese traditions. She presents an argument for using the lens of the rhetorical concept of deliberation for examining the Confucian tradition, fully aware of the difficulty of looking for equivalent concepts; her argument for using this lens is based on current speculation that Confucian philosophy may prove supportive of the developing democracy in China and on democracy's dependence on processes of deliberation.

Lyon's analysis focuses attention on the Confucian valuation of silence and remonstration, explaining each with close reference to the *Analects.* This value of silence, as she points out, goes far beyond the issue of speech, but is grounded in the need for maintaining strong relationships with others and with the world. In the *Analects,* action matters more than words, and respect for others is more desirable than persuading them to any point of view. Silence offers respect and space for growth, and promotes positive relationships. Remonstration involves the act of demonstrating by one's own behavior, by modeling actions. Remonstration leaves others to recognize the value of the action and to decide how to proceed. As with silence, Lyon argues, the Confucian *Analects* presents remonstration as preserving relationships and human connections.

Yameng Liu, in his provocative reappraisal of classical Chinese rhetoric, examines what the various ancient Chinese ideological communities had in common, the underlying rhetorical conditions that enabled their productive critical engagement. In his chapter, "'Nothing Can be Accomplished If the Speech Does Not Sound Agreeable': Rhetoric and the Invention of Classical Chinese Discourse," Liu argues persuasively for a way to restructure our view of classical Chinese rhetoric by taking a rhetorical approach rather than the traditional philosophical or linguistic approaches common to Sinology. Liu finds in the various ideological schools shared assumptions, values, criteria, techniques, and terms. He points out that a restrictive equation of rhetoric with "argumentation" or "naming" limits our understanding. Instead, looking at rhetoric as a "productive architectonic art," and applying postmodern perspectives on the production of discourse, he demonstrates that the invention of classical Chinese discourse was dependent on the common assumptions of a highly developed rhetoric.

Biblical Rhetoric

Of all of the ancient rhetorics addressed in this volume, biblical rhetoric has received the most scholarly attention, largely due to the cultural influence of the Bible on the West. A large number of books and articles offer rhetorical criticism and rhetorical analysis of the Hebrew Bible and the New Testament. The dominant approach in these studies resembles literary criticism—examining the use in the Bible of tropes and techniques and styles defined in classical rhetoric. Such a tradition was evident as early as the Renaissance, with the work of Judah Messer Leon in the fifteenth century. In a study entitled Nophet Suphim, Messer Leon applied Aristotelian and Ciceronian categories to the Hebrew Bible, showing that it exemplified "perfect speech." In recent years, biblical scholarship has taken on other directions in rhetorical studies, engaging with political and cultural issues involved in the biblical text. David Metzger's contribution to this collection exemplifies this new direction of research, examining the matrix of power relations among the groups involved in the biblical narrative, looking at the ways the text of the Bible offers persuasion for the dominance of one of these groups in particular. Such a reading of the rhetoricity of the Bible addresses the Bible as an ideological text, providing warrants for a particular position. This reading exemplifies the type of scholarship called for in a collectively constructed book from Yale University Press entitled The Postmodern Bible, published in 1997 (Burnett et al.).

In his study of the rhetoric of the Pentateuch, the first five books of the Hebrew Bible, David Metzger points out the difficulties of such study. We do not know who wrote the Pentateuch, or when it was written/redacted/compiled. We do not know the purposes or audiences. Entitled "Pentateuch

Rhetoric and the Voice of the Aaronides," Metzger's essay builds on the nineteenth-century documentary or Graf-Wellhausen hypothesis. This hypothesis sees the Pentateuch as composed of four different strands by different authors, representing different traditions. Metzger's essay argues that the Pentateuch is not just a combination of different voices; instead, he argues that the editor rhetorically orchestrates the voices of a number of competing power groups: the priestly group who were descendants of Aaron, the descendants of the patriarchs, the Levite priests, the prophets, the descendants of the kings. Metzger demonstrates a way to conduct rhetorical examination despite the gaps of knowledge, by determining for specific sections which power group would speak that way, which would benefit by such an argument, and when would such a presentation have been beneficial. He shows that the Aaronidic priestly strand dominates in the Pentateuch and argues that the redactor would have had to be a descendant of Aaron, or associated with the interests of the descendants of Aaron. To illustrate this, Metzger analyzes a crucial section from the Book of Numbers, the fourth book of the Pentateuch, where the voice of Aaron is legitimized against the voices of the ancestral houses and the Levites.

Alternative Greek Rhetoric

In an essay entitled "The Art of Rhetoric at Rhodes: An Eastern Rival to the Athenian Representation of Classical Rhetoric," Richard Leo Enos explains the political and cultural conditions on the Greek island of Rhodes that shaped the development of a system of rhetoric that rivaled the Athenian approach, remaining popular through the Roman Republic and into the Roman Empire. Enos points out that while Athenian rhetoric is normally thought of as representing the rhetorical approach throughout Greece, in fact references occur in ancient texts to other approaches, particularly to Rhodian rhetoric. Yet scholarship has not given much attention to this rhetorical system. The essay by Enos addresses this gap, looking at why this particular rhetorical system emerged when and where it did, why it endured, and describing its characteristics. Enos points out that such a study demands different methodologies than those employed by scholars trained in the study of Athenian rhetoric; study of Rhodian rhetoric requires investigation of primary sources, often nontraditional in nature. He finds the Rhodian system particularly flexible, suitable for interaction with a wide range of foreign cultures. The originator— Aeschines—left Athens to introduce the formal study of rhetoric on the island of Rhodes. His school of rhetoric stressed the skill of communication with those from diverse cultural backgrounds and languages, as required for the commercial interaction typical of an island strategically located to interact with other seafaring peoples. Rhodian rhetoric was especially suited for declamation and was seen as a moderate alternative to the direct Attick style and the emotional Asiatic style.

Cross-Cultural Rhetorical Studies

Two essays study rhetorical usage across cultural boundaries, looking at similarities and possibilities of cultural diffusion. James Watts analyses rhetorical conventions over a range of cultures and periods in the ancient Near East. In an essay entitled "Story-List-Sanction: A Cross-Cultural Strategy of Ancient Persuasion," Watts examines a particular combination of genres that he finds in examples from Mesopotamia in the third millennium B.C.E.; from ancient Egypt, Babylonia and Mesopotamia in the second millennium B.C.E.; and from Egypt, Mesopotamia, Syro-Palestine and Anatolia in the first millennium B.C.E., among others. At times, all three elements of the story-list-sanction pattern appear, while often only two of the three are used. Watts finds the pattern in texts as widely ranging as dedicatory inscriptions, law codes, treatises, and the Hebrew Bible. Most of the examples were written for public presentation and are royal in origin. Watts points out that each of the three parts in the structure serves a particular purpose meant to enhance the persuasive power: on the whole, the lists draw attention to the current time, the story draws attention to the past, and the sanction focuses on the future. While the development of Greek rhetoric denigrated the use of stories and sanctions for persuasive purposes in argument, Watts traces the continuing appearance in western culture from medieval times on.

Two approaches to rhetorical study inform Jan Swearingen's analysis of women's songs and lamentations in the ancient Near East. Her chapter, "Song to Speech: The Origins of Early Epitaphia in Ancient Near Eastern Women's Lamentations," combines *etic* and *emic* methods. The first involves application of conceptual tools from the field of rhetoric, while the second examines the Near Eastern and ancient Greek cultures through terms and concepts internal to these cultures. As Swearingen points out, such a view through the terms of another culture can help us see the blind spots of our own terminology and can help us to envision other possibilities. Through examination of biblical and Homeric texts, as well as Greek tragedies, Swearingen looks to the genres of song and speech originally practiced by women on occasions involving birth and death. This investigation reveals traces of what later became the epitaph genre in Greek rhetoric. The essay provides a possible explanation for the fact that the leadership role of women speakers in the early periods was lost with the development of Athenian rhetoric. Swearingen's careful examination of the *topos* of Athenian citizenship in the Menexenos reveals a formula of metaphors that characterized Athenian citizens as "motherless children," born not of women but from the soil of the public space of the polis—a space for males. Such metaphors became integral to the developing Athenian rhetorical system, silencing women and their voices. As Swearingen concludes, the Greek enlightenment proved an endarkenment for women.

Suggestions for Teaching Ancient Rhetorics

The final section of the volume includes teaching units submitted by the authors of each individual chapter. This section will be particularly valuable for faculty who want to begin to teach any of the rhetorics and cultures discussed in this collection. The authors provide information about some of the basic references necessary for background on each culture and period discussed, as well as on the particular issues and types of texts addressed. Some authors, such as David Metzger and Rich Enos, make specific teaching suggestions. For example, Metzger takes the reader through an actual undergraduate course, and then a graduate course. He explains some of the approaches he took, such as ways of comparing texts such as Plato's *Phaedrus* and the Shir HaShirim (Song of Songs), both of which deal with love. Another comparison he describes involves pairing Deuteronomy with Books I and II of Aristotle's *Rhetoric;* here his example entails looking at the models for communal language use presented in each text. Enos gives a thorough discussion of the goals for a unit on the rhetoric of Rhodes, suggesting topics for discussion and offering a list of suggested readings.

As Jan Swearingen and Arabella Lyon note in their teaching guides, most of the primary texts from the ancient world are fragments or short pieces, or are written in small segments. Many are aphoristic in nature. Thus these texts invite close reading and lend themselves to examination in class discussion. Because the absence of women's voices and texts proves so pervasive throughout the ancient world, Swearingen suggests using historical novels to help undergraduates fill the gap left by the available corpus of male-authored and male-oriented texts.

Several authors invite faculty and students to read broadly, offering a wide range of suggestions for individual choice. For instance, William Hallo provides sources in the areas of biblical rhetoric, Sumerian literature and rhetoric, Akkadian rhetorical literature generally, the Gilgamesh epic, and on the use of colloquial language in the ancient world. Grant Boswell and Paul Hoskisson suggest readings on the Assyrian Empire and its placement within the ancient world; they also provide references relating to the major ancient texts from this culture and to study of the culture in general.

Thus the teaching unit chapter offers rich resources to help faculty introduce ancient rhetorics to their students. The authors suggest questions for class inquiry and offer ideas for juxtaposing texts and topics that can encourage fruitful discussion and thinking for both undergraduate and graduate levels.

Notes

1. John Poulakos points out that the term *rhetorike* in forms other than the nominative singular was in use before the period of Plato or Aristotle, from the seventh century B.C.E. See "Interpreting Sophistical Rhetoric: A Response to Schiappa." *Philosophy and Rhetoric* 23 (1990): 218–228.

2. For a range of definitions of rhetoric, see the website of Professor James Comas at the University of Missouri: http://www.missouri.edu/~engine/rhetoric/defining_main.html.

3. See definitions by Steven Mailloux ("rhetoric [is] the political effectivity of trope and argument in culture") [p. xii] and Jacques Derrida ("rhetoric, as such, depends on conditions that are not rhetorical. . . . The effects of rhetoric depend on certain situations: political situations, economical situations—the libidinal situation, also.") [Olson, pp. 15–16].

4. This discussion is deeply indebted to the work of Ph.D. student Jon Benda, a dissertator in the Composition and Cultural Rhetoric Graduate Program at Syracuse University.

Works Cited

Adams, Richard E.W. *Ancient Civilizations of the New World.* Boulder, CO: Westview Press, 1997.

Assmann, Jan. *The Mind of Egypt: History and Meaning in the Time of the Pharaohs.* New York: Metropolitan Books, Henry Holt and Co., 1996.

Biesecker, Barbara. "Coming to Terms with Recent Attempts to Write Women into the History of Rhetoric." In Takis Poulakos, ed. *Rethinking the History of Rhetoric: Multidisciplinary Essays on the Rhetorical Tradition.* Polemics Series. Boulder, CO: Westview Press, 1993.

Bizzell, Patricia. "Feminist Methods of Research in the History of Rhetoric: What Differences Do They Make?" *Rhetoric Society Quarterly* 30 (Fall 2000): 5,–17. Editor, Special Issue on Feminist Historiography in Rhetoric. *Rhetoric Society Quarterly* 32 (Winter 2002).

Burkard, G. *Textkritische Untersuchungern zu Agyptischen Weirheitslehren des Alten und Mittleren Reiches. Agyptologische Abhandlungen O. Harrasowitz* Vol. 34. Weisbaden 1977.

Burnett, Fred, Robert Fowler, David Jobling, Elizabeth Castelli, eds. *The Postmodern Bible.* New Haven, CT: Yale University Press, 1997.

Calame, Claude. *Choruses of Young Women in Ancient Greece: Their Morphology, Religious Role, and Social Functions.* Lanham, MD: Rowman & Littlefield, 1997.

————. *The Poetics of Eros in Ancient Greece.* Ithaca, NY: Cornell University Press, 1999.

Campbell, Karlyn Kohrs. *Man Cannot Speak for Her: A Critical Study of Early Feminist Rhetoric.* V. 1. Contributions in Women's Studies, No. 101. New York: Greenwood Press, 1989.

Enos, Richard Leo. "Recovering the Lost Art of Researching the History of Rhetoric." *Rhetoric Society Quarterly* 29 (Fall 1999): 7–20.

————. "The Archaeology of Women in Rhetoric: Rhetorical Sequencing as a Research Method for Historical Scholarship." *Rhetoric Society Quarterly* 32 (Winter 2002).

Forster, John. *Echoes of Egyptian Voices: An Anthology of Ancient Egyptian Poetry.* Norman: University of Oklahoma Press, 1992.

Fox, Michael. "Ancient Egyptian Rhetoric." *Rhetorica* 1 (Sping1983): 9–22.

Gale, Xin Liu. "Historical Studies and Postmodernism: Rereading Aspasia of Miletus." *College English* 62 (January 2000): 361–201.

Glenn, Cheryl. *Rhetoric Retold: Regendering the Tradition from Antiquity through the Renaissance.* Carbondale: Southern Illinois University Press, 1997.

————. "Comment: Truth, Lies, and Method: Revisiting Feminist Historiography." *College English* 62 (January 2000): 387–389.

Harpine, William. "Epideictic and Ethos in the Amarna Letters: The Witholding of Argument." *Rhetoric Society Quarterly* 28 (1998): 81–116.

Jarratt, Susan, ed., Special Issue: Feminist Rereadings in the History of Rhetoric. *Rhetoric Society Quarterly* 22 (Winter 1992).

Jarratt, Susan. "New Dispositions for Historical Studies in Rhetoric." In Gary Olson, ed. *Rhetoric and Composition as Intellectual Work.* Carbondale: Southern Illinois University Press, 2002.

————. *Rereading the Sophists: Classical Rhetoric Refigured.* Southern Illinois University Press, 1997.

Kennedy, George. *Comparative Rhetoric.* New York: Oxford University Press, 1998.

Lesko, Barbara. *"The Rhetoric of Women in Pharaonic Egypt." In Molly M. Wertheimer, ed.* Listening to their Voices. Columbia: University of South Carolina Press, 1997.

Lewis, Mark Edward. *Writing and Authority in Early China. SUNY Series in Chinese Philosophy and Culture.* Albany, NY: State University of New York Press, 1999.

Lichtheim, Miriam. *Ancient Egyptian Literature: The Old and Middle Kingdoms.* Vol. 1. Berkeley: University of California Press, 1973.

Lipson, Carol. "Ancient Egyptian Medical Texts." *Journal of Technical Writing and Communication* 20 (4:1990).

Liu, Yameng. "To Capture the Essence of Chinese Rhetoric: An Anatomy of a Paradigm in Comparative Rhetoric." *Rhetoric Review* 14 (1996): 318–35.

Lu, Xing. *Rhetoric in Ancient China, Fifth to Third Century B.C.E.: A Comparison with Classical Greek Rhetoric.* Columbia: University of South Carolina Press, 1998.

Mailloux, Steven. *Rhetorical Power.* Ithaca, NY: Cornell University Press, 1989.

Martin, Henri-Jean. *The History and Power of Writing.* Chicago: University of Chicago Press, 1994.

Meeks, Dimitri, and Christine Favard Meeks. *Daily Life of the Egyptian Gods.* Ithaca, NY: Cornell University Press, 1996.

Miller, Thomas P. "Reinventing Rhetorical Traditions." In Theresa Enos, ed. *Learning from the Histories of Rhetoric: Essays in Honor of Winifred Bryan Horner.* Carbondale: Southern Illinois University Press, 1993.

Neel, Jasper. *Aristotle's Voice: Rhetoric, Theory, and Writing in America.* Carbondale: Southern Illinois University Press, 1994.

_____. *Plato, Derrida, and Writing.* Carbondale: Southern Illinois University Press, 1988.

"Octalog I: The Politics of Historiography." *Rhetoric Review* 7 (1988): 5–49.

"Octalog II: The (Continuing) Politics of Historiography." *Rhetoric Review* 16 (Fall 1997): 22–44.

Oliver, Robert. *Communication and Culture in Ancient India and China.* Syracuse, NY: Syracuse University Press, 1971.

Olson, Gary, "Jacques Derrida on Rhetoric and Composition: A Conversation." *Journal of Advanced Composition* 10.1 (1990): 1–21.

Poulakos, John. "Interpreting Sophistical Rhetoric: A Response to Schiappa." *Philosophy and Rhetoric* 23 (1990): 218–228.

_____. *Sophistical Rhetoric in Classical Greece.* Columbia: University of South Carolina Press, 1994.

Robb, Kevin. *Literacy and Paideia in Ancient Greece.* New York: Oxford University Press, 1994.

Rosendale, Laura Gray, and Sibylle Gruber. *Alternative Rhetorics*. Albany: State University of New York Press, 2001.

Said, Edward. *Orientalism*. New York: Vintage, 1978.

Schiappa, Edward. "Neo-Sophistic Rhetorical Criticism or the Historical Reconstruction of Sophistic Doctrines?" *Philosophy and Rhetoric* 23 (1990): 192–217.

_____. "History and Neo-Sophistic Criticism: A Reply to Poulakos." *Philosophy and Rhetoric* 23(1990): 307–315.

Shankman, Steven, and Steven W. Durrant. *Early China/Ancient Greece: Thinking Through Comparisons*. Albany: State University of New York Press, 2002.

Thomas, Rosalind. *Oral Tradition and Written Record in Classical Athens*. Cambridge: Cambridge University Press, 1989.

Welch, Kathleen. *Electric Rhetoric: Classical Rhetoric, Oralism, and a New Literacy*. Cambridge, MA: MIT Press, 1999.

Whitburn, Merrill. *Rhetorical Scope and Performance: The Example of Technical Communication*. Ablex, ATTW Contemporary Studies in Technical Communication Series, 2000.

Williams, R. J. "The Sages of Ancient Egypt in the Light of Recent Scholarship." *Journal of the American Oriental Society* 101.1 (1981):1–19.

Worthington, Ian, ed. *Voice into Text: Orality and Literacy in Ancient Greece*. Leiden: E. J. Brill, 1996.

The Write Stuff. January 19, 1999. http://whyfiles.org/079/writing.

Zaba, Zbynek. *Les Maximes de Ptahhotep*. Prague: Editions de L'Academie Tchecoslovaque de Sciences, 1956.

The Birth of Rhetoric

William W. Hallo

Rhetoric, long thought of as an invention of classical Greece, has for some time been held to have had a prior existence in ancient Israel. A whole school of "rhetorical criticism" has grown up in biblical studies since at least 1969,[1] while individual scholars have analyzed specific biblical texts from a rhetorical perspective.[2] Assyriologists (and Egyptologists)[3] have been somewhat slower to take up the challenge.

Some basic problems beset a rhetorical approach to cuneiform literature: how to distinguish fiction from nonfiction,[4] how to identify a usually unknown author,[5] how to divine his (or her!)[6] intention,[7] how to assess the impact on a presumed audience.[8] Cuneiform literature does not, as in the case of classical literature, provide us with a neatly prepackaged corpus of theoretical prescriptions or practical illustrations of the art of persuasion in public speaking. It does not, as in the case of biblical prophecy, preserve impassioned orations inspired by firm belief, addressed to the innermost circles of power, and transmitted in virtually stenographic transcripts by secretaries such as Baruch son of Neriya,[9] whose seal impression, recently recovered (albeit from unprovenanced context), lends new historicity and authenticity to Jeremiah's words.[10] The preserved literature of Sumer and Akkad would not yield readily to the pioneering analyses of the prophetic art of persuasion by Yehoshua Gitay,[11] nor to the whole line of biblical exegesis that goes by the name of rhetorical criticism,[12] and that has most recently been conveniently surveyed by Watson and Hauser.[13] It would not answer to "a forensic understanding" such as newly and effectively applied by Edward Greenstein to the Book of Job,[14] or to the narratological analyses advanced by him[15] and such other literary critics as Adele Berlin[16]. It would not resonate to the combination of narratology and rhetorical analysis championed by Meir Sternberg[17] and

Mary Savage,[18] nor yet to a novel thesis on the "power of the word" put forward by the late Isaac Rabinowitz.[19]

The reasons for these negative assessments are inherent in the nature of the cuneiform evidence, which differs fundamentally from both the Classical and the biblical models. Whether we look at the literature in Sumerian and Akkadian as I intend to do, or in Hittite and in Ugaritic, each follows its own canons—and forms its own canons, as we shall see. For all that, some tentative efforts have been made, in the fairly recent past, to subject portions of the cuneiform canons to rhetorical analysis. I will review them here briefly, before attempting a programmatic statement of further possibilities.

It will not, I trust, be considered unduly immodest if I begin the survey with myself! In 1968, in collaboration with J. J. A. van Dijk, I published a first critical edition of a Sumerian poem that we entitled "The Exaltation of Inanna."[20] It is expressly attributed to the first nonanonymous author in Mesopotamian history, perhaps in all of history: the princess Enheduanna (ca. 2285–2250 B.C.E.), known also by other poetic works and by monumental remains.[21] The poem's division into 153 lines represents a feature original to the composition, for these line divisions agree in all of the poem's numerous exemplars, and the total is carefully counted in the colophon of at least one complete recension.[22] In our edition, we grouped these lines into eighteen stanzas and three "rhetorical" parts and defended these groupings in a literary analysis without claiming that they too necessarily represented "original feature(s) of the composition."[23] The rhetorical parts we called "exordium" (or "proemium"),[24] "the argument," and "peroration" respectively and equated them with stanzas i–viii (lines 1–65), ix–xv (lines 66–135) and xvi–xviii (lines 136–153). Fifteen years later, I applied a similar rhetorical analysis to the first Epic of Lugalbanda ("Lugalbanda in the Cave of the Mountain").[25]

While these examples have not been widely followed, it is at least worth noting that the term "proem" has been used to describe the first two stanzas of another Sumerian hymn to the goddess Inanna in its latest translation by Thorkild Jacobsen[26] and the first three lines of an Akkadian prayer to the god Nanna as translated by William Moran.[27] And at the sixth biennial conference of the Rhetoric Society of America held in May 1994 at Old Dominion University in Norfolk, Virginia, a paper was presented on "Enheduanna's 'The Exaltation of Inanna': Toward a Feminist Rhetoric."[28] The author of the paper, Roberta Binkley, has since then completed a doctoral dissertation on this subject at the University of Arizona.

To return to my survey, in 1973 Stanley Gevirtz found evidence of "Canaanite rhetoric" in the Amarna letters. While heavily indebted to West Semitic (Ugaritic and Hebrew) models, these letters at least introduced rhetorical flourishes into Akkadian.[29] In 1978, Adele Berlin explored "shared rhetorical features in biblical and Sumerian literature."[30] She was not concerned with any one composition or genre, but with the whole gamut of Sumerian poetry, and particularly with a feature it shares with biblical poetry, namely parallelism. Within this broader technique, she noted especially two rhetorical features, one "the particularizing stanza" and the other an ABAB word order pattern.

In his 1980 dissertation, Robert Falkowitz chose to define rhetoric still more widely. Rather than the prevalent classical definition of rhetoric as the art of persuasion in oratory, he preferred the medieval conception in which rhetoric formed a trivium, with grammar and dialectic, within the seven liberal arts, and as such applied to poetry and epistolography as well as to preaching. It was, in short, intended to inculcate the ability to communicate in a lofty idiom distinct from common parlance, let alone colloquialism,[31] and was therefore a proper subject of instruction in the schools. By this criterion, the curriculum of the scribal schools of Old Babylonian Mesopotamia could likewise be described as an exercise in rhetoric. That curriculum first required the Akkadian-speaking students to master the intricacies of cuneiform writing and the basic vocabulary of Sumerian by means of primers constituting syllabaries and vocabularies. But it then went on to connected texts in Sumerian and these typically began with the proverb collections, which Falkowitz accordingly renamed "The Sumerian Rhetoric Collections."[32]

Piotr Michalowski uses rhetoric almost synonymously with stylistics in discussing negation as "a rhetorical and stylistic device."[33] Historians of Mesopotamian art have expanded the definition even more, freeing rhetoric of its verbal associations entirely—for better or worse—and extending it to the realm of nonverbal communication.[34]

More recent studies have tended to return to a narrower definition of rhetoric and to its epistolary setting. Thus Jack Sasson has singled out the emissaries of Zimri-Lim, the Old Babylonian king of Mari (ca. 1780–1760 B.C.E.) for reporting to their sovereign "individually, massively, and often." Their letters "contain dozens of long lines and, in rhetoric, can match the best of biblical prose, full of vivid phrasing, lively pacing, and a terrific sense of structure."[35] Richard Hess has studied the longest letter of the many sent by the Egyptian pharaoh at Amarna to his restless vassals in Asia during the Amarna period. He concludes that its elaborate argument and stylistic sophistication constitute "a creative use of rhetorical persuasion in order to counter the arguments of a vassal and set forth the pharaoh's case."[36] He has also applied rhetorical standards to the Amarna letters from Shechem and Jerusalem.[37]

Kirk Grayson has termed Assyrian rhetoric a "conquering tactic," citing both biblical and Assyrian evidence.[38] Moran documents the classical preference for "the plain style" or what in Greek is called *ho ischnos charactér* and in Latin *subtilis oratio* or *genus tenue* to signal its use in an Old Babylonian prayer to the moon-god.[39] This plain style should not, however, be confused with colloquialism. Moran regards the justly famous letter of a schoolboy to his mother (Zinu) as probably showing "colloquial speech" in Akkadian.[40] It has also been detected in Sumerian, both in wisdom literature[41] and in an incantation,[42] in Akkadian depositions in court,[43] and in biblical Hebrew.[44]

The most recent attempt to apply the canons of classical rhetoric to cuneiform literature is also the most massive one. In a doctoral dissertation written at the Hebrew University under the direction of Aaron Shaffer, Nathan Wasserman has discussed *Syntactic and Rhetorical Patterns in Non-Epic Old-Babylonian Literary Texts* (1993). In nine chapters, he treated in detail the techniques of hendiadys, merismus, rhyming couplets, geminatio, gradatio, hypallage, enumeratio, the hysteron-proteron sequence, zeugma sentences and extraposition sentences. Ten years later, he published an expanded version of the first three phenomena, adding epic texts and discussions of similes (cf. already Wasserman 2000) and two other rhetorical devices which he identified by their Akkadian and Arabic names as *damqₚam-inim* and *tamyiz* respectively (Wasserman 2003).

One should also take note of some recent studies that investigate essentially rhetorical aspects of cuneiform literature without actually using the term. Thus Dietz Edzard has dealt with monologues in Akkadian literature.[45] Laurie Pearce has addressed the question of authorial intention, or "why the scribes wrote."[46] Barbara Porter has raised the issue of "impact on a presumed audience" with respect to neo-Assyrian royal inscriptions.[47] The possible Mesopotamian background of specifically *political* rhetoric has been investigated by Claus Wilcke for older Babylonia and by Peter Machinist for later Assyria. Wilcke regards "rhetorical forms" as just one subject among many others in the scribal-school curriculum, which he, like me, equates with the "canon" (pp. 66f.); Machinist alludes to rhetoric early and often (pp. 77, 88, 103) and defends the wider sense of "political" (pp. 103f. and 383f.).[48]

Even this hasty survey, which has undoubtedly sinned by omission, suggests that there are, after all, some potential insights to be gained by a rhetorical approach to cuneiform literature. In what follows, I will attempt to identify some other directions that this approach might usefully take. I will not stop to dwell on the peculiarities of cuneiform documentation, except to emphasize at the outset how it can best be classified.[49] Using both formal and functional criteria, it can be divided into archives, monuments, and canons. Archives include a vast corpus of letters, accounts, contracts, and other documents of daily life preserved on clay tablets in the hundreds of thousands and constituting some 80 percent of the surviving documentation. Although they play a crucial role in the reconstruction of ancient society and of the wellsprings of our own contemporary institutions, these documents—sometimes disparagingly referred to by Assyriologists as "laundry lists"—qualify for rhetorical analysis only in the case of certain letters.[50] A smaller corpus—perhaps 10 percent of the documentation—consists of royal and other inscriptions that serve us as building blocks in the reconstruction of ancient history. Such texts are typically inscribed on monuments and can be regarded as "monumental." In the best of circumstances, such as the royal inscriptions of the neo-Assyrian empire, they may qualify as examples of rhetoric.[51] The remaining 10 percent of the documentation—inscribed on clay surfaces of various shapes and often recovered in multiple copies—is literary in the broad sense of the term and has its place in the formal curriculum of the scribal schools where, after the primers and the proverbs referred to earlier, the students learned to read and copy out the entire received canon of Sumerian (and later Akkadian) texts of diverse genres that creatively captured the whole range of human experience and the reaction of human beings to the world about them. These texts were literary in the narrower sense but not by any means always belletristic, for they included religious, scientific, philological, and other genres not intended simply to edify or to entertain but first of all to educate. Since the curriculum embodied at any given time all those texts—and only those texts—that were thought necessary and proper to this pedagogic end, I have argued long and hard in favor of labelling these texts as "canonical" and their totality at any given period of history as the canon of that era.[52] I would now be prepared to suggest that they might equally well be labelled "rhetorical," using that term in the broader, medieval connotation cited earlier, but extending it far beyond only the proverb collections that stand near the beginning of the school curriculum.

Proverbs are only one genre among the several that are collectively referred to, on the analogy of the biblical example, as "wisdom literature." That literature was concerned with common mortals, not with gods or kings, and it often offered practical instructions in agriculture and other common human pursuits. Much of it is clearly oral in origin, and intended for oral delivery. Among the wisdom genres that would particularly lend themselves to a rhetorical analysis are three that are usually classified by Assyriologists as dialogues, diatribes, and disputations respectively.[53] Dialogues tend to take place between scribes or between scribal students and their masters or parents;[54]) diatribes may involve men or women of various walks of life outdoing each other in inventive invective.[55] (Some scholars consider dialogues and diatribes a single genre.)[56] Disputations are the most artful of the three genres, and the only one identified as such in the native terminology; the Sumerian term *a-da-man* (Akkadian *teṣītu* or *dāṣātu*) recurs in cultic and archival texts, indicating the occasions when the disputations were performed.[57]

The disputations pit two parties against each other in formal debate.[58] The parties are typically antithetical phenomena from the natural or social environment—summer and winter, bird and fish, silver and copper, hoe and plow, for example. Each party rehearses its advantages first and then the shortcomings of the antagonist in a series of arguments and rebuttals that may reach three or more "rounds" before the final judgment is rendered by the deity or, occasionally, the king, depending apparently on whether the setting of the disputation was conceived of as the scribal school attached to the temple or as the palace.[59] Typically (though not invariably) the palm goes to the party that, at the outset, might have appeared the weaker, as if in recognition of the persuasiveness of its argumentation. (My colleague Victor Bers reminds me of the fifth-century cliché regarding the victory of the weaker argument—*hētton logos*—over the stronger—*kreitton logos,* "supposedly a mark of sophistic skill and immorality.") Thus the lowly hoe triumphs over the lordly plow, perhaps even receiving a token gift for his pains in what van Dijk described as an anticipation of the enigmatic *qesiṭa's* and gold rings awarded to Job at the end of his disputation.[60]

It seems, then, that the disputations have a stronger claim than the proverbs to be regarded as true exercises in rhetoric. In the view of H. L. J. Vanstiphout, one of their principal current interpreters, they "developed out of the abstract and neutral 'debate situation' primarily as an exercise in 'rhetorical skill'. . . . the debate, as a literary and rhetorical form, is in itself and as such the primary reason for being."[61] And "in most cases the victor wins on *rhetorical* points: he is the cleverest debater."[62] Hypothetically, we can reconstruct a kind of dramatic presentation in which two speakers (or actors or rhetors) assumed the respective roles. The preserved texts represent the libretti; their contents consist almost entirely of spoken parts, and the narrative interpolations constitute little more than "stage directions."

Much the same could be said of some of the other genres that followed the wisdom literature in the scribal curriculum and which, unlike that literature, focused on kings and gods. What then are some of the rhetorical and stylistic devices that can be detected in these genres? I will confine myself to epic (including myth), not only because it is evidently omitted from Wasserman's aforementioned thesis (though included in his book), but also because, of all cuneiform genres, this is the one that, even in translation, continues to have the widest appeal.[63] Who has not heard of the Epic of Gilgamesh?

What is perhaps less familiar is that to this day we still do not have any complete recension of the epic! Its rediscovery began in 1872 with the publication of *The Chaldaean Genesis* by George Smith, which included much of the story of the Flood in what proved to be Tablet XI of the epic; it created so much excitement in England that the *Daily Telegraph* supplied Smith with the funds to return to Kuyunjik (which turned out to be a part of ancient Nineveh, and included the royal libraries) and find many more fragments of the epic. But in spite of more than 130 years of additional discoveries, the epic remains fragmentary. Even its very first line is broken and subject to different restorations and translations. The latest suggestion is based on a join made in 1998[64] that "yields the first significant new evidence for the opening of the Epic of Gilgamesh to appear since . . . 1891"[65] and leads to the translation: "He who saw all, (who was) the foundation of the land"[66] or, alternatively, "He who saw the Deep, the country's foundation."[67] Earlier renderings included: "Let me proclaim to the land him who has seen everything"[68] and "Him who saw everything, let me make known to the land,"[69] thus inviting the audience to listen.[70] And indeed here and in the next four lines, the audience is tempted by the inducement of sharing in the knowledge of someone who had travelled widely in the world and experienced much—like Odysseus *polutropon hos mala polla* . . . (I) (1). In the next line, this geographical breadth is matched by chronological depth, for Gilgamesh is said to have "brought back information from before the flood."[71]

But Gilgamesh is not alone among Akkadian epics in thus anticipating classical epic by attempting to attract the attention of a presumed audience at the outset. Claus Wilcke has studied the exordia of Akkadian epics and identified at least four other examples in which the poet steps forward to announce in the first person (typically in the cohortative mood) his intention to sing of a certain subject—a veritable *arma virumque cano* (Aeneid I) (1)—often followed by exhortations to the audience to listen.[72] Among them are Old Babylonian examples thought to be hymnic-epic celebrations of Hammurapi's campaigns against the north[73] and the south,[74] and a hymn to Ishtar as Agushaya, "the mad dancer in battle."[75] Only one example dates from the late period, namely the canonical Anzu Epic).[76]

Still others of the later compositions substitute for this exordium a circumstantial temporal clause that sets the stage for the narrative to follow, a kind of fairy tale beginning with "once upon a time." The Akkadian conjunction is *enuma/inuma/inumi,* "when," which breaks down etymologically into *in umi,* "on the day that," and as such is a throwback to the Sumerian u_4 . . . *a-a,* "on the day that; when," which is such a standard incipit of Sumerian epic and other genres that it became the preferred form of the personal names that identified the antediluvian sages with the works of literature attributed to them.[77] In its Akkadian form it is most familiar from the incipit of the so-called "Epic of Creation," *enuma elish.*[78] Other examples include the much-debated incipit of the (Late) Old Babylonian flood story of Atar-hasis,[79] and the Middle Babylonian myth of Nergal and Ereshkigal.[80]

A third rhetorical solution to introducing epic is to begin with a hymnic apostrophe to the royal or divine protagonist—a useful reminder that myth and epic do not constitute separate genres in cuneiform but only a subset of hymns to kings or gods.[81] With Wolfram von Soden (inspired by Benno Landsberger), it has therefore become customary to describe the Akkadian of early examples of the subset as the "hymnic-epic dialect."[82] The Epic of Erra and Ishum, for example, begins with a hymnic apostrophe to Ishum.[83] Rarest of all is the epic that begins *in medias res,* as in the case of the story of Etana, both in its Old Babylonian and its late recensions[84]

But enough of the proems of Akkadian epics. Let us look also at their perorations, and let us begin once more with the Epic of Gilgamesh. It has twelve chapters, or tablets, a pleasingly round number in Mesopotamian tradition. Perhaps that is why a twelfth chapter was added to the epic, for length of composition, whether in terms of chapters or of lines, was a significant factor in cuneiform poetry. Not only was it one of the few data regularly recorded in the otherwise laconic colophons,[85] but compositional lengths of 200, 480, and 1080 lines may not be wholly accidental.[86]

In fact the twelfth tablet is "an inorganic appendage to the epic proper," as E. A. Speiser put it.[87] C. J. Gadd[88] and S. N. Kramer[89] had recognized it long ago as the straightforward translation of a Sumerian original, a virtually unique occurrence in the long history of Sumero-Akkadian bilingualism.[90] Shaffer's edition[91] shows, in detail, how its 151 lines correspond to the second half of the Sumerian epic of "Gilgamesh, Enkidu and the Netherworld." [92] This second half, as we now know, is represented by two exemplars newly excavated in the Jebel Hamrin area, one of which ends with the incipit of another Sumerian Gilgamesh episode, namely Gilgamesh and Huwawa (Gilgamesh and the Land of the Living).[93]

The latest study on the subject argues otherwise, contending that the twelfth tablet is an organic part of the epic, a "necessary epilogue . . . , and a final affirmation of the truth of what has been revealed," i.e. Gilgamesh's essential humanity.[94] But this study fails on at least two counts. For one, it overlooks the fact that, outside the epic if not within it, Gilgamesh does achieve a measure of immortality, albeit as god of the netherworld. As Tzvi Abusch has shown, the twelfth tablet (along with the sixth) was added to the epic precisely to make that point.[95] Moreover, there is ample and incontrovertible evidence for the gradual growth of the epic over time.

In point of fact the Gilgamesh epic in the final form that is the basis of most modern translations is the product of a millennial evolution, an evolution that has been conveniently traced by Jeffrey Tigay.[96] At an earlier stage, it undoubtedly concluded with Tablet XI for, to quote Speiser again, "the last lines of Tablet XI are the same as the final lines of the introduction of the entire work (I, i 16–19)." [97] The effect is one of "framing" the entire composition with an invitation to inspect the great walls of Uruk built, as we know from elsewhere, by Gilgamesh himself.[98] Such a framing effect, or *inclusio,* familiar in the Bible from the Book of Job (and elsewhere), is lost by the addition of Tablet XII.[99]

But the frame is not an original part of the epic either! The incipit of its Old Babylonian recension is "supreme above kings" (*šutur eli šarri*) as should have long been seen from the colophon of Tablet II but in fact was not realized until the discovery of a new fragment of Tablet I at Kalah and its publication by Donald Wiseman.[100] There, as noted by Shaffer, the words in question occur at the beginning of line 27 of the first column.[101] That implies that the first 26 lines of the canonical recension, including the entire passage about the walls of Uruk, were not originally part of the proemium—nor, probably, of the peroration. The oldest recoverable recension of the Akkadian epic began, not with the bard speaking in the first person and addressing the audience in the second, but with a standard hymnic introduction of the protagonist in the third. This hymnic introduction typically begins with epithets and keeps the audience in supposed suspense before revealing the hero by his proper name. It is thus an example of the rhetorical device that we noted earlier and to which Berlin has given the label of "particularizing parallelism." [102] It is a device much favored at the beginning of Akkadian and especially of Sumerian poems.

What this rapid survey of the evolution of the Akkadian Gilgamesh Epic suggests is that it involved such essentially rhetorical devices as self-introduction of the "speaker," invitation to the audience, hymnic apostrophe to the protagonist, partial repetition of the proemium to achieve a frame effect and closure, and mechanical addition of an extraneous addendum to arrive at a preferred length. The evolution of the composition thus proceeded, at least in part, by successive expansions at its borders. This is a process with possible analogues in the evolution of the biblical corpus, notably in the case of literary prophecy as proposed by David Noel Freedman.[103] I have similarly advanced the notion of "a central core of Deuteronomy which gradually grew by accretion at both ends in what can almost be described as concentric circles." [104] Of course it was not the only means of expansion. A comparison of Old Babylonian and neo-Assyrian recensions of Gilgamesh and other compositions shows expansion likewise in the interior—not always with an equally happy result from a modern esthetic point of view—[105] as well as juxtaposition of originally discrete compositions to form a greater whole.[106]

But we have not yet traced the evolution of the Gilgamesh Epic back to its earliest stages. In fact the unified epic was preceded by a series of discrete, episodic tales not, as yet, organized around the central theme of human mortality. Whether these discrete episodes were already unified in the earliest Akkadian recension remains a matter of debate, with Tigay favoring this view of matters[107] and Hope Nash Wolff questioning it.[108] What has hitherto been beyond dispute is that the earlier Sumerian episodic tales were *not* integrated. The new evidence from Me-Turan raises the possibility that they were beginning to be.[109] We have already encountered one-half of one of them pressed into service for Tablet XII of the Akkadian epic.[110] But with the exception of "Gilgamesh and Agga" and "The Death of Gilgamesh," [111] the others too were bequeathed to the Akkadian poet, not in the form of mechanical or slavish translations but creatively adapted to fashion an entirely new composition.

The technique of blending discrete compositions into a larger cycle did not necessarily involve adaptation of a Sumerian original in a new Akkadian context, nor did it begin with Gilgamesh—though it is easier to recognize it there. But let us return where we began, to the princess-poetess Enheduanna. She is said to be the author of, among other compositions,[112] at least three hymns to the goddess Inanna, each with its own theme. We have already encountered "The Exaltation of Inanna," which commemorates the earthly triumphs of her father Sargon over his enemies within Sumer and Akkad, and sublimates them into cosmic terms. The poem "Inanna and Ebih" does the same for Sargonic triumphs over enemies on the northeastern frontier as symbolized by Mount Ebih (Jebel Hamrin).[113] Finally, the poem "Stout-Hearted Lady" (*in-nin šà-gur₄-ra*) tells of the submission of the whole world to Sargonic hegemony as symbolized by its acknowledgement of Inanna's supremacy in every field of endeavor.[114] In this sequence, we move from Sumer and Akkad to the frontier and thence to the whole world. If we reverse the sequence, we can see the action coming ever closer to home, in a manner worthy of an Amos.[115] And it is precisely this reverse order in which all three compositions are listed together at the beginning of a literary catalogue of Old Babylonian date.[116]

If, then, the three great hymns by Enheduanna in honor of Inanna are taken as forming an integrated cycle, then they constitute a thematic counterpart to her other principal work: the cycle of short hymns to all the temples of Sumer and Akkad.[117] For while the former may be said to celebrate the theme of "the king at war," the latter reflects "the king at peace," solicitously caring for the temples of all the country in a major attempt to satisfy the traditional requirements of Sumerian religion.[118] It achieves in exalted poetry what "the Standard of Ur," found by Sir Leonard Woolley in the Royal Cemetery, had achieved in pictorial terms some three centuries earlier. This precious object, variously interpreted as a wooden box,[119] a desk or lectern[120] or, most recently, as the sound-box of a harp, has four inlaid panels, of which the two largest show the king at war and at peace respectively, presiding over battle on one side and over libations on the other.[121] It thus shows the king at war and in peace or, to put it another way, the ruler as king (*lugal*) and high-priest (*en*), his two principal roles,[122] and one could claim for the beginning of the Mesopotamian record, as Irene Winter has said of the end, that royal rhetoric embraced art as well as literature.

In conclusion, it must seem somewhat audacious to defend the notion of "the birth of rhetoric in Mesopotamia," given that the more conventional view looks for the origins of rhetoric in classical Greece.[123] And indeed, I admit that this notion, or at least this title, was Professor Gitay's, not mine.[124] But I *am* prepared to defend it, along with the related notion that the idea of *humanitas* goes back to Sumerian precedent. It has been said that "the humanities were born in a rhetorical manger. The first recorded use of the word *humanitas* is in the *Rhetorica ad Herrenium,* a text roughly contemporaneous with Cicero."[125] But Latin *humanitas* may fairly be described as a kind of calque or loan translation of Sumerian *nam-lú-ulu₆*, an abstract noun formed from the Sumerian word for "man, human being" (*lú*), perhaps via its Akkadian loan translation *amelūtu.* Like the Latin abstract, the Mesopotamian terms have a double meaning, referring both to "humanity" in the sense of humankind in the aggregate, and to "humanity, humanism," in the sense of that special quality of breeding and deportment that distinguishes the educated person from the masses.[126] A single quotation among many may serve to illustrate. A dialogue[127] in which a father berates his perverse son for nearly all of its 180-odd lines, includes this couplet: "Because you do not look to your humanity, my heart was carried off as if by an evil wind / You are unable to make (your) words pay any attention to your humanity."[128] The first recorded use of the Sumerian term antedates Cicero by two millennia, but shares one of his firm convictions: linguistic ability was at the heart of the scribal curriculum of Hammurapi's Babylonia, as much as it was to be the essence of the Roman rhetorician's *facilitas.*

I cannot resist ending with a saying from the Jerusalem Talmud cited by Richard Steiner in a study of colloquial Hebrew.[129] In Megilla 71b we read that "Greek is good for singing, Latin for warfare, Aramaic for lamentation, and Hebrew for (divine) speech."[130] Had the sages, like Daniel's friends, mastered the "literature and script of the Chaldaeans" (Dan. 1:4), they might well have added that Sumerian and Akkadian are good for rhetoric!

Notes

This is an updated version of the chapter by the same name in William W. Hallo, *Origins: the Ancient Near Eastern Background of Some Modern Western Institutions* (Studies in the History and Culture of the Ancient Near East 6) (Leiden/New York/ Köln: Brill, 1996), 169-187. For details of documentation, the reader is referred to this book, cited hereinafter by short title (*Origins*), page and footnote number. (The original version of this paper was presented to the First African Symposium on Rhetoric: Persuasion and Power, Cape Town, July 12, 1994, Yehoshua Gitay presiding.)

1. Dozeman and Fiore 1992. Add especially Jackson and Kessler 1974.

2. Gitay 1981; 1991.

3. Michael V. Fox, "Ancient Egyptian Rhetoric," *Rhetorica* 1 (1983), 9–22; John

Baines, "Feuds or Vengeance: Rhetoric and Social Forms." Pp. 11–20 in *Studies Wente* (below, p. 236) (1999).

4. *Origins* 169–170.

5. Ibid. 144–148.

6. Ibid. 262–270.

7. Pearce 1993.

8. Barbara N. Porter, "Language, Audience and Impact in Imperial Assyria," in S. Izre'el and R. Drory, eds., *Language and Culture in the Near East* (Israel Oriental Studies 15) (Leiden: Brill, 1995), 51–72.

9. For this patronymic in the inscriptions see previously David Diringer, "Three Early Hebrew Seals," *Archiv Orientální* 18/3 (1950), 66–67; Emil G. Kraeling, *The Brooklyn Museum Papyri* (New Haven: Yale University Press, 1953), No. 13:6.

10. *Origins* 146–147, n. 12 and 268; J. H. Tigay in *COS* 2 (2000) 197–198.

11. Above, n. 2.

12. Cf. above, n. 1.

13. Watson and Hauser 1993.

14. Greenstein 1996.

15. Greenstein 1981; 1982.

16. Berlin 1986; 1994.

17. Sternberg 1983; 1985.

18. Savage 1980.

19. Rabinowitz 1993.

20. Hallo and van Dijk 1968. Latest translation by Hallo in *COS* 1 (1997), 518–522. Latest edition by Annette Zgoll, *Der Rechtsfall der En-hedu-Ana im Lied nin-me-šara* (AOAT 246) (Münster: Ugarit-Verlag, 1997).

21. Hallo and van Dijk 1968, ch. 1. See in detail *Origins* 263–266.

22. Hallo and van Dijk 1968, 35.

23. Ibid., 45.

24. Ibid., 53.

25. *Origins* 172, n. 145.

26. Jacobsen 1987: 113.

27. Moran 1993: 117; cf. below, at note 39.

28. *Origins*, n. 148.

29. Stanley Gevirtz, "On Canaanite Rhetoric: the Evidence of the Amarna Letters from Tyre," *Orientalia* 42 (1973), 162–177. For some of these models, cf. Moshe Held, "Rhetorical Questions in Ugaritic and Biblical Hebrew," *Eretz-Israel* 9 (1969), 71–79.

30. Berlin 1978.

31. See below at notes 39–44 and 129.

32. Falkowitz 1982.

33. Piotr Michalowski, "Negation as Description: the Metaphor of Everyday Life in Early Mesopotamian Literature," *Aula Orientalis* 9 (1991), 134.

34. Winter 1981.

35. Jack M. Sasson, "The King and I: a Mari King in Changing Perceptions," *Journal of the American Oriental Society* 118 (1998), 458; For an example from the third millennium, cf. Benjamin R. Foster, "The Gutian Letter Again," *N.A.B.U.* 1990:31, No. 46.

36. Hess 1990.

37. Richard Hess, "Smitten Ant Bites Back: Rhetorical Forms in the Amarna Correspondence from Shechem," in J. C. de Moor and W. G. E. Watson, eds., *Verse in Ancient Near Eastern Prose* (AOAT 42, 1993) 95–111; idem, "Rhetorical Forms in the Amarna Correspondence from Jerusalem," *Maarav* 10(2003), 221–244.

38. A. K. Grayson, "Assyrian Rule of Conquered Territory in Ancient Western Asia," *CANE* 2 (1995), 961; for the parallel see already H. W. F. Saggs, *Iraq* 17 (1955), 47; 18 (1956), 55; Hallo, "From Qarqar to Carchemish: Assyria and Israel in the Light of New Discoveries," *BASOR* 23 (1960), 59.

39. Moran 1993; cf. *Origins* 173, n. 155.

40. ANET 629.

41. Hallo 1979; cf. Ibid., n. 157.

42. Hallo 1985; cf. Ibid., n. 158.

43. Hallo, "The Slandered Bride," in R. D. Biggs and J. A. Brinkman, eds., *Studies Presented to A. Leo Oppenheim* (Chicago: Oriental Institute, 1964), 96–97. For *bī innam* as "a colloquialism" or "an idiomatic locution" see *CAD* A/1:377d and B 216f. respectively.

44. Below, n. 130.

45. Edzard 1990.

46. Pearce 1993.

47. Above, n. 8.

48. C. Wilcke, "Politik im Spiegel der Literatur, Literatur als Mittel der Politik im alteren Babylonien," in Kurt Raaflaub, ed., *Anfänge politischen Denkens in der Antike,* (Schriften des Historischen Kollegs, Kolloquien 24, 1993), 29–75; P. Machinist, "Assyrians on Assyria in the First Millennium B.C.," ibid., 77–104.

49. For the most recent defense of my taxonomy, see Hallo in *COS* 2 (2000), xxi–xxii.

50. Cf. above, nn. 29, 35–38.

51. See above, n. 8.

52. For details, see *Origins* 144–153, esp. p. 151.

53. Alster 1990; cf. *Origins* 175, n. 164.

54. Ibid., n. 165; Herman L. J. Vanstiphout "Disputations" and "School Dialogues," in *COS* 1 (1996), 575–593. Cf. below, n. 127.

55. Cf. e.g. Sjöberg 1971–72.

56. E.g. Vanstiphout 1991:24 and n. 4.

57. Hallo *apud* Alster 1990: 13.

58. See in detail Vanstiphout 1990, 1992; Brock 2001.

59. *Origins* 176, n. 170.

60. Job 42: 11; cf. van Dijk 1957. For later survivals of the genre, see G. J. Reinink and H. L. J. Vanstiphout, eds., 1991: *Dispute Poems and Dialogues in the Ancient and Mediaeval Near East* (OLA 42); S. Brock, "The Dispute Poem: from Sumerian to Syriac," *Journal of the Canadian Society for Syriac Studies* 1 (2001), 3–10

61. Vanstiphout 1991: 24, n. 5; previously H. L. J. Vanstiphout, "On the Sumerian Disputation Between the Hoe and the Plough," *Aula Orientalis* 2, (1984) 249–250.

62. Vanstiphout 1990: 280.

63. *Origins* 177, n. 174..

64. T. Kwasman, "A New Join to the Epic of Gilgameš Tablet I," *N.A.B.U.* 1998/3:89, No. 99.

65. A. R. George, "The Opening of the Epic of Gilgameš," *N.A.B.U.* 1998/3:90, No. 100.

66. Ibid.

67. Idem, *The Epic of Gilgamesh: A New Translation* (New York: Barnes and Noble, 1999), 1.

68. *CAD* N/1:111.

The Birth of Rhetoric 39

69. J. Tigay, *The Evolution of the Gilgamesh Epic* (Philadelphia: University of Pennsylvania Press, 1982), 141.

70. *Origins* 177, n. 175.

71. Ibid., n. 176.

72. Claus Wilcke, "Die Anfänge der akkadischen Epen," *ZA* 67 (1977), 153–216; cf. Wolfram von Soden, "Mottoverse zu Beginn babylonischer und antiker Epen, Mottosätze in der Bibel," *Ugarit-Forschungen* 14 (1982), 235–239.

73. *Origins* 178, n. 178.

74..Ibid, n. 179.

75. Ibid., n. 180.

76. Wilcke 1977: 175–9; most recent edition Hallo and Moran 1979; latest translations by Foster 1993: 469–485, 1995: 115–131.

77. Hallo 1963: 175–6.

78. Wilcke 1977: 163–175; latest translation by B. R. Foster in *COS* 1 (1997), 390–402.

79. Wilcke 1977: 160–163. Latest translation by Foster in *COS* 1 (1997), 450–453. For the incipit see B. Groneberg, *Archiv für Orientforschung* 26 (1978–79), 20 (with previous literature); M.-J. Seux, "Atra-hasis I,I,1," *RA* 75 (1981), 190–191; von Soden, "Mottoverse," 235–236.

80. Wilcke 1977: 159; latest translation by Stephanie Dalley in *COS* 1 (1997), 384–389.

81. Cf. above, n. 63.

82. *Origins* 179, n. 186, and above, notes 73–75.

83. *Origins* 179, n. 187; latest translation by Dalley in *COS* 1 (1997), 404–416.

84. *Origins* 179, n. 188; latest translation by Dalley in *COS* 1 (1997), 453–457.

85. *Origins* 179, n. 189; cf. above, note 22.

86. Ibid., n. 190. Cf. perhaps the 200 "lines" of Lamentations 1–3 according to the calculations of D. N. Freedman and J. C. Geoghegan, "Quantitative Measurement in Biblical Hebrew Poetry," in R. Chazan et al., eds. *Ki Baruch Hu: . . . Studies in Honor of Baruch A. Levine* (Winona Lake, IN: Eisenbrauns, 1999), 229–249, esp. pp. 232–233.

87. ANET 97.

88. *Origins*, n. 192.

89. Ibid., n. 193.

90. Ibid. 160.

91. Ibid. 179, n. 194.

92. Ibid., n. 195.

93. Ibid. 180, n. 196; see now Antoine Cavigneaux and Farouk al-Rawi, "La fin de Gilgameš, Enkidu et les enfers d'après les manuscrits d'Ur et de Meturan," *Iraq* 62 (2000), 1–19; Gianni Marchesi, "*í-a lùllum$_x$ ù-luh-ha sù-sù:* on the incipit of the Sumerian Poem Gilgameš and Huwawa B," in S. Graziani, ed., *Studi . . . dedicati alla memoria di Luigi Cagni* (Naples: Istituto Universitario Orientale, 2000), vol. 2:673–684.

94. Vulpe 1994. For dissenting opinions see Kilmer 1982 and Parpola 1993: 192–196.

95. *Origins* 180, n. 198.

96. Ibid., n. 199.

97. ANET 97.

98. *Origins,* n. 201; cf. R. J. Tournay, "Inscription d'Anam, roi d'Uruk et successeur de Gilgamesh," in H. Goedicke, ed., *Near Eastern Studies in Honor of William Foxwell Albright* (Baltimore/London: Johns Hopkins Press, 1971), 453–457.

99. *Origins* 180, n. 202.

100. Ibid., n. 203.

101. Ibid., n. 204; cf. also C. B. F. Walker, "The Second Tablet of *ṭupšenna pitema,*" *JCS 33* (1981), 191–195, esp. p. 194.

102. Above, note 30.

103. Freedman 1991, esp. pp. 57–55; 1984.

104. *Origins,* n. 207.

105. Ibid., n. 208.

106. Ibid., n. 209.

107. Ibid. 182, n. 210.

108. Wolff 1969.

109. Above, note 93.

110. *Origins* 182, n. 213.

111. Ibid., n. 214.

112. For the Enheduanna texts not further treated here, see *Origins* 263–266.

113. Ibid. 182, n. 216. Cf. now Pascal Attinger, "Inana et Ebih," *ZA* 88 (1998), 164–195.

114. *Origins* 182, n. 217.

115. Ibid. 183, n. 218.

116. Mark E. Cohen, "Literary Texts from the Andrews University Archaeological Museum," *RA* 70 (1976), 131–132, lines 1–3.

117. *Origins* 183, n. 220. For a different view see now J. A. Black, "En-hedu-ana not the composer of *The temple hymns*," *N.A.B.U.* 2002:2–4.

118. Hallo, "Sumerian Religion," in A.F. Rainey, ed., kinattūtū ša dārâti: *Raphael Kutscher Memorial Volume* (Tel Aviv: Tel Aviv Univ. Institute of Archaeology, 1993), 15–35, esp. 17.

119. *Origins* 183, n. 222.

120. Ibid., n. 223; cf. J.-C. Margueron, "L'Étendard d'Ur': récit historique ou magique?" in *Collectanea Orientalia. . . Études offertes en hommage à Agnes Spycket* (Neuchatel/Paris: Recherches et Publications, 1996) 159.

121. Ibid.

122. Donald P. Hansen, "Art of the Royal Tombs at Ur: A Brief Interpretation," in R. L. Zettler and L. Horne, eds., *Treasures from the Royal Tombs of Ur* (Philadelphia: University of Pennsylvania Museum of Art and Archaeology and Anthropology, 1998), 47.

123. See e.g. Thomas Cole, *The Origins of Rhetoric in Ancient Greece* (Baltimore/London: Johns Hopkins University Press, 1991); I. Worthington, ed., *Persuasion: Greek Rhetoric in Action* (London/New York: Routledge, 1993). On the possible Mesopotamian background of specifically *political* rhetoric, see above, n. 48.

124. See above, unnumbered note.

125. *Origins* 184, n. 226.

126. Van Dijk 1953; cf. Henri Limet, "'Peuple' et 'humanité' chez les Sumériens," G. van Driel et al., eds., zikir šumim: *Assyriological Studies Presented to F. R. Kraus . . .* (Leiden: Brill, 1982), 258–267.

127. For this genre see above, n. 54.

128. *Origins* 184, n. 228.

129. Steiner 1992.

130. *Origins,* n. 230.

Works Cited (either explicitly or by reference to *Origins*)

Alster, Bendt, 1990: "Sumerian Literary Dialogues and Debates and their Place in ancient Near Eastern Literature." In E. Keck et al., eds., *Living Waters: . . . Stud-*

ies Presented to Dr. Frede Løkkegaard (Copenhagen: Museum Tusculum), 1–16.

Berlin, Adele, 1978: "Shared rhetorical features in biblical and Sumerian literature." *Journal of the Ancient Near Eastern Society* 10:35–42.

———, 1986: "Narrative Poetics in the Bible." *Prooftexts* 6:273–284.

———, 1994: *Poetics and Interpretation of Biblical Narrative*. Reprint. (Winona Lake, IN: Eisenbrauns).

Brock, S., 2001: "The Dispute Poem: From Sumerian to Syriac." *Journal of the Canadian Society for Syriac Studies* 1, 3–10.

Cole, Thomas, 1991: *The Origins of Rhetoric in Ancient Greece* (Baltimore/London: Johns Hopkins University Press).

Dozeman, Thomas B. and Benjamin Fiore, 1992: "Rhetorical Criticism," *Anchor Bible Dictionary* (New York etc.: Doubleday) 5:712–719.

Edzard, Dietz O., 1990: "Selbstgespräch und Monolog in der akkadischen Literatur." In T. Abusch et al., eds., *Lingering Over Words: Studies . . . in Honor of William L. Moran* (Cambridge: Harvard Semitic Studies 37), 149–162.

Falkowitz, Robert S., 1982: *The Sumerian Rhetoric Collections* (Ann Arbor, MI: University Microfilms).

Foster, Benjamin R., 1993: *Before the Muses: An Anthology of Akkadian Literature* (2 vols.). (Bethesda, MD: CDL Press).

———, 1995: *From Distant Days: Myths, Tales, and Poetry of Ancient Mesopotamia* (Bethesda, MD: CDL Press).

Fox, Michael V., 1983: "Ancient Egyptian Rhetoric." *Rhetorica* 1:9–22.

Freedman, David N., 1991: *The Unity of the Hebrew Bible* (Ann Arbor: University of Michigan).

———, 1994: "The Undiscovered Symmetry of the Bible." *Bible Review* 10/1 (February) 34–41, 63.

———, and Jeffrey C. Geoghegan, 1999: "Quantitative Measurement in Biblical Hebrew Poetry." In R. Chazan et al., eds., *Ki Baruch Hu: . . . Studies in Honor of Baruch A. Levine* (Winona Lake, IN: Eisenbrauns), 229–249.

George, Andrew, 1999: *The Epic of Gilgamesh: A New Translation* (New York: Barnes and Noble).

Gevirtz, Stanley, 1973: "On Canaanite Rhetoric: The Evidence of the Amarna Letters from Tyre." *Orientalia* 42:162–177.

Gitay, Yehoshua, 1981: *Prophecy and Persuasion: A Study of Isaiah 40–48* (Forum Theologiae Linguisticae 14) (Bonn: Linguistica Biblica).

_____, 1991: *Isaiah and his Audience: The Structure and Meaning of Isaiah 1–12.* (Studia Semitica Neerlandica 30) (Assen/Maastricht: van Gorcum).

Greenstein, Edward L., 1981: "Biblical Narratology." *Prooftexts* 1:201–216.

_____, 1982: "An Equivocal Reading of the Sale of Joseph." In Kenneth R. R. Gros Louis, ed., *Literary Interpretations of Biblical Narratives,* vol. 2 (Nashville, TN: Abingdon), 114–125 and 306–310.

_____, 1996: "A Forensic Understanding of the Speech from the Whirlwind." In M. V. Fox et al., eds., *Texts, Temples, and Traditions: A Tribute to Menahem Haran* (Winona Lake, IN: Eisenbrauns), 241–258.

Hallo, William W., 1963: "On the Antiquity of Sumerian Literature," *Journal of the American Oriental Society* 83:167–176.

_____, 1979: "Notes from the Babylonian Collection, I. Nungal in the Egal: An Introduction to Colloquial Sumerian?" *Journal of Cuneiform Studies* 31:161–165.

_____, 1985: Back to the Big House: Colloquial Sumerian, Continued." *Orientalia* 54:56–64.

_____, 1996: *Origins: The Ancient Near Eastern Background of Some Modern Western Institutions* (Studies in the History and Culture of the Ancient Near East 6) (Leiden/New York/ Koln: Brill).

_____, and J. J. A. van Dijk, 1968: *The Exaltation of Inanna* (Yale Near Eastern Researches 3) (Repr. New York: AMS Press, 1982).

_____, and W. L. Moran, 1979: "The First Tablet of the SB Recension of the Anzu-myth." *JCS* 31:65–115.

Held, Moshe, 1969: "Rhetorical Questions in Ugaritic and Biblical Hebrew." *Eretz-Israel* 9:71–79.

Hess, Richard, 1990: "Rhetorical Forms in EA 162." *Ugarit-Forschungen* 22:137–148.

_____, 2003: "Rhetorical forms in the Amarna correspondence from Jerusalem." *Maarav* 10:221–244.

_____, 1993: "Smitten Ant Bites Back: Rhetorical Forms in the Amarna Correspondence from Shechem." In J. C. de Moor and W. G. E. Watson, eds., *Verse in Ancient Near Eastern Prose (ATOT 42),* 95–111.

_____, 1998: *"The Mayarzana Correspondence: Rhetoric and Conquest Accounts."* Ugarit-Forschungen 30:333–351.

Hunger, Hermann, *Babylonische und assyrische Kolophone.* (AOAT 2).

Jackson, Jared J., and Martin Kessler, eds., 1974: *Rhetorical Criticism: Essays in Honor of James Muilenburg* (Pittsburgh: Pickwick Press).

Jacobsen, Thorkild, 1987: *The Harps That Once . . .: Sumerian Poetry in Translation* (New Haven/London: Yale University Press).

Kilmer, Anne D., 1982: "A Note on an Overlooked Word-play in the Akkadian Gilgamesh." In G. van Driel et al., eds., Zikir Šumim: *Assyriological Studies Presented to F. R. Kraus . . .* (Leiden: Brill), 128–132.

Kramer, Samuel Noah, 1957: "A Father and His Perverse Son," *National Probation and Parole Association Journal* 3:169–173.

Krstovic, J., et al., eds. 1989: *Classical and Medieval Literature Criticism* 2 (Detroit: Gale Research).

Limet, Henri, 1982: "'Peuple' et 'humanité' chez les Sumériens," G. van Driel et al., eds., Zikir Šumim: *Assyriological Studies Presented to F. R. Kraus . . .* (Leiden: Brill), 258–267.

Machinist, Peter, 1993: "Assyrians on Assyria in the First Millennium B.C." In Raaflaub 1993:77–104.

Michalowski, Piotr, 1991: "Negation as Description: The Metaphor of Everyday Life in Early Mesopotamian Literature." *Aula Orientalis* 9:131–136.

Moran, William L., 1993: "UET 6, 402: Persuasion in the Plain Style." *Journal of the Ancient Near Eastern Society* 22:113–120.

Murphy, James J., ed., 1982: *The Rhetorical Tradition and Modern Writing.* (New York, Modern Language Association).

Parpola, Simo, 1993: "The Assyrian Tree of Life." *JNES* 52:161–208.

Pearce, Laurie E., 1993: "Statements of Purpose: Why the Scribes Wrote." In M. E. Cohen et al., eds., *The Tablet and the Scroll: Near Eastern Studies in Honor of William W. Hallo.* (Bethesda, MD: CDL Press), 185–193.

Porter, Barbara N., 1995: "Language, Audience and Impact in Imperial Assyria." In S. Izre'el and R. Drory, eds., *Language and Culture in the Near East.* (Israel Oriental Studies 15) (Leiden: Brill), 51–72.

Raaflaub, Kurt, ed., 1993: *Anfänge politischen Denkens in der Antike.* (Schriften des Historischen Kollegs, Kolloquien 24).

Rabinowitz, Isaac, 1993: *A Witness Forever: Ancient Israel's Perception of Literature and the Resultant Hebrew Bible.* (Bethesda, MD: CDL Press).

Reinink, G. J. and H. L. J. Vanstiphout, eds., 1991: *Dispute Poems and Dialogues in the Ancient and Mediaeval Near East.* (OLA 42).

Sasson, Jack M., 1998: "The King and I: A Mari King in Changing Perceptions." *JAOS* 118:453–470.

Savage, Mary, 1980: "Literary Criticism and Biblical Studies: A Rhetorical Analysis of the Joseph Narrative." In C. D. Evans et al., eds., *Scripture in Context.* (Pittsburgh: Pickwick Press), 79–100.

Sjöberg, Åke, 1971–72: "'He is a Good Seed of a Dog' and 'Engardu, the Fool.'" *JCS* 24:107–119.

———, 1973: "Der Vater und sein missratener Sohn," *JCS* 25:105–169.

Steiner, Richard C., 1992: "A Colloquialism in Jer. 5:13 from the Ancestor of Mishnaic Hebrew." *Journal of Semitic Studies* 37:11–26.

Sternberg, Meir, 1983: "The Bible's Art of Persuasion: Ideology, Rhetoric, and Poetics in Saul's Fall." *Hebrew Union College Annual* 54:45–82.

———, 1985: *The Poetics of Biblical Narrative: Ideological Literature and the Drama of Reading.* (Bloomington: Indiana University Press).

Van Dijk, J. J. A., 1953: *La Sagesse Suméro-Akkadienne.* (Leiden: Brill).

———, 1957: "La découverte de la culture littéraire sumérienne et sa signification pour l'histoire de l'antiquité orientale." *L'Ancien Testament et l'Orient.* (Orientalia et Biblica Lovaniensia, 1) 5–28.

Vanstiphout, Herman L. J., 1984: "On the Sumerian Disputation between the Hoe and the Plough." *Aula Orientalis* 2:239–251.

———, 1990, 1992: "The Mesopotamian Debate Poems." *Acta Sumerologica (Japan)* 12:271–318; 14:339–367.

———, 1991: "Lore, Learning and Levity in the Sumerian Disputations: A Matter of Form, or Substance?" In Reinink and Vanstiphout 1991:23–46.

———, 1996: "'Disputations' and 'School Dialogues.'" *COS* 1:575–593.

Von Soden, Wolfram, 1982: "Mottoverse zu Beginn babylonischer und antiker Epen, Mottosätze in der Bibel." Ugarit-Forschungen 14:235–239.

Vulpe, Nicola, 1994: "Irony and unity of the *Gilgamesh Epic.*" *JNES* 53:275–283.

Walker, C. B. F., 1981: "The Second Tablet of *Ṭupšenna pitema.*" *JCS* 33:191–195.

Wasserman, Nathan, 2000: "Sweeter than Honey and Wine . . .: Semantic Domains and Old Babylonian Imagery." *RAI* 44/3: 191–196.

———, 2003: *Style and Form in Old Babylonian Literary Texts.* (Leiden/Boston: Brill/Styx).

Watson, Duane J. and Alan J. Hauser, 1993: *Rhetorical Criticism of the Bible: A Comprehensive Bibliography with Notes on History and Method.* (Biblical Interpretation Series 4) (Leiden: Brill).

Wilcke, Claus, 1977: "Die Anfänge der akkadischen Epen." *ZA* 67:153–216.

———, 1993: "Politik im Spiegel der Literatur, Literatur als Mittel der Politik im älteren Babylonien." In Raaflaub 1993:29–75.

Winter, Irene, 1981: "Royal Rhetoric and the Development of Historical Narrative in Neo-Assyrian Reliefs." *Studies in Visual Communication* 7:2–38.

Wolff, Hope Nash, 1969: "Gilgamesh, Enkidu and the Heroic Life." *JAOS* 89:392–398.

Zgoll, Annette, 1997: *Der Rechtsfall de En-hedu-Ana im Lied nin-me-šara. (AOAT 246)* (Münster: *Ugarit-Verlag).*

Abbreviations

BASOR = Bulletin of the American Schools of Oriental Research

CAD = The Assyrian Dictionary of the Oriental Institute of the University of Chicago

CANE = J. M. Sasson, ed., *Civilizations of the Ancient Near East* (4 vols.) (New York: Scribner's 1995).

COS 1 = W. W. Hallo and K. L. Younger, Jr., eds., 1996: *The Context of Scripture I: Canonical Compositions from the Biblical World* (Leiden/New York/Koln: Brill).

COS 2 = W. W. Hallo and K. L. Younger, Jr., eds., 2000: *The Context of Scripture II: Monumental Inscriptions from the Biblical World* (Leiden/New York/Koln: Brill).

JAOS = Journal of the American Oriental Society

JCS = Journal of Cuneiform Studies

JNES = Journal of Near Eastern Studies

N.A.B.U. = Nouvelles Assyriologiques Brèves et Utilitaires

OLA = Orientalia Lovaniensisa Analecta

RA = Revue d'Assyriologie et d'Archéologie Orientale

RAI 44 = L. Milano et al., eds., *Landscapes . . . Papers Presented to the XLIV Rencontre Assyriologie Internationale* (Padua: Sargon srl, 2000)

ZA = Zeitschrift für Assyriologie

The Rhetoric of Origins and the Other:
Reading the Ancient Figure of Enheduanna

Roberta Binkley

Working with the rhetoric of cultures outside the traditional rhetorical canon, particularly cultures more ancient than the Greeks, while it increases the complexity of research, it also illuminates the particular embeddedness that shapes and formulates the eurocentric tradition of rhetoric, particularly the "politics and poetics of representation" (Hallam, 2). Crossing disciplinary boundaries, I find that embedded within the methodologies of my own area of rhetoric are often unstated, and frequently unconscious, theoretical assumptions. Among these governing assumptions is the conception of the nature of origins, one which focuses on the origination of rhetoric in the Greek classical period of the late 5th and 4th centuries B.C.E. Embedded in this conceptualization of rhetoric as beginning with the Athenian Greeks are particular discursive conceptualizations of the Other—the Other of another period, place, culture, gender, and spiritual tradition. An example that illuminates how these assumptions operate is the ancient Mesopotamian figure of Enheduanna, a priestess, a princess, poet, and certainly a consummate rhetorician writing near the beginning of literacy ca. 2300 B.C.E.

As the first named historical author, Enheduanna exhibits a strong self-consciousness when she speaks of herself and rhetorically reflects on her process of invention in *The Exaltation of Inanna*. Writing in an alien ancient (pre-Greek) oriental culture, she stands at the beginning of written tradition, a notable exception to the early western canonical tradition in which women are virtually nonexistent. Certainly, her work, her documented existence, and her ethos problematize rhetorical assumptions of origins and the Other in rhetorical historiography and in Assyriology (a general term for the discipline that studies ancient Mesopotamia).

I begin with a sketch of the Mesopotamian context of Enheduanna; I then focus on a section of her best-known work, *The Exaltation of Inanna.* While I use the traditional conceptual terminology of Aristotelian rhetoric, I define rhetoric as inscribing the relationship of power and language (Glenn, 1-2). This study is informed by anthropological reflexive studies (Clifford; Hallam, and Street) and in general by postcolonial and postmodern theorists such as Bernal, Cassin, Said, and Van der Mieroop, who have raised important questions of cannon and representation. It is also influenced by rhetorical theorists who have engaged with the question of the representation of the Other, such as Glenn and Swearingen, as well as the femininist and postmodern Assyriologists Asher-Greve and Bahrani. This text, then, moves on to briefly discuss origins, the stories we tell ourselves about our beginnings; how these stories are reflected in scholarship that represents the Other within the disciplines of canonical rhetorical historiography and Assyriology. I focus particularly on the origin assumptions, as they represent the Other in three areas: the geographic Other, the gendered Other, and the sacred Other. Finally, I sum up how these factors influence my own theoretical approaches, as I attempt to locate and to read Enheduanna within the disciplines of Assyriology and canonical rhetorical historiography.

Enheduanna and Her Rhetorical Context

Mesopotamia, a definition of convenience for an ancient historical area includes present-day Iraq and northeastern Syria and some additional bordering areas, and is in the general geographic area defined by the term, Middle East. Cuneiform script, writing characterized by the use of a stylus and cross-hatching on clay, developed early in this area and came to be used for the next three thousand years as the script for a number of languages. Its utility and flexibility as well as its durability—much of the writing was done on small clay pillows allowed to harden in the sun or fired—created an enormous number of artifacts. Unlike the papyrus and vellum of the Egyptians and the Greeks, clay tablets are much more permanent. The huge number of extant artifacts means that much remains to be translated. Because of this abundance of material, scholars in Assyriology will continue to catalog and translate much of this material for the next several generations.

Among the artifacts discovered, and comparatively recently translated, are the works of the earliest known writer, Enheduanna. She lived and wrote, around 2300 B.C.E., almost two thousand years before the "golden age" of Greece. The corpus of her work so far discovered includes at least two and possibly three major works, hymns, composed to be sung.[1]. They are directed to the goddess Inanna as major theistic works. She also composed and edited a collection of shorter hymns to a number of Sumerian temples and their deities, several of these hymns were added by later scribes.

The extensive existence of scribal schools (the *eduba*) throughout the history of the ancient world insures that any important work will have numerous copies. For example, Hallo and van Dijk used fifty exemplars to translate *The Exaltation of Inanna* by Enheduanna in 1968. Recently German scholar Annette Zgoll completed a new translation and discussion of the text in which she mentioned that since the translation of Hallo and van Dijk in 1968, the text base has "increased by 49 pieces . . . two of which have been joined together" (29). In addition Zgoll mentions that C. Wilcke has identified ten further text documents from newly publicized texts at Istanbul (30). All of the artifacts upon which translations of Enheduanna's work are based come from the Old Babylonian period nearly a half-millennium after her existence.

Enheduanna's works are rhetorically complex sophisticated compositions, and they challenge the traditional canon of rhetoric and thereby many of the origins stories and foundational assumptions of the humanities. Yet she is barely known outside of the discipline of Assyriology. Within the discipline of Assyriology she has either largely been ignored or treated as a footnote. There are many reasons for this. There are problems with this particular text. According to German scholar Annette Zgoll,[2] it is among the most difficult texts handed down in the literature of the Sumerian language (30). Other problems I treat here in general terms of some of the disciplinary methodological assumptions that operate in Assyriology, methodological assumptions that also appear to be operative in rhetorical historiography.

In *The Exaltation of Inanna, Enheduanna* begins the 153-line hymn with carefully arranged epithets and descriptions of the goddess Inanna to illustrate the characteristics of the goddess that become part of the unfolding story carefully building to the declaration that Inanna is supreme among the gods. As she continues the hymn, she interweaves cultural references to the myths of the goddess, gradually bringing her closer. Then she steps forward in first person to tell her own interweaving story of a political rebellion, and her banishment. As a result of this rebellion, she is driven from the temple and exiled to the steppes. She calls on the moon god whom she directly serves as high priestess and also the other gods to restore her to her position. Only the goddess Inanna heeds her plea. Near the conclusion of the hymn, with the rebellion apparently quashed, she sings of her restoration as high priestess and praises the goddess Inanna. In this powerful narrative are the strong elements of emotional appeal (*pathos*). She clearly establishes her own *ethos* by stepping forward in the first person to tell her own story, naming herself. The argument, the underlying the *logos* of the narrative, has variously been interpreted as political (Hallo) and as a court case (Zgoll).

Moving narratively from the third to first person, Enheduanna also tells of her personal creative process. There is a strong authorial presence, one that helps us to understand the ancient continuum of female authorship that C. Jan Swearingen traces in this volume in her article "Song to Speech." Enheduanna is self-consciously present in the process of writing and in the poem/hymn. I read her description of her creative process as a very purposeful receiving. The collaborative "I" of the creatrixes, Enheduanna and Inanna, merge. Enheduanna explains that she heaps the coals in the censer and prepares the lustration to receive her greater self, her transcendent self, the goddess. For a time in the middle of the night, they seem to become one, perhaps in the ancient sense of the relationship with the muses, and out of that union comes the song that will be performed before the audience at noon.

Her process of invention is further complicated by the mention of the nuptial chamber, alluding to the sacred marriage service that was a cultic ceremony about which little is known and much has been speculated. As Cooper says, it offers a "titillating scenario." Enheduanna likely participated in some such service as high priestess. Some scholars believe that it was sexual.[3] However, it appears to have a cosmic dimension in that the writer, as Enheduanna describes herself, communes (receives) the sacred energies of the goddess or god. Thus, the sacred marriage was really between the individual and the sacred. Steinkeller, reviewing the evidence for the sacred ceremony, quotes with approval Copper's assessment that it was "a way for the king and through him the people, to establish personal social ties with the gods." (135). Certainly, in this case, the high priestess, Enheduanna, seems to imply her own personal ties to the goddess, as she talks about her invention process.

136	One has heaped up the coals (In the censer),	prepared the lustration
137	The nuptial chamber awaits you.	Let your heart be appeased!
138	With "It is enough for me, it Is too much for me! I have given birth	oh exalted lady, (to this song) for you.
139	That which I recited to you	at (mid)night
140	May the singer repeat it to you	at noon!

She seems to be describing a process of invention characterized as the "Mystical Enthymeme." As Ryan J. Stark describes it, the mystical enthymeme requires participation from the Audience/Cosmos to work.[4] Authorship becomes a tri-part communion among the writer, the audience, and Cosmos (in this case Inanna as representative of the cosmos). Thus, as Sappho, Plato, and other ancient authors invoked the muse(s), so too Enheduanna invokes the muse in the form of the goddess Inanna calling her, if not to participate in her invention process, at least to witness the birth of the song.

This ancient passage in particular raises questions of origins and the Other. These questions seem to me to go to the heart of the theoretical stances and approaches of traditional rhetorical historiography and to a certain extent the approaches of Assyriology. Certainly, if one searches for origins, her existence and work seem to be a logical place to begin.

Origins in Assyriology and Rhetoric

Origins are also those narratives that constitute the foundations of a discipline, helping to determine the theoretical approaches and stances. They are often based on assumptions that operate in unconscious ways. For example, within the discipline of rhetoric, there exists the prevailing assumption that rhetoric was refined by the Greeks and that its definition by Plato and Aristotle constitute the locus of its origins. In Assyriology, the narratives around origins become problematized by the beginning of the discipline itself in the nineteenth century with its early scholarly roots embedded in nationalism and colonialism.[5] How these theoretical influences operate, in terms of the available material, seems to favor particular approaches and the interpretive emphases, or lack thereof, as exhibited by the way the ancient figure of Enheduanna is represented within the prevailing scholarly standards.

Assyriology and the Mesopotamian Record

The rhetoric of Assyriological scholarship in the main has tended to treat Enheduanna as an individual historical figure in terms of the 19th century Enlightenment's singular self. In this vein some scholars (Alster, Black, and Civil) have questioned her existence.[6] However, her existence and authorship appear to be generally accepted within the discipline, where she is viewed as a specific historical figure, notable as the daughter of Sargon of Akkad, the creator of the first-known empire. The methodological approach within the discipline of Assyriology is generally characterized as predominantly that of philology. Internal challenges within the discipline illuminate some of the problems with this dominant approach. William Hallo, who made the first English translation of *The Exaltation of Inanna* in 1969 and whose chapter on Mesopotamian rhetoric is included in this volume, points out that cuneiform texts "provide the most abundant archival documentation before the European Middle Ages" ("Scepticism," 192). Nevertheless, he goes on to note that the view among many of his colleagues is that the textual record is not complete enough to reconstruct Near Eastern history. Yet, he argues, "we should not expect to know more than the ancient sources knew, but we can hope to know more than they chose to *tell* (emphasis in original, 189).

Recently scholars Marc Van De Mieroop and Zainab Bahrani have argued from a postmodern position, an uncommon approach in Assyriology. Van De Mieroop in his book, *Cuneiform Texts and the Writing of History*, begins with the statement that "the discipline is exceedingly empirical in its approach" (3). In his introduction he notes that although the book may sound critical at times, "it is because the discipline seems often stuck in a nineteenth-century approach that does not properly credit, in my opinion, what Mesopotamia has to offer us" (3). He notes the paradox of the approaches to Mesopotamian history, both within the discipline and without, in which it is seen as the "birth of the West" on one hand and on the other, that "Mesopotamia is the East, the hostile Other as seen by the two cultures that form the cornerstones of the Western tradition: ancient Greece and Judah" (165).

Zainab Bahrani extends this critique in her recent book, *Women of Babylon: Gender and Representation in Mesopotamia*, calling for a "theoretically informed scholarship," which she says is "long overdue in this field" (12–13). She explains that "[a]ny study of the Near Eastern past is hampered at the start by a number of preconceptions that have long since become embedded into the discourse as scientific or empirical facts" (12). Some of these preconceptions center around the conception of gender and the roles of women.[7] "In near Eastern studies, there has been a general reluctance to engage in anything beyond cataloguing references to, or representations of women" (5). And that much of the existing scholarship has been based on "simplistic binaries of male power/female subordination" (6). There has been very little feminist influence on the scholarship of Assyriology.

This philological approach with its nineteenth-century roots influences how subjectivity and agency are conceptualized and the Other defined. For example, the primary controversy around Enheduanna appears to be whether or not she existed as an actual person. Thus the implications of her context, her work, herself, and her rhetorical context have not been explored to any great extent. Except for William Hallo, those who have dealt with her work in any depth are quite naturally women scholars, Joan Goodnick Westenholz and Annette Zgoll. Yet interestingly, outside of Assyriological scholarship, Enheduanna has attracted a popular following.[8] However, within the context of Assyriological historiography she remains viewed as a voice whose influence and themes, while part of the Sumerian-Mesopotamian tradition, remain a curious, isolated artifact.

Rhetoric and the Mesopotamian Record

Although Assyriologists have written about Mesopotamian rhetoric, and William Hallo lists many of the articles in this volume, among rhetoricians the topic of Mesopotamia is virtually ignored. Two articles published in the

'70s by speech communication faculty (Wills and Evans) examine the public speaking arenas of ancient Mesopotamian assemblies from the viewpoint of their similarity to Greek and Roman assemblies populated by male representatives. The underlying assumptions of these articles appears to be based in the eurocentric rhetorical tradition that women did not participate in power (no agency) and had no voice (no subjectivity).

Thus far the only rhetorician who has treated Mesopotamian rhetoric as whole is George Kennedy in his book, *Comparative Rhetoric,* where he gives a brief overview of Mesopotamian rhetoric in Chapter 6, "Literacy and Rhetoric in the Ancient Near East." There Kennedy summarizes features of Mesopotamian writing, such as the limited use of simile in a poetry characterized as highly metaphorical; he speaks of public address and assemblies, and then discusses at some length the rhetoric in *The Epic of Gilgamesh* before turning to the Egyptian Amarna letters. Again, the governing assumption

Limestone disk of Enheduanna, from Ur, diameter 26 cm. Courtesy of the the University of Pennsylvania Museum, Philadelphia (neg. #139330).

seems to be that women, although present in *The Epic of Gilgamesh,* had limited agency. He does not mention, nor seem aware of, the previous existence of Enheduanna. However, a scholarly review of Mesopotamian literature and the scholarship around it would not have led him to her figure. Nor has the figure of Enheduanna been treated extensively beyond occasional mention in the scholarship of rhetoric. A few scholars, such as Andrea Lunsford, Jackie Jones Royster, and Jan Swearingen, have added her to their graduate course reading lists. Yet the fact remains that neither Mesopotamia nor Enheduanna have anything to do with the formation of rhetoric nor any relevance to the origins of rhetoric.

Rhetoric's Origins and the Other

Evolutionary models of the western tradition beginning with the Greeks often act as methodological subtext to historical discussions of rhetoric. While the scholarly community is well aware that the Greeks did not suddenly create a high culture, but were influenced by early Near Eastern civilizations in a myriad of ways, the work in rhetorical historiography appears frequently to be little informed by this realization. Thus, figures, civilizations, texts prior to the classical age of Athens become "prerhetorical" or "protorhetorical." The Other in this binary (rhetoric/protorhetoric) assumes the opposition term as in West/East. As such, the Other, particularly the geographic other, becomes intellectually suspect.

The Geographic Other

Mesopotamia, in the general geographic area defined by the term Middle-East, forms part of the synecdoche of the Orient, the hostile Other (a perception given additional problematic dimensions since the events of September 11, 2001). It is this same area that Van de Mieroop notes, was: "The otherness of the east in antiquity, which provided the Greeks with a means of self-identification" (166). So too, as Edward Said and Martin Bernal have asserted, the East continues to provide the contrasting oriental and racial otherness. Thus the name and the texts attributed to Enheduanna, her position and voice at the beginning of literacy are not only intellectually suspect because of a three-thousand year priority, but also as part of a geographic hostile Other. Yet, it becomes increasingly clear that the civilizations of the ancient world were deeply interconnected, and that much of the Greek literary and intellectual tradition grew out of and were influenced by the larger near eastern world, particularly Egypt and Mesopotamia.

From as early as the third millennium, Mesopotamian kings occasionally campaigned as far as the western sea, boasting of washing their weapons in the Mediterranean. Enheduanna's father, Sargon of Akkad, governed an empire that briefly stretched from the eastern Mediterranean to the Gulf. At the beginning of the second millennium there were Assyrian trading colonies in Anatolia that spread the influence of Mespotomian culture. Recent studies by M. L. West in *The East Face of Helicon* and Walter Burkert in *The Orientalizing Revolution* further document this transmission and the interconnectedness among these ancient civilizations. Akkadian was the *lingua franca* over much of the ancient world in the second millennium based on the remarkably durable written tradition of cuneiform with a continuous schooling tradition traced back to the third millennium. Within the language tradition of Akkadian, great prestige was accorded to written documents in Mesopotamia with traditions in poetry and literature extending back before 2500 B.C.E. This linguistic tradition was not exclusively limited to the work of men, as Hoskisson and Boswell note in this volume. Thus, working with the texts of Enheduanna presents the additional problem of the gendered Other, since she writes as a priestess and to a goddess.

The Gendered Other in Text and Image

Historic Platonic conceptions of identity have become integral to our conceptions of the gendered body and its materiality. Zainab Bahrani explains that we apply Platonic notions of mimesis to the visual objects of Mesopotamian culture, notions that involve assumptions "regarding identity, the body, and difference." (118). The images of eastern women have been presented paradoxically in recent history as well as ancient history. Current images from the recent war in Afghanistan illustrate this paradox. Images of women saturate popular conceptions of "oriental women," women covered in clothing, wearing scarves, their faces obscured by the burka. These images of swathed bodies of the East are in contradistinction to the largely uncovered western female body, an iconic object pervasive in western nineteenth-century depictions. This contrast emphasizes the problematics of what Zainab Bahrani has called "the positioning of the ancient Orient within Western historical discourse" (3). Popular images of the Orient, taken from ancient themes in the nineteenth century and represented in the work of artists such as Ingres, Delacroix, and Ferrier focused on nude odalisques and harems. Edwin Long's 1875 *The Babylon Marriage Market,* an unusually popular painting, was lauded as "extremely accurate in its historical-architectural background, derived from a study of the recent archaeological discoveries in Mesopotamia" (172). Long's topic, taken from Book 1 of Herodotus, described—in what has become an archetypal narrative of Babylonian culture— marriage markets in Babylonian villages, where young women of marriageable age were "auctioned" off to the highest bidder. Thus deeply embedded in Western cultural narratives of origins is this gendered paradox of the "barbarians" vs. the civilized Greeks, reducing the gendered Other of the Orient (both ancient and modern) to a comparative foil, or what Bahrani aptly characterizes as "hieroglyphs that read as Other-than-Greek."

An aspect of this paradoxical and problematic collapse of the images of women in the ancient and the modern Near East raises the question of Platonic conceptions of identity that historically have became integral to our conceptions of the gendered body and its materiality. The Mesopotamian record, particularly Enheduanna, brings into question many western scholarly assumptions regarding the definition of the body, its materiality, and gendered identity, assumptions that became part of the western text. Yet, Enheduanna's description of her invention process, as she creates the poem with the influence of the goddess, points to a different conception of subjectivity, a subjectivity tied to the body and outside of Western dualistic notions derived from the Greeks.

Julia M. Asher-Greve explains that in ancient Mesopotamia, "the mind was still in the body, mind and body were inseparable . . . meaning and understanding were . . . 'embodied'" (432). Heart, body, and mind were a holistic concept, and the mind was not separate from the body as in the Western philosophical tradition (432-34). "Mesopotamians conceptualized the body as the agent of thinking, 'feeling,' experiencing and knowing. The body was the essential ego/being. In the absence of a specific concept of mind the corporeal body was representative of the totality of the individual" (447). Because there was not the split between mind and body that has come to characterize western identity, different conceptions of gender may have existed.

For example, the Sumerian language has no grammatical gender. Certainly Sumerians must have looked at the world in a way different from the Greeks, outside the system of binary gender oppositions that dominates the rhetoric of Aristotle and continues through the western philosophical and intellectual tradition. For Mesopotamians, according to Asher-Greve: "The human body was a divine genderless creation. All humans were created in one process and that process was prior to sex and gender. This concept is corroborated by the archaic sign for person which is a genderless body." Later, in the Atrahasis myth, the two genders were created with a complementary anatomy for procreation. "But gender categories extended beyond the binary concept to multiple gender and social status of persons of ambiguous, or no, sex and castrated men" (453). Within these multiple, fluid gender categories as represented in the sculpture, relief, and seals, spiritual and emotional qualities are equally and evenly present in all genders. Thus in the earliest Sumerian pantheon, goddesses dominated. Sargon of Akkad, (the father of Enheduanna) felt compelled to justify his rule through the agency of the goddess Inanna.

This concept of gender and genderlessness perhaps also played out in the Mesopotamian concept of intelligence, which seems to be different from our own modern conceptualization largely derived from the Western mind/body dualism that locates intelligence in the brain unrelated to the body. Asher-Greve notes that the Sumerian word for intelligence, which signifies understanding and sense, **geštu,** is written with the sign of the ear, ". . . indicates that these faculties were acquired by listening" (434). Enheduanna's description of her invention process speaks to this holistic concept of mind and body, where understanding and sense were acquired by listening, a type of inspiration. She seems to be creatively inspirited by the goddess, Inanna: "I have given birth, oh exalted lady, (to this song) for you." She is inspired as *one* both with the goddess and within herself. Her heart, mind, and body can be interpreted as all part of her inspired composing. She conceives of herself as a whole (spiritual, emotional, physical) in fusion with the goddess (divine) and part of a long tradition.

For example, her portrait on the disk suggests that she may have been part of a long tradition of priestesses. Art historian, Irene Winters, in her study of the disk of Enheduanna, argues that the "weight of significant visual evidence" attests to the existence of the office of en-priestess long prior to written attestation (201). Certainly she is part of a long sacred tradition described by Jan Swearingen in this volume, "Song to Speech."

The Sacred Other

Enheduanna writes to the goddess Inanna, to an image and understanding of the sacred and a tradition that later generations rewrote and which in the western tradition was recharacterized and then erased as Other. By the time of the much later *Gilgamesh Epic,* Gilgamesh curses and reviles Inanna when she offers to make him her lover. Nevertheless, there still exists some connection between women and the arts of civilization, both sacred and profane, since it is the "prostitute" Shamhat who civilizes Enkidu from his animal state, bringing to him knowledge of the arts of civilization and culture. And, the mother of Gilgamesh, Ninsun, represents a wisdom tradition that includes the feminine, as she interprets his dreams and advises him.

The themes and characteristics of the goddess that appear in Enheduanna's work subsequently continue as palimpsest in the Greek and Hellenic polytheistic tradition. In *The Exaltation of Inanna* the characteristics of the goddess, her frightening power, her overwhelming beauty, and her universal power of procreation, announce similar themes that become part of the goddess traditions throughout the ancient world. Inanna/Ishtar becomes Aphrodite and Athena in the Greek/Hellenic tradition.

However, the subsequent Christian and Hebrew tradition corrupt the characterization of Inanna/Ishtar. She becomes the Other, the "whore of Babylon" in the Old and New Testament. Thus, the theistic tradition of most modern major religions locate their origins in a singular male monotheism, replacing a polytheism that becomes the negated binary Other. As Maria Wyke explains: "Ancient Near Eastern societies such as Mesopotamia have persistently been construed by Greeks and Romans (and by modern fans of these cultures) as a primitive, feminized, sexually transgressive Other against which to set a civilized, masculine, moral and by implication, superior West" (428). Polytheism with its sacred goddess traditions becomes that foil characterized as primitive and sexually immoral with marriage markets, eunuchs, temple harlots, and ritual defoliation.

Thus, Enheduanna in *The Exaltation of Inanna* becomes transgressive, an alien, oriental voice that sings to a gendered deity, one subsequent history denigrates. Her gendered ethos and sacred subject matter do not fit the western profile of a singular male subject, a unified agent of discourse, whose themes form the commonplaces of a dominant power group.

The Conundrums of Theory and Enheduanna

Working with the texts and image of Enheduanna, then, problematizes much of the theoretical apparatus of traditional scholarship in both Assyriology and within the rhetorical tradition. I have raised a few of the questions, questions I have only begun to examine. Certainly her enigmatic figure calls into doubt the assumptions of origins not only of the disciplinary theoretical apparatus of canonical rhetorical historiography—focused so narrowly on the culture of the Greeks at Athens primarily in the late sixth and fifth centuries—but also on the concept of origins in general. Whether or not she is the first known author is not really the point; she helps me to read with questioning eyes. That she appears to be part of a much larger and older sacred and intellectual tradition in which women may have been equal participants becomes significant in problematizing the textual canon in the humanities and rhetoric.

The fact of her Otherness, in terms of both geography and gender, also insists on cautionary reading. As I read, I struggle to screen assumptions, popular commonplaces, that often fit everything into an evolutionary framework. The scaffolding of this evolutionary framework remains influential in the academy as an underlying narrative of the steady progression of civilization from the classical age of the Athenian Greeks forward. In this narrative Greek history, characterized as a struggle against the "barbarians" of the Persian empire, evolves into the current struggle against the "evil" empire in the current parlance of geopolitics focused on the Near East.

Gender, in the Greek origins story, becomes identified with "decadence" and the Other—the narratives of Herodotus are foundational to the story of origins forming part of my western vision. Nineteenth-century images, such as those of Ingres's "Odalesque" and Long's "The Babylon Marriage Market," continue the Herodotus vision forming part of our cultural baggage. These images are further reinforced by the textual misogyny of the Athenian Greeks and Aristotle, still the primary ancient rhetorical theorist. According to this story women did not have agency—Aristotle doubts that they have a soul.

Enheduanna appears to be largely regarded in Assyriology as an appendage of her more famous father, Sargon. Yet through her passionate hymns to the goddess, Inanna, she explicates a theology that forefronts the Other, represented by a gendered deity, many of whose characteristics were carried on in the goddess traditions of later Greece and Rome.

Her ethos, while powerful, and her sacred persona remain mysterious. And yet there are her amazing words describing what in current composition theory goes by the name "invention" and which consumes two-thirds of Aristotle's Rhetoric. She speaks of composing as a purposeful invocation and receiving of inspiration, a mingling of the deity and deified self. Little in my theoretical background explains this troubling agency that stands outside of the singular male self-standard for the past two thousand years of history and religious sacred tradition.

Thus the ancient example of Enheduanna helps to provide a vision of future possibilities of an enhanced rhetorical consciousness, one that advocates a more complex inherited literacy—her representation simultaneously works to undermine dominant western discourses of the representation of the Other, while *how* she has been represented maintains those same dominant ideas, both textually and visually. Her ethos acts to expand conceptions of the gendered, geographic, and spiritual Other too narrowly defined by an inherited canonical tradition for the last two thousand years of Western civilization. Certainly, she presents a challenge to the textual Darwinism of the humanities.[9] Finally, her works challenge our definitions and conceptions of the rhetorical Other, offering an invitation to simultaneously enlarge as well as extend the conception of origins two thousand years before the Athenian Greeks.

Notes

1. Enheduanna has written two known works to the goddess Inanna and is quite likely the author of a third. The most accessible versions of these three works are in Betty De Shong Meador's recent book *Inanna, Lady of Largest Heart: Poems of the*

Sumerian High Priestess Enheduanna. Austin: University of Texas, 2000. In addition, Enheduanna is the compiler of the Temple Hymns, a cycle of forty-two hymns of various lengths that speaks directly to the temples of deities. At the end of the hymns she steps forward naming herself as compiler and dedicates it to Sargon, "my lord." The Temple Hymns were translated by Ake Sjoberg in collaboration with E. Bergmann, S.J. in 1969. They appears in *Texts from Cuneiform Sources, Vol. III.* New York: J. J. Augustine, 1969.

2. Page citations that refer to Zgoll's book are not to the published German edition, but rather to a manuscript translation by Tatjana Dorsch.

3. For example, Jacobsen in *The Treasures of Darkness* speculated that the wife of the governor or king probably played the role of the goddess in a local sacred marriage ceremony. Kramer also alludes to this in his book *The Sacred Marriage Rite.*

4. Mystical Enthymeme—At the Rhetoric society Meeting in Las Vegas, 2002, Ryan J. Stark offered this definition of the Mystical Enthymeme: "A type of rhetorical argument in which the writer omits a premise, intentionally, so that the audience and Audience (cosmic powers, angels, etc.) must fill in the missing information. That is, the audience must supply energy and substance to the argument, and the writer leaves room in the argument for that participation. Superlunary powers, including God, Goddesses, angels, and/or mysterious energies participate with the mortal audience in shaping the argument. This sounds strange to the modern academic mind, but it properly describes the style of the mentality of mystical writers themselves from antiquity to the Renaissance. For every text, then, three active elements converge: the author and two kinds of audience co-authors, the mortal audience and cosmic powers."

5. Colonialism became deeply implicated in the nineteenth century intellectual search for origins. This search included changes in philology and the founding of the disciplines of Assyriology and Egyptology under the umbrella of archeology. Archeology necessitated the massive use of funds, bureaucratic organization, and international treaties. As a social enterprise it had to be sold, and one way to sell it became the necessity of exalting the benefits of scholarship to the state. These benefits took the form of material treasures deposited in such places as the British Museum, the Louvre, the Archeological Museum of Berlin and the University of Pennsylvania, Harvard, Chicago, and Yale to name just a few of the institutions with large collections in England, France, Germany and the United States.

This nationalistic focus on archeological treasures centered on the "Greek question" and the neohumanistic tradition of education. To schematize the argument, the Greek (read Athenian) civilization may have borrowed or been influenced somewhat by these older "primitive' cultures, but it was the Greeks who perfected civilization and who were the determining influence of the western intellectual tradition. The ancient Greek view of others as "barbarians" became adapted to nineteenth-century colonial conditions as a convenient concept to explain the antecedents of civilization: the classical past was reappropriated to the new conditions of the age.

6. Miguel Civil asserts that the name Enheduanna is a generic name to designate the priestesses of the moon god at Ur. Jeremy Black explains that all the existing

copies of manuscripts of the works of Enheduanna that self-identify her are from the Old Babylonian period, a half millennium later than Enheduanna and therefore "the historiocity cannot be verified" (43f). He also explains that one of the temple hymns, addressed to the god Nanna at the town of Gaes, was built, according to an inscription of king Amar-Suena, three hundred years later than Enheduanna and therefore implies that she could not have compiled them. Brent Alster in a review of Inanna and Sukale-tudua states the role of Enheduanna has been "widely overrated" and that "the compositions ascribed to Enheduanna could not have been created in her lifetime" (687). However, Zainab Bahrani has argued that this is a clear case that: ". . . issues of authorship and its relation to gender emerge. . . . What is in fact questioned is the possibility of a woman being in a position to write poetry during the third millennium BC. However," she continues, "here is a situation where a woman is clearly recorded as being an author, and we should not rewrite the historical record simply to fit our preconceptions of gendered activities in antiquity" (116).

7. Feminist theory is beginning to impact Assyriology. Mark Van De Mieroop's *Cuneiform Text and the Writing of History,* London/New York: Routledge, 1999, has a whole chapter titled "Gender and Mesopotamian History," and, of course, there is Zainab Bahrani's book, *Women of Babylon: Gender and Representation in Mesopotamia,* London/New York: Routledge, 2001.

8. Enheduanna is now becoming part of the popular culture. Michelle Hart has created an extensive web site <http://www.angelfire.com/mi/enheduana/>

9. In her article, "Who's Afraid of the Sophists? Against Ethical Correctness" in *Hypatia* 15 (2000), French philosopher, Barbara Cassin, traces philosophical textual Darwinism from Parmenides, Plato, and Aristotle to Hegel, Heidegger, and Habermas.

Works Cited

Alster, Brent. "Review of Inanna and Sukaletuda." *Journal of the American Oriental Society,* 119 No. 4 (1999), 687–8.

Asher-Greve, Julia M. "The Essential Body: Mesopotamian Conceptions of the Gendered Body." *Gender and History* Vol. 9, No. 3 (November 1997): 432–461.

Bahrani, Zainab. *Women of Babylon: Gender and Representation in Mesopotamia.* London: Routledge, 2001.

Black, Jeremy. *Reading Sumerian Poetry.* Ithaca, NY: Cornell University Press, 1998.

Burkert, Walter. *The Orientalizing Revolution: Near Eastern Influences on Greek Culture in the Early Archaic Age.* Cambridge, MA: Harvard University Press, 1992.

Cassin, Barbara. "Who's Afraid of the Sophists? Against Ethical Correctness." *Hypatia* 4 (2000).

Civil, Miguel. "Les limites de l'information textuelle." In M. T. Barrelet, ed. *L'archéologie de l'Iraq du début de l'époque néolithique à 3333 avant notre ére.* Paris: Centre National de la Recherche Scientifique, 1980: 225–232.

Cooper, Jerrold S. "Sacred Marriage and Popular Cult in Early Mesopotamia." *Official cult and Popular Religion in the Ancient Near East,* ed. Eiko Matsushima. Heidelberg: Carl Winter Verlag, 1993: 81–96.

Enheudanna. *The Exaltation of Inanna.* Trans. William W. Hallo and J. J. A Van Dijk. New Haven: Yale University Press, 1968.

———. "In-nin sa-gur-ra: A Hymn to the Goddess Inanna by the en-Priestess Enheduanna." Trans. Ake W. Sjoberg. *Zeitschrift fur Assyriologie und Vordesasiatische Archaologie* 65 (1975): 161–253.

———. "The Collection of the Sumerian Temple Hymns." Trans. Ake Sjoberg and E. Bergmann. *Texts from Cuneiform Sources, Vol. III.* New York: J. J. Augustine, 1969.

Evans, Geoffrey. "Ancient Mesopotamian Assemblies." *Journal of the American Oriental Society,* 78 (1958): 1–11.

Geertz, Clifford. *The Interpretation of Cultures: Selected Essays.* New York: Basic Books, 1973.

Glenn, Cheryl. *Rhetoric Retold: Regendering the Tradition from Antiquity through the Renaissance. Carbondale:* Southern Illlinois University Press, 1997.

Hallam, Elizabeth, and Brian V. Street. *Cultural Encounters: Representing "Otherness."* London: Routledge, 2000.

Hallo, William W. "The Limits of Scepticism." *Journal of the American Oriental Society,* 110: (1990) 187–199.

Harris, Rivkah. *Gender and Aging in Mesopotamia.* Norman: University of Oklahoma Press, 2000.

Jacobsen, Thorkild. *The Treasures of Darkness: A History of Mesopotamian Religion.* New Haven: Yale University Press, 1976.

Kramer, Samuel Noah. *The Sacred Marriage Rite; Aspects of Faith, Myths, and Ritual in Ancient Sumer.* Bloomington: Indiana University Press, 1969.

Meador, Betty DeShong. *Inanna, Lady of Largest Heart: Poems of the Sumerian High Priestess Enheduanna.* Austin: University of Texas, 2000.

Mieroop, Marc Van De. *Cuneiform Texts and the Writing of History.* New York: Routledge, 1999.

Steinkeller, Piotr. "On Rulers, Priests and Sacred Marriage: Tracing the Evolution of Early Sumerian Kingship." *Priests and Officials in the Ancient Near East,* ed. Watanabe, Kazuko. Heidelberg: Universtatsverlag C. Winter, 1996.

Swearingen, C. Van. "Song to Speech: The Origins of Early Epitaphia in Ancient Near Eastern Women's Lamentations." *Rhetoric Before and Beyond The Greeks,"* eds. Lipson, Carol and Roberta Binkley. Albany: State University of New York Press, 2004.

West, M. L. *The East Face of Helicon.* New York: Oxford University Press, 1997.

Westenholz, Joan Goodnick. "Enheduanna, En-Priestess, Hen of Nanna, Spouse of Nanna." Eds. Herman Bherens, Darlene Loding, and Martha T. Roth. *Duma-E-Dub-A: Studies in Honor of Ake W. Sjöberg.* Philadelphia: Occasional Publication of the Samuel Noah Kramer Fund, 1989.

Wills, John W. "Speaking Arenas of Ancient Mesopotamia." *Quarterly Journal of Speech.* 56 (1970): 398–405.

Winters, Irene J. "Women in Public: The Disk of Enheduanna, The Beginning of the Office of En-Priestess, and the Weight of Visual Evidence." *La Femme dans le Proche-Orient Antique.* Paris: Editions Recherche sur les Civilisations, 1987.

Wyke, Maria. "Introduction" Special Issue. *Gender and History* Vol. 9, No. 3 (November 1997): 425–431.

Zgoll, Annette. *Der Rechtsfal der En-hedu-Ana im Lied nin-me-sara.* Münster: Ugarit-Verlag, 1997.

Neo-Assyrian Rhetoric:
The Example of the Third Campaign of Sennacherib (704–681 B.C.)

Paul Y. Hoskisson and Grant M. Boswell

Although extensive records from Mesopotamia have been available for over a hundred years now, "the material has been little studied from the point of view of rhetoric."[1] Such studies are long overdue, not just as an academic adventure, but because the ancient Near Eastern material deserves to be recognized in its own right for its rhetorical finesse and refinement. This essay is a modest step in that direction. It is modest because it is limited to only one type of ancient Near Eastern literature, the Assyrian annals, and only a small representative sample at that. It is nevertheless a tentative step toward appreciating ancient Near Eastern rhetoric in its own milieu. Indeed, as we will point out, the annals of Sennacherib's third campaign specifically and Neo-Assyrian royal annals in general indicate a level of rhetorical sophistication and complexity highly particular to the cultural context in which they developed.

For the purposes of this essay, Assyrian rhetoric may be generally defined as the artful use of writing to persuade or influence people.[2] Because the Assyrian annals are many and usually come in several versions, we will limit the discussion to a representative example: the annals that end with the third campaign of the Assyrian king Sennacherib. This essay will discuss the Sitz im Leben, review the question of genre, provide a translation of the introduction and the third campaign, analyze the structure and the rhetorical devices, and suggest a reason for the structure of the annals.

Sitz im Leben

By the time Sennacherib's annals were composed, the Neo-Assyrian Empire was heir to more than two thousand years of writing, history, and culture. During this history Mesopotamia experienced "early, and at times widespread, literacy."[3] Additionally, literacy was not limited to males[4] or professional scribes. Assurbanipal, the grandson of Sennacherib and the last of the great Assyrian kings, claimed that he could read not only Assyrian but also Sumerian, which as a living language had died out over one thousand years before his birth.

The display of texts for public consumption began at least a thousand years before Sennacherib, when perhaps the most widely known ancient Near Eastern text, the Code of Hammurabi, was erected for public display in Babylon. By the time of Sennacherib, the public display extended into the Assyrian palaces, which were "to a greater or lesser degree . . . a showplace for texts."[5] A copy of the annals examined here was carved into one of the two stone bulls that flanked the entrance to Sennacherib's throne room, thus underscoring its intended public consumption.[6]

Historically, these annals were composed fairly early in Sennacherib's reign. The third campaign, the final campaign of this text, took place in 701 B.C. It was also composed near the beginning of what has been called the Pax Assyriaca (721–627 B.C.) and therefore represents Assyrian rhetoric near the height of Assyrian power.[7] It is the last example of Assyrian annals inscribed on stone and put on public display in a palace.[8] The third campaign records, among other events that transpired in the same year, Sennacherib's campaign against the Kingdom of Judah and its king, Hezekiah. Though we will not discuss in any detail the Hebrew Bible version of this campaign, the existence of this account is worth noting.9

Genre

Just what kind of text are the annals exactly? Some scholars have assumed that the annals were historical narratives that recorded the deeds of the Assyrian kings. This assumption, however, presents its own problems because the annals are not constructed in narrative fashion, as we have come to understand narratives in the West. Since Herodotus western narratives have had a beginning, middle, and end. The annals do not have an ending or narrative closure. Therefore, the annals are not formally narratives per se, though they do contain many historical facts melded with nationalistic propaganda and self-aggrandizement.[10] But if the annals are not narratives, what are they? Simplistically stated, the annals form a separate genre. They are annalistic.

Translation[11]

The following translation presents the introduction to Sennacherib's annals and the Third Campaign. The lines between the parts of the translation represent actual lines drawn on the clay cylinders separating the introduction, the first campaign, the second campaign, and the third campaign. For the purposes of this article on Assyrian rhetoric, a more literal rendering seemed advisable, including a more or less successful attempt to line up the English lines with the Assyrian ones. However, because a tight translation would at best read awkwardly, the rendering below is not strictly literal.

Sennacherib

Column I

1. [I am] Sennacherib, the great king
2. the powerful king, the king of all there is, the king of the city and land of Assur,
3. the king of the four quarters, the capable shepherd,
4. the favored of the great gods, the protector of truth,
5. a lover of uprightness, an accomplisher of aid,
6. the companion of the disadvantaged, the striver after goodness,
7. the perfect man, the heroic male,
8. the foremost of all kings, the one who yokes
9. the unwilling, the dasher of my enemies.
10. The god Assur, the great mountain, bestowed on me
11. kingship without compare. Above all
12. who sit on my throne he enlarged my weapon.
13. From the upper sea of the setting of the sun,
14. to the lower sea of the rising of the sun,
15. he caused all of humanity to bow at my feet.
16. The mighty nobles feared the battle.
17. They left their districts and
18. fled like a bat alone to a hidden corner,
19. a place with no entrance.
    [First campaign, comprising column I, lines 20–64]
    [Second campaign, comprising column I, line 65 through column II, line 36]

Column II

1. In my third campaign I surely went
2. to the land of Hatti [Syria and Palestine]. The fearful splendor of my kingship

3. overcame Lulli, king of Sidon. He fled
4. into the midst of the distant sea and disappeared forever.
5. As for greater Sidon and lesser Sidon,
6. the city of Bit-Zitti, the city of Zarephat, the city of Mahalliba,
7. the city of Ushu, the city of Akzibi and the city of Akko,
8. strong, walled cities, places of food
9. and drink for his garrisons, the terror of the weapon of Assur,
10. my lord, overpowered them and they bowed at my feet.
11. Tubalum I set on the royal throne
12. over them, and I imposed a tribute on him,
13. yearly without cessation, of a talent, a gift for my lordship.
14. Concerning Minhimmu of the city Samsimuruna,
15. Tubalum of the city Sidon,
16. Abdi-li'ti of the city Arvad,
17. Uru-milki of the city Byblos,
18. Mitinti of the city Ashdod,
19. Pudu-il of the land of Beth-Ammon,
20. Chemosh-nadbi of the land of Moab,
21. Ayarammu of the land of Edom,
22. all of them are kings of the Amorites, they brought
23. extensive tribute, lavish gifts, fourfold,
24. to me. They kissed my feet. And Sidqa,
25. King of Ashkelon, who did not submit
26. to my yoke, the gods of the father's house, himself, his wife,
27. his sons, his daughters, his brothers, all the seed of his father's house,
28. I exiled and deported to the land of Assur.
29. Sarru-ludari the son of Rukibti, their previous king,
30. I enthroned over the people of Ashkelon.
31. I imposed on him the giving of an offering of gifts of my lordship, and
32. he pulls my yoke. In the further course of my campaign
33. the city Beth-Dagon, the city Joppa,
34. the city Bana-barqa, the city Azuru, the cities
35. belonging to Sidqa, which did not submit
36. at my feet quickly, I surrounded, captured, and plundered their treasures.
37. The officials, the nobles, and the people of Ekron,
38. who put their king, Padi, ruler by an oath and covenant
39. with the land of Assur, in fetters of iron, and
40. to Hezekiah of the land of Judea
41. they delivered him. Because they had acted with villainous enmity,

42. their heart grew afraid. To the kings of the land of Egypt—
43. the troops, the bowmen, the chariots, the horses
44. of the king of the land of Meluhhi (Ethiopia), a force without counting—
45. they appealed; and they came to their aid.
46. In the plains of Eltekeh
47. they arrayed themselves before me in ranks;

COLUMN III

1 they whetted their weapons. With the trust of Assur,
2. my lord, I strove with them and inflicted
3. defeat on them. The lord of the chariots and the sons of the king
4. of Egypt together with the lord of the chariots of Meluhhi
5. in pitched battle my own two hands
6. captured alive. Ektekeh and Timnah
7. I surrounded, captured and plundered their treasures. I proceeded to
8. Ekron and had the guilty officials
9. and nobles killed, and on all of the towers
10. of the city I hung their bodies. The citizens of the city
11. who acted treacherously I reckoned as plunder.
12. The rest of them who had not committed crimes
13. and who were not guilty
14. I declared to be free. Padi, their king,
15. I brought from Jerusalem and
16. set him on the throne of lordship over them.
17. I imposed on him the tribute of my lordship.
18. And as for Hezekiah of the land of Judea,
19. who did not submit to my yoke, forty-six of his fortified cities,
20. walled outposts, and countless villages
21. in their districts, I surrounded with packed earth
22. and with siege engines, with battle troops,
23. sappers, miners, and shock troops and I sacked them.
24. 200,150 people, small and large, male and female,
25. horses, mules, donkeys, camels,
26. cattle, and flocks without counting I drove out from their midst
27. and reckoned as plunder. Himself like a caged bird
28. within Jerusalem, his royal city,
29. I enclosed him, and encircled it with a siege wall.
30. Anyone coming out of the gate of his city I made loathsome. His cities
31. which I had sacked, I separated them from his land and

32. gave them to Mitinti, king of Ashdod,
33. to Padi, king of Ekron and to Silli-bel,
34. king of Gaza and reduced his land.
35. I added to the former tribute a yearly assessment,
36. putting tribute presents(?) of my kingship
37. on his back. As for this Hezekiah,
38. the fearful splendor of my kingship overcame him. And
39. the army, the elite troops which he had stationed
40. for the reinforcement of Jerusalem, his royal city, and
41. the mercenaries he had hired, afterwards he sent to me,
42. to the midst of Nineva, my royal city, with 30 talents of gold,
43. 800 talents of select silver, antimony,
44. large blocks of carnelian, ivory inlaid couches,
45. ivory inlaid chaises, elephant skins, ivory,
46. ebony, boxwood, all kinds of splendid treasure,
47. and his daughters, the women of the palace, male singers, and
48. female singers. To present the gifts
49. and to effect his servitude he sent me his messenger.

Structure and Rhetorical Devices

The Introduction

The excerpts above from Sennacherib's annals are typical of the Assyrian annals in general. They begin with a listing of the king's titles, powers, and general accomplishments comprising nineteen lines. After the introduction, the text provides the details of Sennacherib's first three campaigns. The complete text of these annals, the introduction, and the three campaigns comprise about 213 lines.

The clay cylinders present a clear physical structure to the inscriptions. Between the introduction and the report of the first campaign, there is a horizontal line drawn across the column. A similar line is drawn between the first and the second campaign, and again between the second and third.

Stylistically, the introduction is the most interesting, because it employs several rhetorical figures of repetition. The first nine lines of the introduction are a list of Sennacherib's epithets, figures of speech detailing his kingly qualities.[12] The use of introductory, at times formulaic, epithets in Assyrian annals reflects traditional Mesopotamian titulary that can be traced back at least 1,500 years before Sennacherib.

Formulaic, however, does not mean the epithets are without conscious structure. As Liverani has demonstrated, variants in Sennacherib's titles evidence a purposeful accumulation that relates to his claims to kingship. Furthermore, it is likely that there is a definite pattern in the accumulation of titles over the course of Sennacherib's annals.[13] What the titlulary demonstrates is that the titles the king claims have to be earned by campaigns and are thus evidence of his right to be the king.[14]

The Campaigns

The report of the campaigns also demonstrates internal coherence, strategies of transition, and internal ordering. Typically each campaign is introduced by a phrase announcing the beginning of the campaign. Within each description of a campaign there are three catalogues listing treasure plundered, deeds performed, cities sacked, and tribute exacted, divided according to the different phases of the campaign. The third campaign, in addition to listing the items that Sennacherib seized while campaigning in Hezekiah's kingdom, also contains a subcatalog listing the tribute that Hezekiah sent afterwards as appeasement to Assyria.

Beyond internal ordering of the different phases of a campaign, the campaign units themselves exhibit an ordering principle among them. This feature moves us beyond stylistic features to the rhetorical canon of arrangement. The three campaigns of these annals seem to be arranged from the most decisive to the most problematic in terms of Sennacherib's dominance as the "great king." Thus in Sennacherib's third campaign the annals report the most resistance. It is true that at the time of the composition of the annals being studied here, the third campaign was the most recent and would therefore have contained more detail. As Van De Mieroop points out, the annals were constantly being revised, not as revisionist history, but in order to account for "the situation that existed at the time of the writing, not the situation of the past which had no relevance any longer."[15] As Sennacherib continued to mount campaigns and the third campaign fell into the past, the text was abbreviated in subsequent versions. Nevertheless, Sennacherib's annals up to the third campaign exhibit the pattern of moving from the least problematic to the most difficult.

The third campaign is interesting for two reasons. First, like the arrangement of the three campaigns from seemingly easiest to hardest, the three catalogues of the third campaign also seem to be arranged from least difficult to most problematic. Luli had rebelled, but at the approach of Sennacherib fled out of fear and was destroyed. Sidqa initially resisted, but was forced into submission by Assyrian military might. Last of all, though Hezekiah's resistance was not completely broken by military force, he did eventually submit and pay tribute.

Second, the third narrative unit of Sennacherib's third campaign functions as an apology for those who might dispute Sennacherib's claim to pre-eminence. That is, perhaps a foreign dignitary could make the counterclaim that Sennacherib was not the king of all kings he claimed to be because he did not destroy or subdue every king in the region. Hezekiah would then become the counterexample to Sennacherib's claim to kingship. Anticipating this rhetorical move, Sennacherib's annals offer a refutation of the counterclaim. Although King Hezekiah was not captured or killed or forced to flee, as other kings mentioned in the earlier campaigns, his country was razed, with the exception of Jerusalem, and in the end he did acknowledge Sennacherib's overlordship by paying him tribute.

In summary, the structure of Sennacherib's annals gives evidence for several important features of Neo-Assyrian rhetoric. The text is structured rhetorically to exhibit narrative units with internal coherence. It exhibits stylistic features that increase the presence and immediacy of Sennacherib's claim of kingship through various repetitive figures. The text demonstrates a sense of global arrangement of its narrative units to form an inductive argument in support of Sennacherib's claim in the titulary to supreme kingship. Furthermore, the global arrangement serves the function of what would become in classical rhetoric *the confirmatio,* or supporting evidence, as well as the *confutatio,* or anticipation of counterarguments. That is, Neo-Assyrian rhetoric already shows significant evidence for logical development and form that includes inductive inference in support of a claim, anticipation and rebuttal of counterclaims, strategic arrangement, and stylistic emphasis.

Literary Considerations

Given Assyria's general cultural dependence on Babylon, it is not surprising that the Assyrian texts composed under Sennacherib exhibit clear debt to previous cuneiform literature. The similarities exist first of all on the word and phrase level, where stock combinations of words that appear in previous royal inscriptions were incorporated into Sennacherib's inscriptions. By doing so, Sennacherib was able to proclaim, without explicitly stating the case, "that he was part of the long line of Assyrian rulers" who had succeeded in subduing large parts of the Near East.[16]

On a much deeper level than phrases and word combination, themes were borrowed from Mesopotamian literature. For instance, works such as the great Babylonian creation epic, "Enuma Elish" (in its later attested Assyrian form), were appropriated to provide a propagandistic undertone to Sennacherib's accounts, particularly of a battle between Assyrian forces and a rebellious southern Mesopotamian alliance that included Babylon.[17] The effect of using the subtle reminders of this great Babylonian epic when recording the details of the battle that took place in traditional Babylonian territory was to cast the war as a fight between the forces of good—i.e, Assyria as a type of the heroic Babylonian national god Marduk, against the forces of evil—i.e., the southern Babylonian alliance as a type of the evil goddess Tiamat, who was bent on destroying the order of heaven. The effect would not have been lost either on the Assyrians, who considered themselves the champions of the gods in maintaining peace and order, or on the Babylonians, who would be reminded through the references to their own national creation epic of the need for order in the universe.

The Absence of an Ending

In typical ancient Near Eastern fashion, the annals stand by themselves; that is, they do not have a conclusion. They contain a beginning: the grandeur of the king is declared. There is a middle: his accomplishments are blazoned. But there is no ending. This lack of culmination has bothered some occidental critics who want to see, in typical western style, an introduction, a body, and a conclusion to the annals. We propose that there may be two reasons the Assyrians did not create an ending, and had they been instructed how to create a conclusion or ending to the annals, would have scratched their heads and asked why anyone would want one. The first reason has to do with rhetorical style, and the second concerns the rhetoric of kingship.

With no formal ending to the annals, the reader is left to draw the intended conclusion. Not unlike enthymematic reasoning explained in Aristotle, visitors to Sennacherib's palace would supply the conclusion they were supposed to draw, namely, submission to the greatness, the glory, and the power of Sennacherib was the only sane and logical course of action. Any course to the contrary, as the annals bore ample witness, would produce disastrous consequences for those who acted contrary to Sennacherib's will.

There is at least one example, though, of the Assyrians drawing the obvious conclusion. The Hebrew Bible account of the siege of Jerusalem during Sennacherib's third campaign explicitly mentions the intent of Assyrian rhetoric: intimidation. When Sennacherib realized, after razing the rest of the kingdom of Judah, that he might not be able to begin or complete a siege of Jerusalem during the third campaign, he wrote a letter to King Hezekiah. In the letter, Sennacherib explicitly stated what was only implicit in his annals, namely, that resistance was useless and futile. In a very short paraphrase of the gist of his annals, but with the addition of a concise statement of what the Assyrians intended with their annalistic rhetoric, Sennacherib wrote, "Surely you have heard what the kings of Assyria have done to all countries, exterminating their people; can you hope to escape? Did their gods save the nations which my forefathers destroyed, Gozan, Harran, Rezeph, and the people of

Betheden living in Telassar? Where are the kings of Hamath, of Arpad, and of Lahir, Sepharvaim, Hena and Ivvah?"[18] The message was clear: continued resistance meant sure destruction. Hezekiah and the inhabitants of Jerusalem could not escape the obvious intent of Assyrian rhetoric. Though Jerusalem was never captured by the Assyrians, Assyrian rhetoric produced the desired results: Hezekiah submitted to Assyrian hegemony, as the end of Sennacherib's third campaign states and the Hebrew Bible clearly confirms.

We therefore propose that a stated conclusion to the written annals was superfluous. In fact, within context of the annals, the absence of an ending creates a powerful instance of subtle understatement and rhetorical sophistication.

The second reason for not having a conclusion concerns the rhetoric of Assyrian culture, or more specifically, of Assyrian kingship. A perusal of Assyrian letters quickly demonstrates that at least in the genre of the letter, the Assyrians had a strategy for signaling the end of discourse. Other narrative texts composed in the Neo-Assyrian period also exhibit clear conclusions. There can be no doubt that the Assyrians knew about, had a sense for, and employed endings. Assuming that rhetorical forms reveal something significant about the cultural understanding of the people who used them, the culture of Assyrian kingship could supply the reason the annals forego a conclusion.

Van De Mieroop notes that Assyrian kings conducted nearly annual campaigns, and when they finished the campaigns they almost always commemorated the campaigns with some sort of public memorial.[19] The account of the campaigns is therefore cumulative, emphasizing not the completion of a campaign but the continuity of a process. The commemoration of the third campaign would therefore involve a recitation of the first and second campaigns but would focus specifically on the relevant details of the most recent, third campaign. With each new annual campaign, the annals of the previous campaigns would be adjusted. For this reason, the annals were never finished but simply revised to reflect the conditions then prevailing. By extrapolation, Sennacherib's annals of his deeds would end only when he ceased to be king.

Therefore, it is also possible that an Assyrian king's claim to the throne was a process and not an event. The frequent military campaigns, the building projects, the performance of religious duties, the hunting exploits depicted so beautifully in the Assyrian bas reliefs, all these proclaimed the fitness of a person to be king. Therefore, instead of seeing the invocation of epithets as merely formulaic, the titulary served a key rhetorical function with respect to various audiences.20 It is reasonable to conclude, therefore, that Sennacherib had the annals written with specific rhetorical force in mind. As has been enumerated for the case of Sennacherib's son, the annals served the purpose, among other things, of fulfilling the obligation to claim title to kingship, of realizing the duty to commemorate deeds at a public works ceremony, of increasing the credibility of his reign to his subjects, and to placate religious and secular audiences.[21]

The annals can therefore be analyzed as an inductive argument in support of the king's claim to kingship. The task of Sennacherib and other Assyrian kings was to claim title to the throne. Part of this obligation to assert one's kingship was to conduct campaigns, subdue enemies, perform required religious duties, and realize building projects for the public good. That is, Assyrian kingship was performative in that Assyrian kings continuously legitimized their claim to the throne by performing the acts required of a king.

If Assyrian kingship was performative in this sense, rather than stative, the necessity for an Assyrian king to perform as a king throughout his reign would explain the lack of a conclusion in the annals. Each version of the annals was merely another performance claim to the throne, an ongoing obligation that had no end. To have added a conclusion or an ending to Assyrian annals would have been tantamount to adding an ending to the kingship claim of that king.

Conclusion

Neo-Assyrian annalistic rhetoric, by extrapolation from the small sample of Sennacherib's annals treated above, exhibits sophisticated rhetorical awareness and complex culturally situated rhetorical devices. The annals are structured along carefully devised patterns that reflect awareness of a rhetorical progression. The same structure that is present between the three campaigns is repeated within the third campaign, but with the addition of a climactic variant. The body of the annals provides the evidence for the kingship claims of the introduction. There is no need for an ending, because the reader provides the enthymematic conclusion. In addition, as long as the king was alive, there could be no end to the king's annals. Certainly, Assyrian rhetoric flourished in ways not accounted for in the classical tradition.

Notes

1. See George A. Kennedy, "Literacy and Rhetoric in the Ancient Near East," *Comparative Rhetoric: An Historical and Cross-Cultural Introduction* (Oxford: Oxford University Press, 1998): 118. Kennedy is right that little rhetorical scholarship has been done on texts from the ancient Near East. Kennedy reviews Fox and Wills, cited below: Michael V. Fox, " Ancient Egyptian Rhetoric," *Rhetorica* 1 (1983): 9–22. John W. Wills, "Speaking Arenas of Ancient Mesopotamia," *Quarterly Journal of Speech* 56 (1970): 398–405. In addition, O'Connor looks at the rhetorical structure of

a Western Phoenician text in M. O'Connor, "The Rhetoric of the Kilamuwa Inscription," *Bulletin of the American Schools of Oriental Research* 226 (April 1977): 15–29. And most significantly, ancient Near Eastern rhetoric is treated by Katz. Katz's work is problematic, but remains the only book-length treatment of material from the region. See Ronald C. Katz, *The Structure of Ancient Arguments: Rhetoric and Its Ancient Near Eastern Origins* (New York: Shapolsky/Steimatzky Publishers, Inc., 1986).

2. Compare Carl Joachim Classen, *Rhetorical Criticism of the New Testament* (Tübingen: Mohr Siebeck, 2000), 99, where he states that rhetoric "is the theory of the most effective use of the possibilities of language, of the great variety of expressions and their functions, [and] the ways and means to apply them in practice with the greatest possible effect."

3. William W. Hallo and William Kelly Simpson, *The Ancient Near East: A History* (New York: Harcourt Brace Jovanovich, 1971), 166. Not all Assyriologists would agree with this rather liberal view of the extent of literacy.

4. If an extrapolation from the example of the Middle Bronze Age city of Mari can be applied generally, women served as scribes. See Nele Ziegler, "Le Harem de Zimri-Lim," *Florilegium Marianum* 4, Mémoires de N.A.B.U. 5 (Paris: SEPOA, 1999), 91–92. For this reference we would like to thank Jack Sasson of Vanderbuilt University.

5. John Malcolm Russell, *The Writing on the Wall: Studies in the Architectural Context of Late Assyrian Palace Inscriptions* (Winona Lake, Indiana: Eisenbrauns, 1999), 1. Russell has greatly facilitated the present study by collecting and synthesizing the Neo-Assyrian inscriptional material. This paper would have been much more difficult to complete without his synthesis. Much of what follows is indebted to his excellent monograph.

6. In addition to the version carved into the bull, there are other versions impressed on clay cylinders that were fired and then imbedded in the walls of the palace. These texts were obviously placed in protected places to preserve them from destruction, so that future remodelers of the palace would find them, read about Sennacherib, and be duly impressed enough to preserve his memory in the remodeled palace. For an overview of the extant versions of the texts of Sennacherib's reign, see Table 1 in Eckart Frahm, "Einleitung in die Sanherib-Inschriften," *Archiv für Orientforschung,* Supplement 26 (Vienna: Institut für Orientalistik der Universität Wien, 1997), 6. For the question of hidden texts, see Russel, 127.

7. Hallo and Simpson, 138.

8. Russell, 218, "To my knowledge, no annalistic text of [Sennacherib's successors, Esarhaddon or Assurbanipal] has been found inscribed on stone."

9. 2 Kings 18:13 – 19:37. See also the nearly word-for-word identical account in Isaiah 36–37.

10. Marc Van De Mieroop, *Cuneiform Texts and the Writing of History* (London and New York: Routledge, 1999), 17, 45–48, 55.

11. This translation was by one of the authors from the transcription in Riekele Borger, *Babylonisch-assyrische Lesestücke* (Rome: Pontificium Institutum Biblicum, 1963). This transcription is from the Rassam cylinder with variants from other texts, including the bull.

12. Ronald C. Katz, *The Structure of Ancient Arguments: Rhetoric and Its Ancient Near Eastern Origins* (New York: Shapolsky/Steimatzky Publishers, Inc., 1986), 131.

13. Mario Liverani, "Critique of Variants and the Titulary of Sennachirib," in *Assyrian Royal Inscriptions: New Horizons in Literary, Ideological and Historical Analysis,* ed. F. M. Hales (Rome: Instituto per l'Oriente, 1981), 235.

14. Liverani, 236.

15. Van De Mieroop, 47.

16. Frahm, 279. Translation from the German of this passage and of subsequent paraphrases were made by Paul Hoskisson.

17. It is beyond the scope of this essay to present this campaign of Sennacherib. For the evidence of this level of borrowing from literary works into Sennacherib's annals and into other genres, see Frahm, 279–280.

18. 2 Kings 19:10–13, *New English Bible.*

19. Van De Mieroop, 25–27.

20. Barbara Nevling Porter, *Images, Power, and Politics: Figurative Aspects of Esarhaddon's Babylonian Policy* (Philadelphia: American Philosophical Society, 1993), 80–81.

21. Ibid., 99–105; see also Barbara Nevling Porter, "Language, Audience and Impact in Imperial Assyria," *Israel Oriental Studies* 15 (1995): 51–72.

Works Cited

Borger, Riekele. *Babylonisch-assyrische Lesestücke.* Rome: Pontificium Institutum Biblicum, 1963.

Classen, Carl Joachim. *Rhetorical Criticism of the New Testament.* Tübingen: Mohr Siebeck, 2000.

Frahm, Eckart. "Einleitung in die Sanherib-Inschriften." *Archiv für Orientforschung.* Supplement 26. Vienna: Institut für Orientalistik der Universität Wien, 1997.

Hallo, William W., and William Kelly Simpson. *The Ancient Near East: A History.* New York: Harcourt Brace Jovanovich, 1971.

Katz, Ronald C. *The Structure of Ancient Arguments: Rhetoric and Its Near Eastern Origins.* New York: Shapolsky/Steimatzky Publishers, Inc., 1986.

Kennedy, George A. "Literacy and Rhetoric in the Ancient Near East." In *Comparative Rhetoric: An Historical and Cross-Cultural Introduction,* 115–40. Oxford: Oxford University Press, 1998.

Liverani, Mario. "Critique of Variants and the Titulary of Sennachirib." In *Assyrian Royal Inscriptions: New Horizons in Literary, Ideological and Historical Analysis.* Ed. F. M. Hales, 225–57. Rome: Instituto per l'Oriente, 1981.

Porter, Barbara Nevling. *Images, Power, and Politics: Figurative Aspects of Esarhaddon's Babylonian Policy.* Philadelphia: American Philosophical Society, 1993.

_____."Language, Audience and Impact in Imperial Assyria." *Israel Oriental Studies* 15 (1995): 51–72.

Russell, John Malcolm. *The Writing on the Wall: Studies in the Architectural Context of Late Assyrian Palace Inscriptions.* Winona Lake, Indiana: Eisenbrauns, 1999.

Van De Mieroop, Marc. *Cuneiform Texts and the Writing of History.* London and New York: Routledge, 1999.

Ziegler, Nele. "Le Harem de Zimri-Lim." *Florilegium Marianum* 4. Mémoires de Novelles Assyriologique Brèves et Utilitaires 5. Paris: Société pour l'Étude du Proche-Orient Ancien, 1999.

Ancient Egyptian Rhetoric:
It All Comes Down to *Maat*

Carol S. Lipson

This study examines aspects of the rhetorical system developed in ancient Egypt. While the visual representations created in this culture are quite familiar today, the textual practices are little known to rhetoricians. Fewer than a half dozen articles or chapters have appeared in the field of rhetoric and composition in the last twenty years.[1] I will here look at the ways that ancient Egyptian rhetoric built upon a central cultural concept—that of *Maat*. I will address four claims regarding the close relationship between ancient Egyptian rhetoric and the values that surrounded the concept of *Maat*:

1. A number of the popular textual genres present *Maat* as content—that is, they teach *Maat*.
2. In the letter genre, common in the everyday life of the culture, the rhetorical form embodies *Maat*: the written texts serve as rhetorical performances of *Maat*.
3. The letters use *Maat* indirectly as an instrument of persuasion.
4. *Maat* serves as a Superaddressee in the letters, in Bakhtin's sense of a third voice or participant, an ultimate addressee beyond the writer and the immediate receiver.

To address the first claim, I will briefly discuss the major genres of wisdom texts and autobiographies. However, the bulk of this study examines the letter genre, important to the day-to-day operations of the vast state bureaucracy. At first glance, such business letters would seem unlikely to either teach *Maat* or perform *Maat*, given their reporting functions. Yet I argue that even this mundane genre has been constructed rhetorically to ritually enact and reinforce major cultural values.

Depiction of judgment scene in the hall of *Maat.* Photo by E. Lipson of papyrus owned by C. and E. Lipson.

What is *Maat*?

Most readers would recognize the image above as depicting the ancient Egyptian judgment of the dead.[2] Here the heart of the deceased, on the left scale in a jar, is weighed against the symbol for the goddess *Maat,* on the right side of the scale. The symbol used for *Maat* here is the feather that appears in the goddess's headdress. If the heart weighs the same as does the feather—is equated to *Maat* in effect—then the deceased can proceed to the afterlife. If not, the deceased is devoured and ceased to exist. This judgment scene is known mainly from New Kingdom sources, dating from 1550 to 1070 B.C.E.[3] The goddess *Maat* does appear on early artifacts, and references to a divine tribunal that judges access to the afterworld occur in late Old Kingdom sources (about 2200 B.C.E.). In Late Period sources (~500 B.C.E.), the judgment scene takes place in the Hall of *Maat.* Often the figure of *Maat* appears above the central pole of the scales, offering a redundant reinforcement of *Maat*'s centrality in this crucial cultural practice. Thus, across all periods of pharaonic history, a final judgment scene is omnipresent in the culture's understanding of passage to the afterlife, and from the Middle Kingdom on, *Maat* was associated with that final determination.

In this culture, and in this particular mortuary mythology, *Maat* functions as both a goddess and a concept. The goddess is represented either as a tall slender figure with a large feather headdress, as a seated statue with the feather headdress, or as above, simply as the feather headdress. There is comparatively little mythology surrounding this goddess; she is the daughter of the Sun God Ra, and the wife of the God of Wisdom and Truth (Thoth), the god who invented writing. *Maat* exists mainly as a concept, which has no direct English translation. The concept was first presented explicitly in the Middle Kingdom (~ 2100 B.C.E.), and remained prominent thereafter. Often *Maat* is referred to as truth, justice, or order. I will translate *Maat* as 'what is right,' since it is clear from a variety of contexts that the judgment scene presents a determination whether the deceased has done what is right, or has behaved properly according to the cultural precepts. The deceased is measured against *Maat* as a standard for behavior.[4] Jan Assmann describes *Maat* as "connective justice," involving a collection of social norms that govern how individuals should interact with others to form communities (Assmann 1996, 127).

Yet *Maat* is not simply a stand-alone set of behavioral precepts. *Maat* is tied to the natural order of the motion of the sun, moon, and stars, as well as to the motion of the river Nile, all of which provided the conditions for life in Egypt. The concept of *Maat* is based on the premise that humans must not disturb the balanced state of creation, but instead must respect and live in accord with the cosmic harmony and the natural order. Kings are often shown offering to the gods small statues of the seated *Maat* goddess, as a way of attesting that they are upholding the order of the universe as willed by the gods. The very nature of the concept focuses on the culture's understanding of the interconnected order of the cosmic, divine, natural, and human worlds, as well as to its understanding of the need to preserve that order. The concept is a fundamentally conservative one, bent on preservation rather than on change.

Without doubt, the concept of *Maat* carries a strong ethical dimension. To do *Maat* meant to behave in certain ways towards others in order "that your conduct may be blameless" (Lichtheim 1973, *Instructions of Ptahhotep*, p. 64). The available artifacts can inform us only of the elite's view of what constitutes "blameless" conduct, and much of what we learn comes from the written texts.

How Did the Elite Learn What It Means To Do *Maat*?

When we look at the genres of writing that developed in this culture, we see a wide range of types—from hymns to love songs to mortuary rituals to lists of accounts. But one of the most prominent of the forms involved texts that offered advice on how to comport oneself in this society. A common type of advice text was the instructions text, similar in some ways to the Hebrew proverbs that are better known in our society. The instructions give advice on how to behave as part of the elite. The instructions also concern themselves with appropriate communication in various situations; in many ways, they constitute rhetorics, offering concrete principles and guidelines for speech and behavior. They do not, however, offer analytic systems categorizing speech or behavior. Instead, they're highly situational and practical.

One of the primary uses for the instructions was in the education system. A small percentage of the population was taught to read and write; traditional estimates indicate that about 1 percent of the Egyptian population was literate. Although these were not all born to the elite group, acquiring the skills of reading and writing served as a gateway for mobility to the elite. Such training offered the possibility of a lifetime of state support; one's fortune would be tied to that of the ruler and his government bureaucracy (Forman and Quirke, 17). Reading and writing were taught by having the students memorize, recite, sing, and copy the didactic instructions texts, among other genres. The students were being taught the content—appropriate behaviors for members of the elite—while they were also learning to interpret and form hieroglyphs and the cursive hieratic script. Such students would have been almost exclusively male, though there does seem to be evidence of some literacy among females (Feucht, 332). On the whole, the instructions texts were created for the education of future male bureaucrats and for the enjoyment of functioning bureaucrats.

Typically, the instructions present themselves as having been written by famous figures of great antiquity, addressed to a son; these attributions are generally held to be fictitious. I will illustrate their approach to teaching *Maat* by looking to one of the older, better known such texts: *The Instructions of Ptahhotep.*[5] This text begins with a list of the titles of the aging author, presented as the chief administrator under king Isesi. The opening is addressed to the king: "O King, my lord! Age is here, old age arrived" (Lichtheim 1973, p. 62). This prefatory section seeks the king's 'order' that Ptahhotep create the instructions for his own son, as "a staff of old age." While the text is put forward as Ptahhotep giving his son words of advice, the preface places the king at the forefront. The preface addresses the king with a request to approve the creation of such a project, and then offers the king's words of authorization. Typically, this text is not just an official's discourse to his son, but is also being presented as having been created for the king, to benefit the king and his kingdom: "May such be done for you, So that strife may be banned from the people, And the Two Shores may serve you!" (p. 63). In this world, even a high-ranking father's advice to his son is conveyed as "ordered" by the king and as serving the king. The king's approval frames the presentation: "Said the majesty. . . . Instruct him then in the sayings of the past" (p. 63).

The following two excerpts are taken from the middle of the body of this long document:

> If you are a man who leads,
> Who controls the affairs of the many,
> Seek out every beneficent deed,
> That your conduct may be blameless.
> Great is justice, lasting in effect
> Unchallenged since the time of Osiris.
> One punishes the transgressor of laws,

Though the greedy overlooks this;
Baseness may seize riches,
Yet crime never lands its wares;
In the end it is justice that lasts. . . . (p. 64)

Be generous as long as you live
What leaves the storehouse does not return;
It is the food to be shared which is coveted,
One whose belly is empty is an accuser;
One deprived becomes an opponent,
Don't have him for a neighbor.
Kindness is a man's memorial
For the years after the function. (p. 72)

The picture of *Maat* presented in this early example is one of beneficence—the reader is advised to be generous and kind. However, the argument
for beneficence is not made on the grounds that the poor deserve food, or that
good should be done for its own sake. Instead, the appeal here is to personal
benefit: if you don't feed people, they will prove troublesome, but if you take
care of them, they will take care of your memorial or tomb, and will help ensure your life after death. Other instruction texts present a picture of doing
Maat that is centered more strongly on upright and just behaviors (*Merikare*,
Middle Kingdom), and/or on being silent and patient and speaking only when
needed (*Loyalist Teaching*, Middle Kingdom). In all cases, however, the appeal is based on personal benefit: do *Maat* so you gain respect, so you endure
on earth, so you are remembered, and so you ensure your station in the afterlife.

Other genres were available for reinforcing the importance of behaving
according to *Maat*. Many of these form part of the mortuary practices, such as
what we now call *The Book of the Dead*, the *Pyramid Texts*, the *Coffin Texts*,
or the tomb Autobiographies. There is no evidence that students in the schools
would have copied, read, or memorized most of these texts. But there is evidence that some of these texts formed highly visible parts of ritualized events
that members of communities would have attended. For instance, tomb autobiographies and other mortuary texts would have been recited aloud to the
community congregated for the entombment of a public official. Thus individuals would often have heard recited, or would even have read themselves,
the tomb autobiographies of officials. Such autobiographies offer no personal
information, but provide a list of career titles and assignments, as well as a
proclamation of the deceased's adherence to *Maat* and therefore his suitability
for the afterlife. As with the instructions, the autobiographies reinforced the
understanding of what it meant to do *Maat*.

One typical example of such an autobiography is from the tomb of a Middle Kingdom bureaucrat named Intef. As is common in these texts, the following portion constitutes a generic list of qualities and behaviors; such a list basically serves to offer a justification for going on to the afterlife.

> I was collected, kind, merciful,
> who quietened the weeper with a kind word.

> I was one generous to his dependent,
> who did what was excellent for his equal.

> I was one exact in the house of his lord,
> who knew flattery when spoken.

> I was generous, open-handed,
> a lord of provisions, free from neglect.
> . . .
> I was righteous, the likeness of a balance,
> truly exact like Thoth.

> I was firm-footed, excellent of counsel,
> one faithful to his benefactor.

> I was wise, one who taught himself wisdom,
> who took counsel so as to be asked for counsel.

> I was one who spoke in the office of Truth
> cleverly spoken in occasions of anxiety. (Parkinson, p. 63)

Though this has been considerably excerpted, the two halves of this recital remain apparent. The first half emphasizes kindness, mercy, generosity, open-handedness, friendship, sweetness to the have-nots, and care for the hungry. The second half points to another dimension of *Maat*—honesty, rectitude, righteousness, exactitude, fairness, firmness, patience, and cool-headedness. Again here, the justification for such actions is given as personal benefit: I took counsel, so I would be asked for counsel. The recital, with its long list of virtuous valued behaviors, in effect affirms that 'I have done *Maat* in my life.'

In short, these two popular genres were among the most widely available texts in the culture. The instructions were copied, memorized, and recited. The autobiographies were frequently read at communal occasions. Both of these genres present content designed to inculcate adherence to and enactment of *Maat*. They serve as guidelines for behavior of the elite, presenting the obligation of the elite to help maintain the well-being of the society.

The Letters Perform *Maat*

In ancient Egypt, writing became a significant part of the lives of citizens (Assmann 1996, p. 48). All families were taxed, and their contributions were recorded by scribes. Those serving in the administration would be assigned to duties away from home, at outposts, fortresses at the borders, temples, and tombs in the desert, for example. During flood season, major portions of the population would be assigned to work on large state projects, such as pyramids or tombs. These distant assignments offered frequent occasion for letters. The letters, written and read by scribes, would serve as ways to communicate with superiors and with families, even for those who were not literate. In addition, decrees announcing official policies would be read and posted. Those who felt they warranted legal redress could write, or hire a scribe to write, a petition. Both the decrees and petitions would be written in the form of letters. Letters were thus common in this culture among the administrators who ran the country. According to one prominent Egyptologist, Egyptians became inveterate letter writers (Kemp, 131).

Since 1990, a complete edition of English translations of the letters of ancient Egypt has been available (Wente); collections from particular periods appeared soon thereafter (Murnane 1995; Moran 1992). Examination of these sources shows that the letters often begin with quotes from and references to the previous elements in a dialogue. Even very early letters sent by kings present themselves as responses to another voice, situating themselves as contributions to an exchange among speakers within a practice of turn taking and response to prior turns. The letters use a variety of approaches to recognize and represent the voices being responded to in a dialogue. Often they use direct quotes, but at times they paraphrase, reporting the words of another indirectly. Occasionally, they just refer to the fact of having received such words and immediately move to response.

As Egyptologists Donald Redford and David Silverman point out suggestively, one important basis for all Egyptian written texts involves the oral context in performance (Redford 1992, p. 66; 1995, pp. 2223, 2225; Silverman, 102). They contend that all written texts in ancient Egypt would have been read aloud and thus performed in a sense. And they suggest that the written genres grew out of and remain embedded in oral situations in which such texts arose. For the genre of letters, the evidence suggests that scribes wrote most of the letters, whether the sender was literate or not (Wente, 6). Most letters would also have been read aloud by scribes to the receivers. Thus the letters were public texts, with broader audiences than just the designated receivers. Anyone within hearing range would hear such texts read aloud at the receiving end. Since scribes were involved in both writing and reading the letters, the voices of scribes appear in the genre conventions as well.

The letter below illustrates many of the common conventions of the genre, including the response to prior elements of a dialogue as well as the presence of the scribes in the dialogue. It comes from a king to his chief administrator, from Dynasty 13 in the Middle Kingdom.

[Year 5], third month of the second season, day 20. [Copy of] a royal decree that was brought to the office of the [reporter] of the Southern City (Thebes).

Royal decree [to the] city [prefect], vizier, and overseer of the six great law courts, Ankhu:

Now this decree of the king is brought to you to inform you that the elder of the portal Ibiyau, son of Remenyankh, has made petition saying, "May a warrant be put in writing, drawn up in the pavilion of the King's servant [. . .] against the assistant accountant of prisoners, Pay, who has been making illicit use of the fugitive Sankhu, in having him (Pay) brought to the Residence in order that he may be interrogated about the misappropriation he has committed," so he said.

Now it (the petition) has been granted. Have him [Pay] brought in custody (?) to the Residence so that you may then take action against him.

Now the King, l.p.h., is prosperous [and flourishing].[6]

(Wente, #11, pp. 24–25)

One can see in this letter the habit of quotation, in citing the actual words of the petition to which this decree responds. The statements of the initiator of this legal action, the petitioner Ibiyau, are not just reported here, but they are quoted. The king's decision is not here presented as a quote, though often that is the case. The opening does not say 'I write to inform you,' as a writer might do today. Since a scribe would read this aloud, it would be awkward for a scribe to be presenting himself in the first person, using the king's voice. Instead, the prose accommodates the fact that a scribe writes the decree and reads the decree aloud. The text is thus presented in the third person, explaining that "this decree of the king . . . inform[s] you." The phenomenon of the reading scribe seems to explain the avoidance of the first person in the letters through the Middle Kingdom (Wente 10, 24). The receiver of the letter, the chief administrator, is then told what to do: to have the malcreant brought to the palace, and then to take action against him.

It does not seem inevitable that a royal decree or proclamation be presented as a response to specific words of a specific individual. On the one hand, the letters simulate the crux of an oral situation, which before writing would have involved the petitioner standing before an administrator, voicing his request. The transference of the legal and communication process to writing continues to honor the specificity of that voice. On the other hand, the foregrounding of such voices seems to relate to the culture's emphasis on a sense of the responsibility of the elite for enacting justice and for ethical treatment of others. The genre conventions connect the major voices in the communication situation, presenting them as participating in a dialogue. In the letters, it is not uncommon to see quotes within quotes, if the petition or prior correspondence contained internal quotes. Such a construction, dependent on quotes, grounds itself in a sense of attentiveness to reproduce the voices and particular words of the other.

Another voice makes its appearance in the letters, as seen in the strange last line: "Now the King, l.p.h., is prosperous [and flourishing]." This line ends a letter from a king to his chief administrator. In this closing line, the king seems to declare himself as prosperous; alternately, one can see in this convention that the writing scribe declares the king as prosperous. This line in fact serves as much more than a declaration that 'this has been a great year for the king, increasing the king's personal fortune tremendously.' Instead, I suggest that this voice refers to the value system that governs this culture: *Maat*. This formulaic closing line is entirely conventional, though considerably varied in use. I suggest that it serves as a ritual reaffirmation of the order of things. In the culture's understanding of *Maat*, the king is the symbolic center of his people. For the people and the country to prosper, the king must prosper. The formulaic statement that ends the letter functions as affirmation that the king and thus the state are well. Through the "l.p.h." abbreviation, this line also includes a ritualistic prayer for the king's continued well being and long life. This abbreviation is used by Egyptologists to stand for the ubiquitous prayer-like phrase "may he have a long life, be prosperous, and healthy." The phrase is normally offered by an inferior about a superior, and it would be highly unusual for a king to use it in reference to himself. This ritual prayer reveals the voice of a writing scribe in the text, as the scribe performs an appropriate worshipful ritual on behalf of those serving the king. The very short concluding line offers a shorthand interpretation of the concept of *Maat*: if the king prospers, then he has served *Maat* well, and has served the gods well, along with their ordered creation, and the people. And the line ritually enacts the obligation of the elite, who have to do their part as well to maintain *Maat*. It serves an important epideictic function.

Often the conventions of the beginnings of letters enact a cultural understanding of the hierarchical roles and obligations of societal members, particularly when the letters come from those of lower status than the receivers. In these letters, individual names are not given in the body of the letter, nor are personal pronouns. The avoidance of such individualization renders a highly typified, generic effect. Often the characters involved in the letters occupy what seem to be represented as the major set of roles in the society. There's the king or majesty. There's the lord, which seems to cover anyone of higher status than the writer, except for the king. There's the brother, who seems to represent someone of equal status; and then there's the humble servant, of lower status than the recipient. The body of the letters names these roles, but does not normally name the particular person at the moment occupying that role. When the status differential between writer and recipient was not great, the letters might use second-person forms of address. But up to and including the Middle Kingdom, the first person was avoided (Wente, 10). Though the letters address specific communication situations, the entire effect seems generic. These communication customs distance the participants into nonspecific, hierarchical roles in society. Such letters come across as virtually fill-in-the-blanks exercises. However, what looks for most of a letter to be a routine progress report often turns out in the end to be something very different, as can be seen dramatically in the following letter from the New Kingdom, during the reign of Ramesses III, around 1160 B.C.E..

The fan-bearer on the king's right, the city prefect and vizier To. The scribe Neferhotep communicates to his lord: In life, prosperity and health! This is a missive to inform my lord.

A further communication to my lord to the effect that I am calling upon Amon-Re, King of the Gods, Mut and Khonsu, upon Pre-Harakhti, upon Amon of Menset, upon Nofretari of Menset, upon Amon of the Thrones of the Two Lands, upon Amon of the Beautiful Encounter, upon Ptah of Ramesses-miamon, upon Ptah of the Place of Beauty (Valley of the Queens) to the south of the Village, upon Hathor, mistress of the West, to its north, and upon Amenophis, who takes his set in the vicinity of the West Side, to keep Pharaoh, l.p.h., my good lord, healthy and to let him celebrate millions of jubilees as great ruler of every land forever and ever while you continue to be in his favor every day.

A further communication to my lord to the effect that I am working on the princes' tombs which my lord commanded to be made, I am working very properly and very excellently with good work and with excellent work. Let not my lord worry about them, since I am working very assiduously and am in no way slackening.

A further communication to my lord to the effect that we are exceedingly impoverished. All supplies for us that derive from the treasury, that derive from the granary, and that derive from the storehouse have been allowed to run out. A load of excavated (?) stone isn't light! Six *oipe*-measures of grain have been taken away from us besides only to be given to us as six *oipe*-measures of dirt.

May my lord provide us with a means of staying alive, since we

are already starving. We are no longer living if nothing whatsoever is
given to us.

(Wente, #56, 50-51; New Kingdom, Dynasty 20)

As can be seen here, the letter conventions are based on principles of
order, on a system of arrangement that enabled the composition of such documents. The pattern of ordering the letters reinforces the strongly hierarchical
basis of the society, emphasizing the roles and functions of members at different levels of society, and their responsibilities to those at higher levels. The
real point of the letter to a recipient of higher status comes only after extensive formulaic opening material. On the one hand, the letters seem to be
loosely structured as a list of separate points. In fact, the list seems to be the
basis of most texts in ancient Egypt (Silverman, 91–92; Forman and Quirke).
On the other hand, the introductory lists are based on a very particular internal
order. Though the opening of the letter above is more elaborate than most,
some version of such an opening is common in all such letters. A writer of
lower status is hereby demonstrating that his place in the order of things is to
serve his superior—his lord—thereby serving his king and the country's gods.
His duty in fulfilling *Maat* is to conscientiously and expeditiously carry out
the tasks assigned to him.

In the above letter, the first two sections suggest business as usual, as the
writer communicates wishes for longevity of the pharaoh and continued success of the recipient in his position as administrator serving the pharaoh. The
writer communicates that he is working diligently, and that the pharaoh and
his chief administrator need not worry about the tombs that the writer is assigned to work on. Only in the third and last entry in this three-part list do we
find the real point of the letter, which is far from business as usual. The workers at this desert location are starving and will die if no food is sent. It is quite
typical in the letters for the real information to be buffered, offered in two or
three lines toward the end. When a disparity in status exists between sender
and recipient, the writer enacts elaborate rituals in the letter before being free
to convey the information that serves as the raison d'etre of the document.
The form suggests a type of metonymic relation with the cultural ideology. In
its pyramidal structure, the letter reflects and reinforces the culture's values:
service to the king and gods are foremost, and service to the state follows
closely. Only then are the needs of individual subjects able to be considered.
The form enacts these principles of *Maat,* reinforcing and reflecting these
principles. Even when the communication need is urgent, the rituals demonstrating devotion to *Maat* must first be performed.

Thus I suggest that the letter-writing conventions involve much more
than formal conventions. The opening sections in the letter above offer no
new information, but function as ritual enactments of the communicator's def-

erence to *Maat,* to the right way. On one level, the writer follows *Maat* in using the appropriate form of a letter. More fundamentally, these formulaic opening statements serve as ritual performances of a subordinate's function in the scheme of maintaining *Maat,* demonstrating the subordinate's role in supporting *Maat* within the ideal functioning of society. These openings show the communicator doing *Maat,* enacting the rituals of *Maat,* carrying out the responsibilities of *Maat,* showing devotion to the principles of *Maat.* They put the message of a subordinate within a framework involving the mutual obligations and responsibilities of those at different levels of power for acting according to the good of society.

Do the Letters Teach *Maat?*

The letters rarely refer explicitly to *Maat.* Yet in many of the letters, covering a broad range of periods, we can see the writers attempting to influence the receivers by defining and interpreting what doing *Maat* might mean. Letters from kings often can be seen to do this, as is the case with the earliest available letters, from King Djedkare-Izezi in Dynasty 5, and letters from King Pepi in Dynasty 6. In these letters the king praises a recipient for doing what the king likes (Wente #2, 18–19), and for telling the truth to Pharaoh (Wente, #3, 20). Similarly, a number of the letters explicitly express a subordinate's desire not to do anything the superior dislikes, obliquely invoking such service as a principle of *Maat.* Here the letters personalize and concretize *Maat* in persuading as to what should be proper behavior, or in persuading that one is following proper behavior. Most commonly, such behavior is understood as pleasing the pharaoh and higher levels of the elite. A Dynasty 12 letter from King Senwosret to his chief treasurer offers a quite representative approach for persuading a subordinate to act. Here the king commands the treasurer to sail to Abydos in order to establish a monument for the god Osiris, referred to as the king's father (Wente, 24). Senwosret writes, **"Now it is in the proper way of doing things** in benefiting (?) my father Osiris that you will do this since . . . Majesty sends you, trusting in your doing everything to justify . . . Majesty's confidence" (emphasis mine). Except for the opening invocation of *Maat* as the proper way, the letter is typical in establishing a sense of personal obligation, as the king cites a range of things that majesty has already done for the receiver, which justifies the receiver's now doing what majesty asks (Wente, 24).

Egyptologist John Baines points out that for most of its history, ancient Egypt had a small, close-knit elite group of a few hundred men running the country (132). In all periods, the estates and positions of the elite "depended on the patronage of the King" (135). In the letters, we see that there was always a chain of command, and a superior on whom an individual administrator's fortunes would depend. The evidence of the letters suggests that in day-to-day functioning, the appeal to moral aspects of *Maat* took a back seat to the pragmatic realities of accountability within a privileged group centered on a strong leader. Especially from superiors to inferiors, the letters show a strong appeal to define *Maat* as identification with the desires of the pharaoh and of his relatively small core elite. The letters from subordinates to superiors also illustrate this desire to show identification and a will to please. The letters from both superiors and subordinates show an appeal to expediency as a part of *Maat*[7]: in this sense, doing *Maat* means giving leaders and subordinates information and materials and time they need to accomplish the important work of the state.

The letters operate in specific contexts, involving specific social interactions among writer and recipient. It was clearly inappropriate for a subordinate to argue with a superior, or to tell his superior outright what was involved in doing *Maat*. However, inferiors do seem to invoke the concept of *Maat* indirectly in the letters, if they need to offer protest to a superior. In the letter below, from Dynasty 8, a lower official attempts to suggest a reinterpretation of what is appropriate behavior of a superior.[8] The writer, Iruremtju, clearly is not satisfied with the superior's response to a situation in which Iruremtju feels victimized.

The count, seal-bearer of the Lower Egyptian king, sole companion, and chancellor of the god, Iruremtju to the sole companion and lector priest, Sobekhotpi's son, Khnumhotpi's son, the commander of troops, Merrenakht:

I have given my considered [attention] to the account of the business concerning which you sent the sole companion and steward Hotep in order that I not do anything you dislike. If the purpose of your writing to me is that you might expose the robbery that has been committed against me, well and good! But if the purpose of your doing this is to break up the fighting because of your seeing two foreign countries [. . .] me (?) [. . .] united, then I shall see whether you like the count, seal-bearer of the Lower Egyptian king, [sole companion], and overseer of scribes of the crews Sabni more than me.

It is, however, better to desire righteousness than prolonged crookedness. Consequently, this is an occasion for attending to every violation on the part of this count, for he is not one who is living off his own possessions. Inasmuch as you and I are in agreement that this count should not brush aside the robbery he has committed, you vouched for me in the Court of Horus (the King).

Morever, the sole companion and steward Hotep has seen that I
am not taking a stand against the troops of the lands of Medja and
Wawat (in Nubia) in order that I [not] do what you dislike.

Address: Iruremtju to the count, sole companion, and overseer of
priests, Re.

(Wente, #67, p. 58; Dynasty 8; emphasis mine)

In this letter, Iruremtju begins with the formulaic announcement of the
titles of his recipient, but also with deferential reference to the recipient's lin-
eage, offering the parents' names. The name of the recipient, Merrenakht, appears last in this honorific introduction. The writer then approaches his attempt to persuade Merrenakht, his superior, by announcing his great care in
reading the superior's correspondence, and his care not to displease the superior. He goes on to put the ideal interpretation on the superior's letter—one
that fits with his own view of the matter. It is clearly not a view he has confidence that his superior adheres to, and he explicitly allows the possibility that
the superior's letter might mean something different. Iruremtju goes on to approach the task of convincing this superior to act as Iruremtju wishes.

This letter buffers dissent with expressions of humility, deference, and a
desire to please. The writer emphasizes the fact that he and his superior have
been "in agreement" about some particulars of the situation in the past, as
well as the fact that the superior had already vouched for the writer in one situation. As much as possible, and typically for this culture, this writer seems to
have tried to turn a disagreement and protest into points of agreement. Significantly, the letter ends on a claim that the writer's action on another matter is
based on a will to please, or more precisely a will not to do anything that will
displease. The construction of this letter involves developing a representation
of unity and concord rather than division. This is a rhetoric of accommoda-
tion, characteristic of the Egyptian approach.

Crucial to the persuasion in this letter is the bolded sentence, where the
writer offers a suggestion for a revised way of thinking about the situation
based on *Maat*—different from the way the superior now approaches it. He
points out that valuing righteous behavior is preferable to valuing crooked behavior, using this ethical principle of *Maat* to redefine what is proper and improper in the particular context under discussion. He translates *Maat* to this
particular setting, offering his analysis of its application, without directly crit-
icizing the position of the superior. The persuasion is indirect.

As seen here, inferiors could and did invoke the concept of *Maat*
obliquely in order to convince superiors to act upon concepts of beneficence,
compassion, righteousness, or justice—all concepts associated with *Maat*
(Assmann, 1989; Lichtheim, 1997). Alternatively, inferiors could and did in-

voke concepts of expediency—for instance, citing the need to save workers' time in order to allow the important work of the state to get done (see Wente, #40, #98, #106). The references to these aspects of *Maat* are often veiled, but they do appear in the letters. These presentations offer ways for writers of lower status to offer ballast for their suggestions of appropriate behavior by superiors. Given that the culture's understanding of *Maat* covered such a broad scope, writers could build on that breadth to suggest alternate interpretations, grounded in considerations of *Maat*, as to what constituted right action in particular situations. Even when the term itself is technically absent, it does seem indirectly present. The letters seem to demonstrate different types of appeals to *Maat* common to and available to different groups at different levels of the power structure. All writers and receivers are part of the elite, but reside at different rungs of the hierarchy. The conventions allow a range of voices to engage in an ongoing pragmatic discussion about what it means to behave according to *Maat*, within a decidedly undemocratic system.

Maat as Superaddressee in the Letters of Ancient Egypt

I have suggested above that writers of the letters often obliquely define *Maat* behavior for their readers. I propose further that a third voice exists in the exchanges, beyond the writer and receiver, beyond the scribes. In Mikhail Bakhtin's terms, I suggest the presence of a voice that Bakhtin labeled the superaddressee. In a notebook entry from Bakhtin's later period, known as "The Problem of the Text," Bakhtin introduced a valuable extension of his earlier notion of addressivity. He offered the new term "superaddressee," which refers to a higher authority that a speaker or writer addresses, beyond the immediate audience. The superaddressee is an audience "whose absolutely just responsive understanding is presumed" (125–26). Bakhtin provided some examples of this imagined higher addressee, which might be "God, absolute truth, the court of dispassionate human conscience . . . [or] science" (126). In the texts of ancient Egypt, I propose that culture's conception of *Maat* functions as a superaddressee. That is, the individual utterances not only invoke *Maat* for rhetorical purposes, but also seem to be putting themselves up for understanding by and assessment before *Maat*.

While in the human realm of ancient Egypt, there may well have been differences of opinion in understanding what constituted proper behavior according to *Maat* in particular circumstances, ultimately the goddess *Maat* was understood to make a judgment in the hall of *Maat*, weighing the heart of the dead. The genre of letters seems to instantiate such a judgment scene, in which writers demonstrate to a fully understanding *Maat* that they are doing

Maat in particular situations. The goddess *Maat* hovers over these texts as the ideal receiver, the final authority, who will understand fully how the texts perform and present adherence to *Maat*. These letters put forth interpretations and enactments of *Maat* for weighing, similar to the weighing of a deceased individual's heart. The rhetorical system has created conventions for letter writing that invite final scrutiny by *Maat*. Often larger portions of the letters seem to be constructed for the third voice, as an appeal to the cultural codes, than are formulated for the needs of the immediate receivers. While the rhetorical system may seem to modern readers to function a-rhetorically for the particular communication situation, the omnipresence of the superaddressee suggests a broader, more complex rhetorical context for these day-to-day administrative communications.

In fact, in the ancient Egyptian culture, writing was highly valued, and written texts were often copied onto the walls of tombs or onto funerary stelae. At other times, letters were copied onto papyri and buried with the dead as treasured objects (Wente, pp. 3, 5, 17). There was not a sense that the administrative letters were transient objects, to be used for the immediate purpose and then discarded. Some of the media used for the letters, such as pottery, tablets, or stone, were viewed as eternal. As Assmann points out astutely, the gods and the world of the dead were considered important audiences for texts and artifacts and were treated as available publics (1996, p. 33). Rhetorically, then the conventions of the letter genre seem to have been based on an understanding of long-term availability for multiple audiences and multiple purposes. These purposes range from persuasion within the immediate context to demonstration of proper performance of *Maat* within a timeless, divine dimension.

Conclusion

This brief glimpse of the instructions and autobiographical genres, as well as the more extensive examination of the letters genre, shows the ways that all of these genres function as reinforcement of the culture's effort to promote the doing of *Maat*. Analysis of the letters genre reveals the conventions as performative, demonstrating the doing of *Maat* for the immediate receiver and for *Maat*, the ultimate receiver. An article-length study of texts covering a 1500-year period inevitably looks to some broad similarities and tendencies, but cannot examine closely the particular forms and approaches in particular periods of Egyptian history. I must emphasize that the conventions were by no means static, nor was the precise understanding of doing *Maat*. Further study will be needed to address the rhetorical changes, to examine the rhetorical conventions in relation to the changes in the culture over time. However, this preliminary study does suggest a close relationship between the ancient Egyptian culture's major values and its rhetorical formulations. The rhetorical system simultaneously reflects and reinforces the cultural system, while also ritually enacting its major values.

Notes

1. These include an analysis by Michael Fox, proposing the five canons of ancient Egyptian rhetoric. George Kennedy's pioneering book on *Comparative Rhetoric* includes a unit on Egyptian rhetoric, focusing on the wisdom texts and the Amarna letters. One article addressed the medical rhetoric (Lipson 1990), while another examined the epideictic element of the Amarna letters (Harpine). A forthcoming article looks at the multimedia nature of ancient Egyptian public texts (Lipson).

2. Photo by E. Lipson of family artifact. At the left, the god Anubis accompanies the deceased to the hall of judgment. Next, the heart is weighed, and the god Thoth records the positive outcome. The Swallowing Monster hovers by the scale, should the verdict prove negative. At the right, the god Horus escorts the deceased to the throne of Osiris.

3. Approximate dates are given for the periods of Egyptian history, based on Barbara Watterson, *The Egyptians*, Oxford, UK: Blackwell, 1997, xix–xx. Egyptian history is traditionally counted in dynasties. The dynasties are further grouped into periods: the major divisions, referred to in this essay, involve the Old Kingdom, the Middle Kingdom, the New Kingdom, and the Late Period.

4. For full studies of *Maat*, see Jan Assmann, *Maat, l'Egypte Pharaonique et l'Idee de Justice Sociale.* Paris: Juilliard, 1989. Also Miriam Lichtheim, *Maat in Egyptian Autobiographies and Related Studies.* Fribourg, Schweiz: Universitatsverlag Freiburg, 1992, as well as Lichtheim, *Moral Values in Ancient Egypt.* Fribourg, Switzerland, University Press of Fribourg, 1997.

5. The oldest manuscript of *Ptahhotep* dates from the Middle Kingdom. Miriam Lichtheim posits that the text was composed in the Sixth Dynasty, at the end of the Old Kingdom, one hundred years before (*Ancient Egyptian Literature,* pp. 6–7).

6. In all letter translations presented in this article, parentheses ( ) indicate the translator's insertion of words that do not appear in the Egyptian text, but which he deems necessary to the sense; this includes clarifying additions as well. Square brackets [ ] indicate the translator's restoration of text; this mostly involves text that the translator deems has been inadvertently omitted by the scribe. A sequence of three dots signals the presence of a portion of damaged or obscure text that cannot be translated. Italics indicate Egyptian words left untranslated.

7. Note the parallels with Kenneth Burke's discussion of identification as the basis of rhetoric. Burke cites Aristotle's analysis of rhetorical tactics, especially the "shift between public and private orders of motivation [in which] in public, one praises

the just and the beautiful, but in private one prefers the text of expediency" (A Rhetoric of Motives. Berkeley: University of California Press, 1969, p. 57).

8. Dynasty 8 falls within the First Intermediate Period, between the end of the Old Kingdom and the start of the Middle Kingdom. The dating would be approximately 2170 to 2160 B.C.E.

Works Cited

Assmann, Jan. *Maat, l'Egypte Pharaonique et l'Idée de Justice Sociale.* Paris: Juilliard, 1989.

_____. *The Mind of Egypt: History and Meaning in the Time of the Pharaohs.* Transl. Andrew Jenkins. New York: Metropolitan Books, Henry Holt and Co., 1996.

Baines, John. "Society, Morality, and Religious Practice." In Bryon Shafer, ed. *Religion in Ancient Egypt.* Ithaca, NY: Cornell University Press, 1993: 123–200.

Bakhtin, M. M. "The Problem of the Text," *Speech Genres.* Austin: University of Texas Press, 1987: 103–126.

Burke, Kenneth. *A Rhetoric of Motives.* Berkeley: University of California Press, 1969.

Donadoni, Sergio, ed. *The Egyptians.* Chicago: University of Chicago Press, 1997.

Feucht, Erica. "Women." In Sergio Donadoni, ed. *The Egyptians.* Chicago: University of Chicago Press, 1997: 315-46.

Forman, Werner and Stephen Quirke. *Hieroglyphics and the Afterlife in Ancient Egypt.* Norman: University of Oklahoma Press, 1996.

Fox, Michael. "Ancient Egyptian Rhetoric." *Rhetorica* 1 (Spring 1983): 9–22.

Harpine, William D. "Epideictic and Ethos in the Amarna Letters: The Withholding of Argument." *Rhetoric Society Quarterly* 28.1 (1998): 81–98.

Kemp, Barry. *Ancient Egypt: Anatomy of a Civilization.* New York: Routledge, 1989.

Kennedy, George. *Comparative Rhetoric.* New York: Oxford University Press, 1998.

Lichtheim, Miriam. *Ancient Egyptian Literature: The Old and Middle Kingdoms.* Vol. 1. Berkeley: University of California Press, 1973.

_____. *Maat in Egyptian Autobiographies and Related Studies.* Fribourg, Schweiz: Universitatsverlag Fribourg, 1992.

_____. *Moral Values in Ancient Egypt.* Fribourg, Switzerland: University Press of Fribourg, 1997.

Lipson, Carol. "Ancient Egyptian Medical Texts." *Journal of Technical Writing and Communication* 20 (1990): 391–409.

_____. "Recovering the Multimedia History of Writing in the Public Texts of Ancient Egypt." in *Eloquent Images,* ed. Mary Hocks and Michelle Kendrick. Cambridge, Mass.: MIT University Press, Forthcoming.

Martin, Henri-Jean. *The History and Power of Writing.* Trans. Lydia Cochrane. Chicago: University of Chicago Press, 1994.

Moran, William, editor and translator. *The Amarna Letters.* Baltimore: Johns Hopkins University Press, 1992.

Murnane, William J. *Texts from the Amarna Period in Egypt.* Atlanta, Georgia: Scholars Press, 1995.

Parkinson, R. B. *Voices From Ancient Egypt: An Anthology of Middle Kingdom Writings.* Norman, Oklahoma: University of Oklahoma Press, 1991.

Quirke, Stephen, and Jeffrey Spencer, eds. *The British Museum Book of Ancient Egypt.* London: Thames and Hudson, 1992.

Redford, Donald. *Egypt, Canaan and Israel in Ancient Times.* Princeton, NJ: Princeton University Press, 1992.

_____. "Ancient Egyptian Literature: An Overview." *Civilizations of the Ancient Near East.* Ed. Jack Sasson. New York: Charles Scribner's and Sons, 1995. Vol. 4.

Shafer, Byron, ed. *Religion in Ancient Egypt.* Ithaca, NY: Cornell University Press, 1993.

Silverman, David, ed. *Ancient Egypt.* New York: Oxford University Press, 1997.

Watterson, Barbara. *The Egyptians.* Oxford, UK: Blackwell Publishers, 1997.

Wente, Edward, trans. *Letters from Ancient Egypt.* Atlanta, GA: Scholars Press, 1990.

Law, Rhetoric, and Gender in Ramesside Egypt

Deborah Sweeney

Introduction

The investigation of rhetoric in ancient Egypt has focused mainly on the elite and on the more formal aspects of eloquence expressed in literary and monumental texts.[1] In this essay, in contrast, I will attempt to trace rhetoric in a more everyday context, in legal texts from the extensive corpus of the Ramesside Period (ca. 1300–1070 B.C.E.). I will investigate two different faces of rhetoric—on one hand, the art of persuasion,[2] and on the other, the stylistic means used to enhance eloquence.[3] I will also contrast women's use of these devices in court with the use men made of them.

Training in Rhetoric

Elite males and scribes in ancient Egypt learned eloquence partly by practice and emulation as trainee administrators, and partly by copying and memorizing instruction texts composed for male members of the elite, which stressed speech norms such as truthfulness and modesty. Women from the elite and scribal classes usually did not hold formal scribal office and thus did not attend school.[4] They may have learned to read and write at home, but it is not clear what exposure they had to the teachings. Conceivably, women who learned to read and write might have copied extracts from them while learning, as did male students. They might also have heard these texts read aloud, since Egyptian literary texts were often performed to an audience.[5]

It is even less certain how well literary texts were known outside the elite. C. J. Eyre argues that only a highly restricted group of people were capable of understanding the literary allusions and interquotations used in royal inscriptions,[6] although elsewhere he suggests that literary texts might have been performed in more popular settings, such as "the ancient equivalent of the coffee-shop, party or public ceremony."[7]

Legal Texts

No comprehensive law codes are known from Egypt at this time. A few royal decrees from the New Kingdom (1550–1070 B.C.E.) are preserved, listing specific measures to eradicate abuses or to protect a given institution. New Kingdom legal practice is mostly known from records of individual cases. These written records tend to summarize the dialogue, weeding out the repetitions and redundancies of spoken language.[8] They do not necessarily represent the exact words uttered.[9]

Many legal records of small-scale interpersonal disputes[10] come from the village of Deir el-Medîna, the home of the workmen who built and decorated the royal tombs of the Valley of the Kings (ca. 1500–1080 B.C.E.). The workmen had their own law court, which settled disputes and legal arrangements between the workmen themselves, and between the workmen and outside parties, generally dealing with private issues,[11] such as failure to pay debts, theft, and property disputes. More serious cases, such as perjury under oath or theft of government property, were referred to the workmen's supervisor, the vizier. Both women and men appear as witnesses, accusers, and defendants, although only very rarely did women form part of the court.[12]

Legal texts were often written on papyri, but in Deir el-Medîna many were jotted down on ostraca (potsherds or small pieces of stone). Ostraca tend to be small, on average about the size of a modern postcard, so the texts written on them are briefer and more summary in style, whereas the papyri tend to include more detail.

Other records of property arrangements and inheritance disputes are known from other sites in Egypt at this period. Several texts feature women prominently. For instance, the Inscription of Mose narrates a long-drawn-out legal dispute over family lands. During the reign of Horemheb a woman named Werel represented this family in administering the family estate, including litigation over the property, and later, during the reign of Ramesses II, the widow Nubnofret from the same family appealed to the vizier to defend her rights to the land. In Papyrus Ashmolean Museum 1945.96 (also known as the Adoption Papyrus) a childless couple, Nanefer and her husband Nebnefer, make various unconventional legal arrangements to dispose of their property. Instead of bequeathing his property to his siblings, which may have been the norm for childless couples, Nebnefer adopts his wife Nanefer as his daughter so that she can inherit his property. After his death, Nanefer frees and adopts three slave children who have grown up in their household and have formed an alternative family for her.[13]

The most dramatic legal texts of this period are undoubtedly the records of the trial of the members of the royal household of Ramesses III (ca. 1153 B.C.E.), who conspired to stage a coup (the "Harem Conspiracy"), and the royal commissions of enquiry during the reigns of Ramesses IX (1126–1108 B.C.E.) and XI (1099–1069 B.C.E.) into the robberies at the royal tombs in the Valley of the Kings and the Valley of the Queens, and the thefts from the royal mortuary temples in Western Thebes.[14]

COURT PROCEDURE

Professional lawyers did not exist in ancient Egypt; generally, everyone spoke for themselves.[15] The plaintiff and defendant might produce witnesses, and the members of the court might ask questions. The court made a decision, announced its verdict, and then the loser swore an oath obliging himself to pay whatever penalty the court demanded, under pain of a severe beating or an additional fine.[16]

In testamentary disputes, the testator explained their intentions. Other interested parties might be obliged to take oaths to honor these arrangements.

In interrogations, such as the tomb robbery enquiries, culprits and witnesses were placed under oath to speak the truth and were questioned by the court. If they refused to speak, they were tortured by beating and by having their hands and feet mangled, either until they gave evidence or until it was plain that they had nothing to say.[17]

Legal Argument

There is no ancient discussion of what might have constituted convincing proof in ancient Egyptian litigation, but it may be inferred from people's attempts to convince the court in legal cases.

Documents might be produced as evidence. For example, in the Inscription of Mes, Nubnofret asks the vizier to produce the official land register, so that she can prove her right to the family holdings (line N7). In P BM 10053 v1.9–10, evidence was submitted in writing by someone who "wrote down every theft he had committed in every inspection of his." This practice is rare in Ramesside legal texts, however.

Either side might produce witnesses to corroborate their account. Alternatively, suspects might also challenge the court to bring someone to accuse them. One woman offers, "I am the fourth wife. The two others are dead and the other one is alive. Have the one who is alive brought so that she can accuse me" (P BM 10052 v15.7–8).

People sometimes appealed to the judgment of the god by inviting the deity's oracle to participate in the legal process.[18] The gods were also considered to intervene of their own accord, by inflicting illness, nightmares, or twinges of bad conscience to encourage witnesses to rescind false evidence or to come forth with information they had previously withheld.[19] On the other hand, personal revelations from the gods had to be verified officially by the god via his oracle. For instance, when a man named Merysekhmet alleged that the god had decreed that he should share in the chapel of Qenna, although he had not lifted a finger to build it, Qenna approached the oracle. The god denied this pronouncement and forbade Merysekhmet from approaching the chapel in the future (O BM 5625).[20] However, Merysakhmet enjoyed a particularly bad reputation as a slippery customer.[21] His claims to have been favored by divine revelations would probably have met with a certain scepticism in any case.

Interrogators, plaintiffs, and defendants used rhetorical questions to highlight assumptions about the case or possible conclusions to draw from the evidence. For instance, one interrogator asks a suspect, "You are the storehouse keeper of the men—how was it that you were standing by them while they were discussing if they did not give you a share?" (P BM 10052 v8.11–12). The interrogator implies that if the thieves allowed the suspect to hear their discussion, he must have been in league with them.

As part of the argument, hypothetical situations might be imagined. During the tomb robbery trials, one of the interrogators suggested, "In the event that I were to go and steal a goat-skin from a stable and someone else went after me, wouldn't I denounce him to make the punishment fall on him as well as on me?" (P BM 10052 r1.19–21).[22]

As counterarguments, the accused might deny all knowledge of the issue, using formulae such as "I didn't see anything whatsoever" (e.g. P BM 10052 r6.13) and "If I had seen, I would have said so" (e.g. P BM 10403 v3.31).[23] Alternatively, a suspect might offer a more innocuous explanation of the facts. One woman suspected of receiving stolen property argued that she received it as the price for food she sold during a famine: "The officials said to her, 'What is the story of the silver which X worked for Y?' She said, 'I got it in exchange for barley in the Year of the Hyenas when there was a famine.'" (P BM 10052 v11.7–8)[24] Occasionally, people provided themselves with alibis—for example, one thief claimed that he was in prison at the time of the thefts, and therefore could not have committed them (P Mayer A v8.21–22).

Culprits might also insist that false accusations had been brought against them out of personal enmity: "As for X, (he is) my enemy, and I quarrelled with him and I said to him, 'You will be mutilated because of this theft which you did in the necropolis,' and he said to me, 'If I go I will take you with me.'" (P BM 10052 r4.8–10)[25] Usually, however, defamation of character seldom appears in the court records as a rhetorical tactic. Damaging remarks about the defendant were recorded only when they happened to be relevant to the case under discussion: for example if a debtor had already defaulted on the same payment several times (e.g. O OIC 12703; O Gardiner 53), or had admitted to being in the wrong out of court (O DeM 580). Maybe this polite behavior is connected to the explicit prohibitions in Egyptian wisdom literature against repeating calumny.[26] Alternatively, the recording scribe may simply have weeded out insults as irrelevant to the proceedings.

Exceptions to an argument might also be invoked. For instance, in Papyrus Abbott, the mayor of Eastern Thebes had brought accusations that the royal tombs had been robbed. After an official commission of enquiry had found most of the kings' tombs intact, the inhabitants of Western Thebes came to jeer at the mayor of Eastern Thebes. The latter tried to squelch his adversaries' jubilation by pointing out that one of the royal tombs had nonetheless been robbed (P Abbott 6.2–3).

Precedents were invoked in court to confirm the verdict, rather than to prove the defendant innocent or guilty. For example, a scribe reporting a theft of state property to the vizier remarks that a woman who made a similar theft in previous years had been severely punished, as a precedent for punishing the current offender severely (O Nash 1 v12–13).

Style and Rhetoric

By and large, Egyptian court records do not record elaborate forensic oratory like that of ancient Greece and Rome. However, the recorded dialogue includes various simple rhetorical devices. Repetition and parallelism were often used for effect. For example, the standard oath formula used during the Ramesside period is reinforced by parallelism, "As Amun endures, and as Pharaoh (life, prosperity and health!) whose power is more terrible than death endures. . ." To some extent, the conflict of two opposing interests in litigation naturally evoked antithesis, and we find formulae such as: "One found the scribe X in the right, and one found the painter Y in the wrong" (O Berlin 12654 r9).[27]

Parallelism and antithesis were used to enable the speaker to open up certain options and exclude others, or to reaffirm the choices they had made or obligations to which they were committed. A man hiring a donkey promised, "Should the donkey die, I will be liable for it. Should it live, I will be liable for it." (O Berlin P. 1121 r7–8).

Parallel constructions and antithesis were particularly common in inheritance cases. Antithesis was often used to explain the background to disinheriting people, contrasting the speaker's generosity and someone else's ingratitude, or one person's helpfulness as opposed to another party's callousness.

For example, Naunakhte, a woman living at Deir el-Medîna, bequeathed her property to those of her children who had supported her in old age, cutting her ungrateful children out of her will.1 "I brought up these eight servants of yours (her children), and I gave them household equipment—everything which one usually does for people like them. Now look, I have grown old. Now look, they are not looking after me in my turn. As for every one of them who has given me a hand, I will give him my property. As for anyone who has not helped me, I will not give him my property." (Naunahkte I col. 2.2–7)[29]

The speaker might also use parallel constructions and antithesis when listing those who would be affected by their will, particularly those excluded who might contest the arrangements. For instance, in the Adoption Papyrus (v3–4) it is stipulated that "should a son or daughter, a brother or a sister of their mother or father dispute with them. . .". A similar declaration states that "neither son nor daughter will speak against it. Their complaints will not be heard." (Naunakhte IV. 3)[30]

Listing someone's property, or someone's misdeeds, also tends to engender parallel constructions. For example, the misdeeds of the chief workman Paneb from Deir el-Medîna included liasons with the wives of several of his subordinates: "He had intercourse with citizeness Tuy when she was the wife of crewman Qenna. He had intercourse with citizeness Hunero when she was with Pendwa. . . He had intercourse with citizeness Hunero when she was with Hesysunebef, and when he had intercourse with citizeness Hunero, he had intercourse with Wabkhet her daughter, and Aapehty his son had intercourse with Wabkhet too." (P Salt 124 r2.2–4)

Pathos was used in inheritance cases, both to blame the ingratitude of relatives who were expected to support the speaker in illness and old age, and to praise the faithfulness of those who offered support. This behavior is represented in a very low-key manner, stating that someone did or did not do good to the speaker, perhaps connected with the Egyptian ideal of not speaking ill of other people. However, these statements would probably have been more significant in an Egyptian setting than they appear to us, since they were linked both to well-established social expectations that one's spouse and children should take care of one in times of need, and to fears of being abandoned to destitution if they failed to do so. For example, the woman Nanefer in the Adoption Papyrus (r18–20) describes the slave children who have become part of her family on an informal basis and whom she now intends to adopt officially: "I have reached this day with them and they have done no harm to me, but they have benefited me, and we have no son or daughter apart from them."

Whereas parallelism, antithesis, and pathos were used frequently, other rhetorical features appear only rarely. For instance, a certain number of metaphors appear, but it is not clear whether they were standard phrases or newly minted by their speakers. The father of one of the tomb-robbers scolds his mates, "As for the noose of . . . which [you] have laid upon the neck of the lad, you have come to take away his share and yet his punishment will overtake him tomorrow." (P BM 10052 r3.14–15)[31]

Hyperbole occasionally appears. For example, during an enquiry into the safety of the royal necropolis, one of the workmen of Deir el-Medîna asserts, "As for all the kings . . . they are intact. They are protected and ensured for eternity." (P Abbott r6.5–7)

Pars pro toto (synecdoche) is sometimes used. For example, one woman promises, "I will prepare a coffin for my husband, I will bury him." (O DeM 225 r5) Since the coffin was the major constituent of a person's tomb equipment,[32] this essential item stands for the remaining food, clothing, items of personal adornment, and ritual items which would also have accompanied her husband to the grave.

Tropes sometimes appear: for instance, in one case a litigant addresses the oracle as "my great light!" (O Petrie 21 r6) The same is true of merismus (one case deals with "access for entry and exit" [O CGC 25555v6)], litotes[33] (during the commission of enquiry into the tomb robberies, one official asserts, "It is no light accusation which this mayor of Thebes made" (P Abbott 6.8–9)) and alliteration (for instance, O CGC 25555 v2 speaks of [*jr n3 ht n t3]jj s.t m sb n s3jj.w n sb3* which can be loosely translated in order to preserve the alliteration, "as for the property in this place, comprising posts and planks at the portal. . .").

Women in Court

Women could bring cases and be sued, make contracts, and hold and bequeath property in their own right. In theory, at any rate, they had exactly the same legal rights and responsibilities as men.[34] In the official record, male officials treat women the same as men, both for good and ill, since the female suspects in the tomb robbery trials were tortured to make them give evidence, just like the men.[35]

However, women were probably at a disadvantage in the legal system. In many societies where public speaking contexts are prestigious, women tend to be granted less opportunity to speak in public.[36] In such cases, men are likely to develop a public speaking voice, whereas women tend to be more forthcoming in private,[37] less so in public. Public contexts are likely to be male contexts, whose rules for procedure tend to be made by men.[38]

Women of the scribal class in the New Kingdom lacked the on-the-job training in eloquence to which men of the same social standing had access, since they seldom held official bureaucratic posts.[39] Women may therefore have been at a disadvantage in male-dominated public forums,[40] although they did undertake other tasks that would have given them practice in public performance, such as officiating as cultic singers.[41] Women of slightly lower social standing engaged in small-scale trading and sold articles in the market,[42] which would have given them some experience in negotiation.

The speech patterns of both sexes in court were fairly similar. Like their male counterparts, women told their stories using chains of past narrative forms headed by a main clause with past time reference: "When the war of the chief priest happened, this man stole the property of my father, and my father said, 'I will not let this man enter my house,' and he became ..." (P BM 10052 13.24–26).

Maybe women made an effort to adopt male speech patterns in order to succeed in a male-dominated environment, but it is also possible that the recording scribes standardized spoken utterances, as they summarized them for the written record.[43]

Women used antithesis, parallelism, and pathos, since many of the cases in which they spoke at length concerned inheritance. They also used repetition for emphasis elsewhere. For example, the speaker in Ostracon Nash 5 (a possible case of wife-beating)[44] says, "He beat me, he beat me!" On the other hand, the utterances attributed to women feature relatively few other stylistic elaborations—almost no metaphors or hyperbole are associated with women. Since these elements are rare in any case, and since fewer utterances by women have been recorded, this distribution may simply reflect the inadequacy of our sources, rather than a genuine gender difference.

In theory, women in ancient Egypt had considerable equality before the law. They could inherit and bequeath property, undertake major property transactions, and summon others to court without needing the permission of husbands or male relatives. In practice, however, women may not have been able to implement their rights.[45] Women initiated fairly few court cases.[46] Maybe only the toughest or the most desperate women took cases to court.

By contrast, Barbara Lesko argues that Egyptian women behaved quite assertively in court and in other informal settings.[47] It is true that women's behavior in these contexts sometimes appears more assertive than the norm of decorum and self-restraint in public speech that wisdom texts prescribe for officials. However, Lesko's suggestion that the women spoke in this way because they had little exposure to wisdom literature is equally true of many of the men who appear in the legal records. The male culprits in the tomb-robbery trials, for instance, express themselves with no less gusto than the women. Actually, even the officials, who had been educated in the wisdom tradition, seldom refer to this tradition in court.

This issue seems to be a difference in genre rather than a gender issue. The norms of performance in court or of recording legal texts were designed to facilitate the outcome of an argument and to record the main facts in the case and its outcome—who owed what to whom, who would inherit what property, and so on. They therefore seldom record rhetoric of the density that appears in literary texts.

Abbreviations

BM   British Museum
CGC   Catalogue Général des Antiquités Égyptiennes du musée du Caire. Nos. 255–1–25832.
HOP   Schafik Allam, *Hieratische Ostraka und Papyri der Ramessidenzeit* (Tübingen: im Selbstverlag des Herausgebers, 1973)
JEA   *Journal of Egyptian Archaeology*
P   Papyrus
O   Ostracon
r   recto
v   verso

Notes

This research was supported by The Israel Science Foundation (grant no. 797/98). Many thanks to Dr. Orly Goldwasser for her comments on a draft of this paper, and to my assistant, Mr. Nir Lalkin, for help in its preparation.

1. Laurent Coulon, "La rhétorique et ses fictions: pouvoirs et duplicité du discours à travers la littérature égyptienne du Moyen et du Nouvel Empire," *Bulletin de l'Institut Français d'Archéologie Orientale* 99 (1999): 103–132, summarising earlier literature. For rhetoric in less formal contexts see Barbara Lesko, "Women's Rhetoric from Ancient Egypt." In *Listening to Their Voices: The Rhetorical Activities of Historical Women,* edited by Molly Meijer Wertheimer, 89–111 (Columbia: University of South Carolina Press, 1997); *idem,* "'Listening' to the Ancient Egyptian Woman: Letters, Testimonials and Other Expressions of Self." In *Gold of Praise: Studies on Ancient Egypt in Honor of Edward F. Wente (Studies in Ancient Oriental Civilization* 58), edited by Emily Teeter and John A. Larson, 247–254. (Chicago: University of Chicago Press, 1999).

2. Friedrich Junge, "Rhetorik." In *Lexikon der Ägyptologie,* vol. V, edited by Wolfgang Helck and W. Westendorf, 250–253. (Wiesbaden: Harrassowitz, 1984); Coulon, "La rhétorique et ses fictions," 103–104.

3. Waltraud Guglielmi, "Der Gebrauch rhetorischer Stilmittel in der ägyptischen Literatur." In *Ancient Egyptian Literature: History and Forms (Probleme der Ägyptologie,* 10) edited by Antonio Loprieno, 465–497. (Leiden, New York and Cologne: Brill, 1996).

4. Gay Robins, *Women in Ancient Egypt* (London: British Museum Press, 1993), 111. For female literacy see Steven Blake Shubert, "Does She or Doesn't She? Female Literacy in Ancient Egypt," *Proceedings of the Near and Middle Eastern Civilizations Graduate Students' Annual Symposia 1998–2000* (Toronto: Benben Publications, 2001), 55–76 and literature cited therein.

5. Christopher John Eyre, "Why Was Egyptian Literature?" In *VI Congresso Internazionale di Egittologia,* vol. II, edited by Gian Maria Zaccone and Tomaso Ricardi di Netro, 115–120. (Turin: Tipografia Torinese—Stabilimento Poligrafico S.p.A., 1993).

6. Christopher John Eyre, "The Semna Stelae: Quotation, Genre, and Functions of Literature." In *Studies in Egyptology presented to Miriam Lichtheim,* 2 vols., edited by Sarah Israelit Groll, 163. (Jerusalem: Magnes Press, 1990).

7. Eyre, "Why Was Egyptian Literature?," 120.

8. Orly Goldwasser, "'Low' and 'High' Dialects in Ramesside Egyptian." In *Textcorpus und Wörterbuch,* edited by Stefan Grunert and Ingelore Hafemann, 312. (Leiden: Brill, 1999).

9. Lesko, "'Listening' to the Ancient Egyptian Woman," 247.

10. For legal texts from Deir el-Medîna, see *HOP* (passim); Andrea G. McDowell, *Jurisdiction in the Workmen's Community of Deir el-Medîna* (*Egyptologische Uitgaven* V.) (Leiden: Nederlands Instituut voor het Nabije Oosten te Leiden, 1990). For additional texts from this site, see most recently Andrea G. McDowell, *Village Life in Ancient Egypt: Laundry Lists and Love Songs* (Oxford: Oxford University Press, 1999) and the texts listed in the Deir el-Medîna Database, at http://www.leidenuniv.nl/nino/dmd/dmd.html.

11. See McDowell, *Jurisdiction,* 156–158 for some exceptions.

12. McDowell, *Village Life,* 169–170.

13. For Ramesside legal texts in general see, *HOP,* passim. For the Inscription of Mose, see Gaballa Ali Gaballa, *The Memphite Tomb-Chapel of Mose* (Warminster: Aris and Phillips, 1977), 22–24, pls. 50–55, 58–62; Schafik Allam, "Some Remarks on the Trial of Mose," *JEA* 75 (1989): 103–112. For the Adoption Papyrus, see Alan Henderson Gardiner, "Adoption Extraordinary," *JEA* 26 (1940): 23–29; Christopher John Eyre, "The Adoption Papyrus in Social Context," *JEA* 78 (1992): 207–221 and literature cited therein.

14. For the Harem Conspiracy, see Adrian de Buck, "The Judicial Papyrus of Turin," *JEA* 23 (1937): 152–164. For the robberies, see Thomas Eric Peet, *The Mayer Papyri A and B. Nos. M. 11162 and M. 11186 of the Free Public Museums, Liverpool* (London: Egypt Exploration Society, 1920); idem, *The Great Tomb-Robberies of the Twentieth Egyptian Dynasty* (Oxford: Clarendon Press, 1930).

15. Possible exceptions being P Cairo JdE 65739 and O Nash 5 (McDowell, *Village Life,* 34).

16. See McDowell, *Jurisdiction,* passim. Her discussion refers to Deir el-Medîna, but the procedure was probably fairly typical of courts at that period.

17. Wolfgang Helck, "Folter." In *Lexikon der Ägyptologie,* vol. II, edited by Wolfgang Helck and Wolfhart Westendorf, 279–280. (Wiesbaden: Harrassowitz, 1977).

18. McDowell, *Jurisdiction,* 107–114.

19. Joris F. Borghouts, "Divine Intervention in Ancient Egypt and its Manifestation (b3w)." In *Gleanings from Deir el-Medîna (Egyptologische Uitgaven,* I), edited by Robert J. Demarée and Jac. J. Janssen, 4–8. (Leiden: Nederlands Instituut voor het Nabije Oosten te Leiden, 1982).

20. Alyward M. Blackman, "Oracles in Ancient Egypt," *JEA* 12 (1926): 176–185; McDowell, *Village Life,* 177–178.

21. Jac. J. Janssen, "Two Personalities." In *Gleanings from Deir el-Medîna (Egyptologische Uitgaven,* 1), edited by Robert J. Demarée and Jac. J. Janssen, 116–123. (Leiden: Nederlands Instituut voor het Nabije Oosten te Leiden, 1982).

22. Also in private conversations—for instance, a woman argues with her husband, who has taken a bribe from a gang of tomb robbers as the price of his silence, "Oh you silly old man whose old age is bad, if you are killed and thrown into the water who will look for you?" (P BM 10052 3.16–17)

23. Both male (e.g. P BM 10403 v3.14) and female (P BM 10052 v10.14 , v11.5; P BM 10403 v 3.28–29, v3.31) suspects denied involvement in this way.

24. Also P BM 10052 11.5–6, P BM 10052 r1.8–13, where the culprit argues that he was given the stolen property to keep by the robbers, rather than stealing it himself from the tomb, and O Ashmolean 1945.37 + 1945.33 + O Michaelides 90 r17–23.

25. Peet, *Great Tomb Robberies,* 141, 161 note 28, explains "by falsely accusing him of the same crimes." In this case, the speaker was released, so he must have succeeded in convincing the authorities of his innocence.

26. E.g. Ptahhotep 149–150, 350–360 (Richard B. Parkinson, *The Story of Sinuhe and Other Ancient Egyptian Poems 1940–1640 B.C.E.* [Oxford: Oxford University Press, 1997], 253, 257–258).

27. Cf. O Gardiner 165 r12–13; P Turin 167 + 2087/219–198 v8. See also McDowell, *Jurisdiction,* 23–24. After interrogation and torture, suspects who had nothing further to tell sometimes protested in despair, "If you bid me lie, I will lie!" (e.g. P BM 10052 v12.18) Suspects also protested their innocence using the formula, "Far from me, far from my body!" (P BM 10052 r4.8, v11.15–16)

28. McDowell, *Village Life,* 38–40; Jaroslav Cerny, "The Will of Naunakhte and the Related Documents," *JEA* 31 (1945): 29–53.

29. Similarly, a man whose wife (or sister?) neglected him during a serious illness declares: "She did not do good for me. The crewman X, my son, he did good for me." (O Petrie 18 r6–7)

110 *Deborah Sweeney*

30. See also Adoption Papyrus r4–5, r19–20, r23, v7–9; Naunakhte IV v5. For further examples of parallelism and antithesis, see P Abbott 5.15; P BM 10052 v12.8; P BM 10403 3.26–7; Adoption Papyrus v5–6; O CGC 25227.

31. See also P BM 10052 r4.23; v14.4; v14.8; v14.20; O OIC 12073 r3.

32. Stuart Tyson Smith, "Intact Tombs of the Seventeenth and Eighteenth Dynasties from Thebes and the New Kingdom Burial System," *teilungen des Deutschen Archäologischen Instituts, Abteilung Kairo* (1992): 197.

33. Waltraud Guglielmi, "Stilmittel." In *Lexikon der Ägyptologie*, vol. VI, edited by Wolfgang Helck and W. Westendorf, 32 (Wiesbaden: Harrassowitz, 1986).

34. Janet H. Johnson, "The Legal Status of Women in Egypt." In *Mistress of the House, Mistress of Heaven*, edited by Anne K. Capel and Glenn E. Markoe, 176–177 (New York: Hudson Hills Press, 1996).

35. Peet, *Great Tomb Robberies*, passim.

36. Janet Holmes, *Women, Men and Politeness* (London: Longman, 1995), 67.

37. Susan Gal, "Language, Gender and Power: An Anthropological Review." In *Gender Articulated: Language and the Socially Constructed Self*, edited by Kira Hall and Mary Buchholz, 169–182 (New York and London: Routledge, 1995).

38. Holmes, *Women, Men and Politeness*, 197.

39. Robins, *Women in Ancient Egypt*, 111.

40. Holmes, *Women, Men and Politeness*, 197.

41. Emily Teeter, "Female Musicians in Pharaonic Egypt." In *Rediscovering the Muses: Women's Musical Traditions*, edited by Kimberley Marshall, 68–91, esp. 89. (Boston: Northeastern University Press, 1993).

42. Eyre, "The Market Women of Pharaonic Egypt," 173–191, in *Le Commerce en Egypte ancienne* (Biliothéque d'Étude 121), ed. by Nicholas Grimal and Bernadette Menu, Cairo, Institute Français d'Archéologie.

43. Apart from the Adoption Papyrus, for which see Sarah Israelit Groll, "A Short Grammar of the Spermeru Dialect." In *Studien zu Sprache und Religion Ägyptens zu Ehren von Wolfhardt Westendorf. Band I: Sprache*, edited by Friedrich Junge, 41–61 (Göttingen: Hubert and Co., 1984). This text seems to be written in the local dialect of the provincial site of Spermeru, where the papyrus was written, whereas most legal texts of this period come from Thebes, where the local dialect was somewhat different.

44. *HOP,* 221–222; McDowell, *Village Life,* 34.

45. Robins, *Women in Ancient Egypt,* 141.

46. In Deir el-Medîna, women usually appear as defendants, rather than claimants (Lynn Meskell, "Deir el-Medîna in Hyperreality: Seeking the People of Pharaonic Egypt," *Journal of Mediterranean Archaeology* 7 [1994]: 210).

47. Lesko, "Women's Rhetoric from Ancient Egypt," and "'Listening' to the Ancient Egyptian Woman."

Works Cited

Allam, Schafik. *Hieratische Ostraka und Papyri der Ramessidenzeit.* Tübingen: im Selbstverlage des Herausgebers, 1973.

Allam, Schafik."Some Remarks on the Trial of Mose." *JEA* 75 (1989): 103–112.

Blackman, Alyward M. "Oracles in Ancient Egypt." *JEA* 12 (1926): 176–185.

Borghouts, Joris F. "Divine Intervention in Ancient Egypt and its Manifestation (b3w)." In *Gleanings from Deir el-Medîna* (*Egyptologische Uitgaven,* I), edited by Robert J. Demarée and Jac. J. Janssen, 1–70. Leiden: Nederlands Instituut voor het Nabije Oosten te Leiden, 1982.

Černý, Jaroslav. "The Will of Naunakhte and the Related Documents." *JEA* 31 (1945): 29–53.

Coulon, Laurent."La rhétorique et ses fictions: pouvoirs et duplicité du discours à travers la littérature égyptienne du Moyen et du Nouvel Empire." *Bulletin de l'Institut Français d'Archeologie Orientale* 99 (1999): 103–132.

De Buck, Adrian. "The Judicial Papyrus of Turin." *JEA* 23 (1937): 152–164.

Eyre, Christoper John. "Crime and Adultery in Ancient Egypt." *JEA* 70 (1984): 92–105.

_____. "The Semna Stelae: Quotation, Genre, and Functions of Literature." In *Studies in Egyptology presented to Miriam Lichtheim,* 2 vols., edited by Sarah Israelit Groll, 134–165. Jerusalem: Magnes Press, 1990.

_____. "The Adoption Papyrus in Social Context." *JEA* 78 (1992): 207–221.

_____. "Why Was Egyptian Literature?" In *VI Congresso Internazionale di Egittologia,* vol. II, edited by Gian Maria Zaccone and Tomaso Ricardi di Netro, 115–120. Turin: Tipografia Torinese—Stabilimento Poligrafico S.p.A., 1993.

Gaballa, Gaballa Ali. *The Memphite Tomb-Chapel of Mose.* Warminster: Aris and Phillips, 1977.

Gal, Susan. "Language, Gender and Power: An Anthropological Review." In *Gender Articulated: Language and the Socially Constructed Self,* edited by Kira Hall and Mary Buchholz, 169–182. New York and London: Routledge, 1995.

Gardiner, Alan Henderson. "Adoption Extraordinary." *JEA* 26 (1940): 23–29.

Goldwasser, Orly. " 'Low' and 'High' Dialects in Ramesside Egyptian." In *Textcorpus und Wörterbuch: Aspekte zur Ägyptischen Lexikographie,* edited by Stefan Grunert and Ingelore Hafemann, 311–328. Leiden: Brill, 1999.

Groll, Sarah Israelit. "A Short Grammar of the Spermeru Dialect." In *Studien zu Sprache und Religion Ägyptens zu Ehren von Wolfhardt Westendorf. Band I: Sprache,* edited by Friedrich Junge, 41–61. Göttingen: Hubert & Co., 1984.

Guglielmi, Waltraud. "Stilmittel." In *Lexikon der Ägyptologie,* vol. VI, edited by Wolfgang Helck and W. Westendorf, 22–41. Wiesbaden: Harrassowitz, 1986.

_____. "Der Gebrauch rhetorischer Stilmittel in der ägyptischen Literatur." In *Ancient Egyptian Literature: History and Forms (Probleme der Ägyptologie,* 10), edited by Antonio Loprieno, 465–497. Leiden, New York, and Cologne: Brill, 1996.

Helck, Wolfgang. "Folter." In *Lexikon der Ägyptologie,* vol. II, edited by Wolfgang Helck and W. Westendorf, 279–280. Wiesbaden: Harrassowitz, 1977.

Holmes, Janet. *Women, Men and Politeness.* London: Longman, 1995.

Janssen, Jac. J. "Two Personalities." In *Gleanings from Deir el-Medîna (Egyptologische Uitgaven,* 1), edited by Robert J. Demarée and Jac. J. Janssen, 109–131. Leiden: Nederlands Instituut voor het Nabije Oosten te Leiden, 1982.

Johnson, Janet H. "The Legal Status of Women in Ancient Egypt." In *Mistress of the House, Mistress of Heaven: Women in Ancient Egypt,* edited by Anne K. Capel and Glenn E. Markoe, 175–186. New York: Hudson Hills Press, 1996.

Junge, Friedrich. "Rhetorik." In *Lexikon der Ägyptologie,* vol. V, edited by Wolfgang Helck and W. Westendorf, 250–253. Wiesbaden: Harrassowitz, 1984.

Lesko, Barbara. "Women's Rhetoric from Ancient Egypt." In: *Listening to their Voices: The Rhetorical Activities of Historical Women,* edited by Molly Meijer Wertheimer, 89–111. Columbia: University of South Carolina Press, 1997.

_____. "'Listening' to the Ancient Egyptian Woman: Letters, Testimonials and Other Expressions of Self." In *Gold of Praise: Studies on Ancient Egypt in Honor of Edward F. Wente (Studies in Ancient Oriental Civilization,* 58), edited by Emily Teeter and John A. Larson, 247–254. Chicago: University of Chicago Press, 1999.

McDowell, Andrea G. *Jurisdiction in the Workmen's Community of Deir el-Medîna (Egyptologische Uitgaven,* V). Leiden: Nederlands Instituut voor het Nabije Oosten te Leiden, 1990.

_____. *Village Life in Ancient Egypt: Laundry Lists and Love Songs.* Oxford: Oxford University Press, 1999.

Meskell, Lynn. "Deir el-Medîna in Hyperreality: Seeking the People of Pharaonic Egypt." *Journal of Mediterranean Archaeology* 7 (1994): 193–216.

Parkinson, Richard B. *The Story of Sinuhe and Other Ancient Egyptian Poems 1940–1640 B.C.E.* Oxford: Oxford University Press, 1997.

Peet, Thomas Eric. *The Mayer Papyri A and B. Nos. M. 11162 and M. 11186 of the Free Public Museums, Liverpool.* London: Egypt Exploration Society, 1920.

_____. *The Great Tomb-Robberies of the Twentieth Egyptian Dynasty.* Oxford: Clarendon Press, 1930.

Robins, Gay. *Women in Ancient Egypt.* London: British Museum Press, 1993.

Shubert, Steven Blake. "Does She or Doesn't She? Female Literacy in Ancient Egypt." *Proceedings of the Near and Middle Eastern Civilizations Graduate Students' Annual Symposia 1998–2000* (Toronto: Benben Publications, 2001): 55–76

Smith, Stuart Tyson. "Intact Tombs of the Seventeenth and Eighteenth Dynasties from Thebes and the New Kingdom Burial System." *Mitteilungen des Deutschen Archäologischen Instituts, Abtailung Kairo* 48 (1992): 193–231.

Teeter, Emily. "Female Musicians in Pharaonic Egypt." In *Rediscovering the Muses: Women's Musical Traditions,* edited by Kimberley Marshall, 68–91. Boston: Northeastern University Press, 1993.

The Use of Eloquence:
The Confucian Perspective

George Q. Xu

In classical China (mid-sixth century to late third century B.C.), as in other ancient nations in what Karl Jaspers called the "Axial Period"—the age of the Greek and Indian philosophers, the Hebrew prophets and Zarathustra, between 800–200 B.C., there was extensive evidence of the indispensable role played by deft use of discourse in the development of civilization.[1] That period, traditionally known as the late Spring and Autumn period and the Warring States period in Chinese history, witnessed dramatic social changes: the old social order was crumbling; the ducal states were fiercely engaged in prolonged bloody wars, combined with treacherous diplomatic maneuvers, in insatiable efforts to expand their territories and political power; and the chaotic situation motivated numerous thinkers, known as the "Hundred Schools," to speculate and discourse about the fundamental issues of human behavior, morality, and government. All these social, political, and cultural fermentations gave a new impetus to the use of discourse. Heated dialogical argumentation between different schools of thought advanced philosophical thinking; compilations of political speeches, pronouncements, and arguments by earlier sage-kings became shared sources of wisdom; and itinerant political operatives employed eloquent persuasion to exercise dramatic influences upon the politics of states at war with each other. Ironically, and perhaps uniquely, however, verbal eloquence was not valorized by classical Chinese thinkers, and on the contrary the views found in their texts reveal a general mistrust of it, a sentiment common to almost all major schools of thought despite their fundamental philosophical differences, but it is most conspicuously and extensively reflected in Confucian texts.

The Daoists, represented by Laozi (sixth century B.C.) and Zhuangzi

(369–286 B.C.), advocated a return to nature and *wu wei* (nonaction), valued humility and quietude, and rejected the folly of pride and self-assertion. From this philosophical stance, they formed their ethical belief about the use of speech: "To talk little is natural. . . . Truthful words are not beautiful; beautiful words are not truthful. Good men do not argue; those who argue are not good."[2] The Mohists—Mozi (ca. 478–ca. 392 B.C.) and his followers, being devout believers in universal love, sought to persuade others by showing a unifying love rather than by gaining a verbal dominance over them. In their view, therefore, "the wise discerns all in his mind but speaks simply. . . . In speech, not quantity but ingenuity, not eloquence but insight, should be cultivated."[3] The Leagalists, represented by Shang Yang (died 338 B.C.), Hanfeizi (ca. 280–233 B.C.) and Lu Bowei (died 235 B.C.), being practical politicians, were interested only in the immediate effectiveness of the mechanisms of government that would consolidate the centralized rule of the emperor. They measured the use of discourse with the yardstick of practical utility. While keenly aware of the usefulness of persuasion in political operations, they disdained "indulgence in argumentation with no useful purpose and flowery eloquence with no practical results," and they even blamed the deterioration of government effectiveness on sophistry that served no practical function.[4]

More than any other school, however, the Confucians condemned "glib talking," vehemently and extensively, creating a particularly poignant irony of eloquent speakers and writers denouncing eloquence. More than any other school, their condemnations were explicitly focused upon the "glib talker's" culpability of violating the social moral code, upsetting the traditional social order, spreading erroneous ideas detrimental to the Confucian project of "saving the world"—in this latter case, furthermore, their condemnations had the effect of silencing dissident views. Again, more than any other school, it is possible to ascertain in the Confucian condemnations of eloquence a systematic expression of a world view of language use. In the later ages, especially after Confucianism became established as the official ideology in Han Dynasty (206 B.C.-A.D. 220), what the Confucians preached against eloquence was reinforced with all the might of an orthodox faith, while their act of eloquent preaching seemed overlooked. No other school's views on speech enjoyed such official sanction and promotion. Consequently, the Confucian devaluation of eloquence has had an especially pervasive, profound influence on communication among Chinese. A careful consideration of this expressed devaluation is indispensable to a proper understanding of Chinese rhetoric, ancient or modern. In the context of this article, rhetoric is broadly defined to include the practice and theory of the use of discourse to accomplish a didactic, aesthetic, or persuasive objective; and eloquence is the skillful, artistic verbal expression for rhetorical effect. In the following pages, I will examine the manifestations of the Confucians' mistrust of eloquence in its sociopolitical context, attempt to reconstruct their world view that underpinned their expressions, expose the irony of the Confucians employing eloquence to denigrate eloquence, and the long-lasting influence of their demonstrated negative attitude toward eloquence.

Glib Talk Violates the Core Values of Confucianism

Confucius (551–479 B.C.), whose doctrines evolved into Confucianism, was the most influential philosopher in Chinese history, and actually his influences are still being felt in China despite the Communists' half-century-long effort to eradicate them. Faced with the fierce political strife and profound social changes of his time, Confucius was the most ardent, among his contemporary thinkers, to advocate a restoration of the old social order and harmony based upon blood kinship of (Western) Zhou Dynasty (11th century-770 B.C.) as a panacea for all the perceived symptoms of degeneration. At the heart of his restorative project was the restitution of *li* (often translated as "rites")—the traditions and conventions that had carried the power of unwritten law—which, in his view, was being neglected or even abandoned.[5] His urgent program of restoring *li* to its former position of dominance in cohering the whole society contained a strict proscription against glib talking because glibness violated the ethical tenets of *li* and *ren* (virtues). The *li* he referred to encompassed the whole system of traditions, customs, ceremonies, and conventions that exercised a compulsory and binding force over every member of the Zhou society, practically comparable to the laws in later ages, and *li* also defined "the cosmic order and its hierarchy of superior-inferior relationships. Parents were superior to children, men to women, rulers to subjects. Each person therefore had a role to perform."[6] And *ren* was the core of Confucius's philosophy, which signified goodness, virtue, benevolence, and ultimately what differentiated humans from animals.[7] Confucius said, "To subdue one's self and return to *li* (rites) is perfect *ren* (human-heartedness, virtue)," which was recorded in the *Analects*.[8] The *Analects*, a collection of Confucius's sayings and anecdotes compiled by his disciples, is one of the primary sources of Confucius's discourse, the others including *The Great Learning* and *The Doctrine of the Mean*, originally two chapters in *The Book of Rites* compiled by his grandson and disciples.

The restoration of *li* and the attainment of perfect *ren*, equated in their valuation—these are the two criteria that governed Confucius's view of language use. He instructed: "Speak not at variance with *li*," thus prescribing both the content and manner of delivery for acceptable speech.[9] Whatever is said has to be within the confines of *li*, and a "true gentleman" "expresses (his cause) with modesty."[10] *Li* included "the principle of order—the attribution to everything of its correct place in the great whole of experience," and Confucius "support[ed] the institutions likely to ensure order—the family, hierarchy, seniority—and due reverence for the many nicely graded obligations between men."[11] Any person speaking out of order, e.g., a subordinate demonstrating eloquence before his superiors, a youngster before his elders, a woman before her husband, would be viewed with resentment and might be punished by censure. A story narrated in the *Analects* gives a concrete representation of the connections between *li,* speech, and manner of delivery in Confucius's mind:

> After three disciples expressed their political aspirations with regard to managing a state, another disciple Zeng Xi asked Confucius: "What do you think of these three students' words?"
>
> Confucius said: "What they did was simply express their aspirations."
>
> Zeng Xi asked again: "But then, Master, why did you sneer at You (one of the students)?"
>
> Confucius replied: "A state has to be managed with *li,* but he spoke without humility. That's why I sneered at him."[12]

Obviously, Confucius disliked the aggressiveness of You's speech, no matter how eloquent it might have been, because he regarded the act of speaking without humility as a violation of *li,* antithetic to the proper management of a state. The preference for conformity to *li* to aggressive eloquence implied in this story is given more explicit expression in this comment: "What's the use of being a glib speaker? Those who deal with people by virtue of a smart tongue are often hated by others."[13] In Confucius's system of social valuation, glib tongues were not a positive asset; on the contrary, they were believed to be liable to procure hatred for themselves. When placed in the context of Confucian emphasis on harmony in human relations, the enormity of such a liability would become all the more striking. In contrast to glib talking, however, slowness in speaking was commended as the standard conduct of nobility: "A true gentleman should be slow in his words and prompt in his action."[14] Slowness with words, actually, was preferred as the manifestation of a deeper, reflective mind that searched inward for the proper motivation, veracity, and appropriateness of the words. Only such words as well considered in the spirit of *li* and *ren* were regarded as conducive to harmonious human relationships and to a harmonious society.

Glib talking was not only resented as an improper personal manner, but, more important, also as an inherent character flaw, a moral carbuncle. "Glib words corrupt the potentiality for virtue," and "glib people are dangerous."[15] Although no direct explanation was provided for the presumed danger, a clue could be found in the opening lines of *Analects:* "Clever talk and an ingratiating manner are seldom signs of *ren* (true virtue)."[16] The danger was believed to lie in the abandonment and absence of *ren,* the most fatal moral flaw a human being could ever have. Thus, the impropriety of eloquence was condemned in terms of the ultimate gravity of the core values in Confucian philosophy. His attitude is equally apparent in what he regarded as a *ren* (virtuous) person's proper verbal behavior. For a truly *ren* person, Confucius repeatedly iterated, "his speech is slow and cautious": "Fortitude, resoluteness, simplicity, and slowness with speech—possessing these qualities is near to *ren*."[17] From the ethical as well as political standpoint of attaining *ren,* Confucius's outburst of indignation at the end of the following dialog is readily understandable:

> Zilu has secured Zigao an appointment as Magistrate of Bi County. The Master said, "You're ruining the young man."
> Zilu said, "There are people (to govern), and there are land and grains (to manage). Why does one have to read books to be learned?"
> The Master said, "This is why I hate glib-tongued people."[18]

Confucius objected to the appointment because Zigao was too young and had not completed his studies. According to Liu Xin (ca. 56 B.C.–A.D. 23)—one of the earliest scholars who chronicled the development of ancient Chinese thought, the Confucianists "delighted in the study of the *Liu Yi* [six classics or six liberal arts] and paid attention to matters concerning human-heartedness (*ren*) and righteousness."[19] With the educational objective being to cultivate *ren* in the students as the basis for learning *li,* the Confucian curriculum was not exclusively based upon book learning; and Confucius and his disciples recognized practical experiences as learning as well.[20] Actually, in the early days of Confucius's teaching career when Zilu was with him, he and his disciples often engaged in political activities as a part of their learning.[21] Therefore, Zilu's argument not only started with an unstated false assumption that Confucius insisted exclusively on Zigao's completing his studies of books, but also treacherously played upon a Confucian tenet that books are not the only source of learning. The argument was glib and clever, straying, in Confucius's view, far from *ren.* No wonder the Master was so infuriated that he uttered the sweeping condemnation, "I hate glib-tongued people."

Sharp Tongues Upset Kingdoms and Families

Furthermore, as Confucius interpreted *li* as an outward manifestation and formalization of the internal human-ness of *ren,* the abandonment and absence of *ren* inevitably became inimical to his project of restoring and preserving *li*—that is, restoring and preserving the idealized social order—for the sake of correcting the evils of his time.[22] From Confucius's point of view, the danger inherent in glib talking went beyond the limits of ethics and morality and had actual political consequences. Such consequences were so enormous that he intoned his condemnation of glib talkers with strong abhorrence: "I detest those who overthrow kingdoms and families with their sharp tongues."[23] In this statement, he recognized the devastating political power of eloquent speech and the damages it could do to the stable hierarchical social order he valued so much, revealing his fundamental negative attitude to the use of eloquence.

This sentiment was echoed by Confucius's illustrious followers, Mencius (ca. 370–ca. 300 B.C.) and Xunzi (ca. 313–238 B.C.), as evidenced by the two works bearing their names, the *Mencius* and the *Xunzi*. By Mencius's time, it became quite apparent that the Golden Age under sage emperors had been irreversibly lost. While he deplored the loss—"Sage emperors are no longer to be seen," he saw the erosion of *ren* and *yi* (righteousness) as both the cause and the effect of current degeneration.[24] Therefore, he vehemently attacked manifestations of such erosion: "the feudal lords are uninhibited in whatever they do, and scholars holding no official position are indulging themselves in extravagant talking."[25] Among the practitioners of extravagant talking, the most conspicuous were the so-called *zongheng jia,* itinerant political strategists who employed their verbal prowess to influence feudal lords, manipulating interstate politics. Mencius's animosity toward them was clearly revealed in a brief exchange of question and answer between him and a student:

> Jing Chun asked, "Weren't Gongsun Yan and Zhang Yi great men? When they became angry, the feudal lords were fearful; and when they remained quiet the land was free from flames of war."
> Mencius said, "How could they be considered great men? Haven't you ever studied *li*? . . . ."[26]

He went on to affirm that only those who practiced *ren, li,* and *yi* (righteousness) could be regarded as great men. It is obvious that he denied that the political strategists were great men, because their extravagant talking for political manipulations was in contradiction to *ren, li,* and *yi* (righteousness). They were exactly what Confucius had characterized as "those who overthrow kingdoms and families with their sharp tongues." They shuttled between states, forming and disbanding political and military alliances to procure greater power for some states at the expense of others, often at the cost of thousands of lives slaughtered in battle. That is why Mencius took it upon himself to "rectify people's hearts, extinguish heresies, oppose extreme behaviors, and banish intemperate discourse."[27] Extravagant talking and intemperate discourse "slandering the Dao of ancient sage kings" and "attacking *li* and *yi* (righteousness)" were particularly seditious and subversive of the ethical and political ideals the Confucians cherished."[28] For the same reasons, Xunzi was weary of "arguments, full of figurative language and eloquence, but not in conformity with *li* and *yi* (righteousness)" for fear that they would destroy "the unifying bond of good government."[29]

Clever Talk Is Placed at the Bottom of the Scale

In both Mencius's and Xunzi's deprecations of eloquent speech that was contradictory to what they believed to be *li* and *yi* (righteousness), we can hear an argumentative tone imbued with strong emotions. A similar tone is also detectable in Confucius's words cited above. A plausible explanation for their emotional denunciations, for their general mistrust of eloquence as evidenced in the foregoing paragraphs, and also for the irony of their use of speech to denounce eloquence can be found in their philosophical view of discourse. In the Confucian system of beliefs, a scale of moral valuation with regard to speech use, ranging from *wu yan* (no speech) to *ning* (clever talk, glib talk), is readily ascertainable. At the very top of the scale is the silent *tian* (Heaven), the perfect ideal. The concept of *tian* "clearly corresponds to [the English] word Heaven and to the German *Himmel* in the sense of Providence, Nature, God."[30] For Confucius, *tian* is supreme: not only the origin of all things, the ultimate source of the life cycles of all things, and also the preserver of the harmony of all things. Confucius says: "Does *tian* (Heaven) speak? The four seasons pursue their courses, and all things are continually being produced, but does *tian* (Heaven) say anything?"[31] In his view, as *tian* (Heaven), although *wu yan* (no speech, silent) wills everything to pursue its course, the infinite power lies in *wu yan* (no speech, silence). *The Doctrine of the Mean* cites a line from *The Book of Songs,* a Confucian classic of over three hundred poems, to illustrate the silent power of *tian:* "'*tian* (Heaven) reigns over all, emitting neither sound nor smell.' That is perfect virtue."[32] Mencius reiterated the same idea: "*Tian* (Heaven) is *wu yan* (no speech, silent), revealing its intentions by its acts and deeds."[33] The Confucians aspired to emulate the doings of *tian* (Heaven). "Therefore, the superior man, even when not taking any action, commands reverence, and even though not speaking a word, he is trusted."[34] The ancient sage kings, according to the Confucians, conducted themselves in perfect conformity with *li,* and therefore acquired the prestige and power to influence the ordinary people without using words: "The ruler is like the wind, the people like the grass; when the wind sweeps across, the grass bends."[35] Confucius also said: "When a ruler's personal conduct is upright, he is effective without giving orders. If his personal conduct is not upright, he may give orders but they will not be obeyed."[36] That is to say, setting upright examples without speech (*wu yan*) is better than *you yan* (speech): the highest ideal of virtuous behavior.

However hard the sages strove to emulate *tian* (Heaven), nonetheless, they were not able to remain silent all the time. Actually, the Confucian classics record numerous speeches supposedly made by the sages, so there is the second notch on the Confucian scale reserved for the sages' articulations of ultimate truths and wisdom.

The third gradation on the scale is designated for the speech of *junzi,* "superior men." The qualifying characteristic of a "superior man's" speech is that it is made righteously, cautiously, selectively, and slowly. It is important that speech is devoted to *li, ren,* and *yi* (righteousness). Confucius said: "When a number of people are together, for a whole day, without their conversation turning on righteousness, . . . theirs is indeed a hard case."[37] For Xunzi, only what is in conformity with the ancient sages' teachings and in conformity with *li* and *yi* (righteousness) is "the superior man's speech."[38] However, even righteous speech, no matter how well it is managed, is still considered inferior to *wu yan* (no speech), according to Confucius: "Among the appliances to transform the people, words and facial expressions are but trivial influences."[39]

The fourth gradation down the scale marks eloquence used as an expediency for practical purposes. When asked about disputation, Mencius said: "Indeed, I do not like disputation. I am compelled to do it."[40] He was forced to resort to eloquent disputation to defend the orthodoxy of the Confucian doctrines. In his comment on the priest Tuo's eloquence, Confucius admits that in his chaotic time, eloquence is an indispensable instrument for surviving.[41] But eloquence as a survival tool is many steps removed from the sanctity of wu yan (no speech) and the sages' righteous speech on the moral scale.

Finally at the lowest end of the scale is so-called *ning* (clever talk), *hengyan* (extravagant talking), or *yinci* (excessive, intemperate discourse), which is despised by the Confucians. As demonstrated above, clever talking was regarded by the Confucians not only as an impropriety of manners and a character flaw, but also, in and of itself, as a deviation from *ren, li,* and *yi* (righteousness).

The scale of moral valuation of speech use gives some clue to unraveling the irony of the Confucians employing speech to denounce eloquence. The Confucians of the ancient times under discussion were masterful speakers and writers themselves, but they resorted to several rhetorical devices to legitimize their own persuasive speech in attacking others' glibness. First of all, they presented themselves as pious worshipers of the *tian* (Heaven), showing an awe at its silent omnipotency by refraining from overuse of speech, and, at least in the case of Confucius, verbal display and extravagance were deliberately avoided. Confucius's description of a truly virtuous person as being cautious and simple with words, as quoted above, can be viewed as a self-portrayal of his own verbal behavior. A disciple thus commented on Confucius's unobtrusive style versus the possible aggressive style in achieving an objective: "By being mild, benevolent, respectful, temperate, and deferential, our Master gets [what he wants]."[42] Secondly, the ancient Confucians often distanced themselves from the use of eloquence by performing the speech act of denying their interest in verbal contention, such as Mencius's claim that he didn't like disputation, although he was an able disputer in fact. This ploy was useful only to the extent that the following two devices were successful. Thirdly, Confucius and his followers positioned their speech toward the upper end of the scale. Confucius claimed that he "merely transmitted (old traditions) without creating anything new [of his own]; believed in and loved ancient traditions."[43] He was merely transmitting the ultimate truths and wisdom developed by the sage kings through their deeds and words in the past Golden Age, when a perfect social order guaranteed peace and harmony. This device accomplished two important things for him. On one hand, more than citing authorities to reinforce his credibility, he projected a sacred image onto himself as the mouthpiece of the sages, thus creating an ethos above reproach and warding off any suspicions of his abusing speech to denigrate eloquence. On the other hand, he obtained a validation of the content of his speech, which was transmitting the sages' benevolent and righteous thoughts, employed in the noble enterprise to eradicate the chaos plaguing the land and to restore the utopian social order of yore. He and his followers thus justified their employing the "superior men's speech" to inveigh against clever talk and extravagant discourse.

Fourthly, another rhetorical device the Confucians employed was speaking from their self-appointed status of superior men: "A superior man differs from other men in that he retains his heart. He retains his heart by virtue of ren (virtue, benevolence) and li (the rites)."[44] They were thus able to set up what Kenneth Burke called a "terministic screen," which defined and controlled the observations of speech making.[45] Armed with those terms as a measure, they could readily sanction their own discourse and screen out the discourse that did not fit their definitions of li, ren, yi (righteousness), exiling the latter to the lower end of their scale of valuation. And they saw good reason to be indignant in their tone when repudiating clever talk and extravagant discourse employed to disseminate what they believed to be ideas deviant from or contrary to the Confucian moralistic tenets. Clever talk and extravagant discourse, being relegated to the bottom of the scale, were objectionable, and became even abominable and dangerous when mingled with erroneous ideas. "Argumentative speech, if used in contradiction to the sage kings and at variance with *li* and *yi* (righteousness), is evil speech."[46] Therefore, both Mencius and Xunzi denounced the itinerant political strategists who they believed "overthrew kingdoms and families with their sharp tongues." They also vehemently rebuked Yangzi, believed to be a predecessor of Daoism, and Mozi as well as their followers for their "extravagant talking" and "intemperate discourse," because their philosophical principles were different from the Confucian system of beliefs. No doubt, such remonstrations against ideological opponents' eloquence are redolent of suppressive intentions and effects of silencing dissident views.

At this point, the politics of the Confucians' rhetoric becomes apparent. Their emotionally charged denunciations of their opponents' eloquent use of discourse revealed the fact that they were still entangled in difficult debates with rival schools of thought. For three hundred years, their views were only one school among many, and they were not able to overpower any of their rivals. Their condemnations of other schools' abuse of eloquence did not help themselves gain much ascendancy. In Qin Dynasty (221–206 B.C.), the Legalists were exclusively in power, while all other schools including the Confucians were marginalized and persecuted and their books burned. Even in the early years of Han Dynasty, the Confucians had a difficult time competing against the Daoists because some powerful members of the royal family favored the latter. However, the tide of affairs turned in favor of the Confucians, when Emperor Wu of Han Dynasty (156–87 B.C.) saw in Confucianism a useful stabilizing influence for the powers that be. The Confucians, claiming to be true preservers of ancient sages' legacy, were ideologically conservative. Their doctrines validated and rationalized the hierarchical structure of society and family and the mandate of the ruling royalty, providing needed defense for the status quo. Therefore, Emperor Wu established Confucianism as the orthodox ideology of the land in 136 B.C. Thus, what the Confucians had not been able to achieve rhetorically, that is, an overall triumph over rival schools of thought, was accomplished by a royal edict. Their position against eloquence, along with their more fundamental teachings, was consolidated and much strengthened. It became one of the social standards for acceptable behavior in public and served as a regulator of discourse use, effectively serving the official need for maintaining the hierarchical social structure of a unified empire. Glib talk, especially in public or in front of one's superiors or elders, was frowned upon for being a breach of good manners; and eloquent expositions upon ideas different from the officially sanctioned doctrines could be labeled as "spreading fallacies to deceive people," and often with dire consequences.

The emperors of later dynasties were repeatedly reminded of the perils that "clever talk" and "extravagant discourse" could entail. In A.D. 1068, when the historian Shima Guang (A.D. 1019–1086) presented his *Zi zhi tong jian (A Comprehensive Mirror in the Aid of Government)* to Emperor Shen Zong (A.D. 1048–1085) of Song Dynasty (A.D. 960–1279), he explained, "The art of the itinerant political strategists [of the Warring States period] is of no help to governance. I recorded their doings in my book simply to show . . . how they overthrew kingdoms and families with their sharp tongues."[47] Since the objective of his book was to use the rise and fall of past dynasties as a mirror to help the emperor in governing the country, the intention of recording the overthrow of kingdoms and families by sharp tongues was obviously to preserve the historical events as a warning for the rulers.[48] And Chinese rulers have paid much heed to this warning and done much to banish sharp tongues, especially those with ideas incompatible with the dominant ideology. They have vigorously promoted the Confucian commandment: "Speak not at variance with *li*," in numerous reincarnations, suppressing many a Chinese person's urge and effort to develop and demonstrate verbal eloquence over the past twenty centuries.

In contemporary China, theoretically Marxism has supplanted Confucianism for more than half a century, but the Confucian tenet remains influential, and the only difference is that *li* has been replaced with the orthodox, or government endorsed, doctrine. Now it is understood as "Don't speak at variance with the official ideology!" And this ideology can be couched in a variety of terms, depending upon the political imperatives at the time, such as "patriotism," "the revolutionary cause," "unity," "stability," and "prosperity," as defined by the authorities. A person speaking eloquently for a cause not endorsed by the government has to be wary of being accused of employing "extravagant talk" to spread "unpatriotic" ideas, undermining "unity" and "stability," against "the best interests of the majority of the people."

The Confucian tenet can still exert a tangible effect today, not only because violating it could possibly incur repudiation or even penalty, but also because Confucian antipathy toward eloquence has deeply penetrated into the collective consciousness of the Chinese people. It became part of accepted wisdom over the centuries, as Confucianism became the dominant controlling ideology in everyday life, and studying and internalizing Confucianism became the only mechanism by which a common person could hope to move up the social ladder. Such attitudes, for example, solidified into common proverbs, such as "Just as bad drama is noisy, so a base person talks much," and are routinely included in the widely read publications of advice to children, such as "It's better to speak less than more," "Don't talk smart," and "Refrain from talking too much when dealing with people."[49] In fact, it has been so inextricably embedded in Chinese culture that a proper understanding of Chinese rhetoric would be all but impossible without taking it into full account.

Notes

1. For a characterization of the "Axial Period," see Karl Jaspers, *The Origin and Goal of History* (New Haven, CT: Yale University Press, 1953), 1–3.

2. *Laozi,* annotated by Wei Yuan, in *zhuzi jicheng* [A Collection of the Works of Pre-Qin Schools of Thought] (Beijing: China Press, 1980), chapters 23 and 81.

3. *Mozi,* annotated by Sun Yirang, in *zhuzi jicheng* [*A Collection of the Works of Pre-Qin Schools of Thought*] (Beijing: China Press, 1980), chapter on "Self-Cultivation."

4. *Hanfeizi,* annotated by Wang Xianshen, in *zhuzi jicheng* [*A Collection of the Works of Pre-Qin Schools of Thought*] (Beijing: China Press, 1980), chapter on "Signs of the Perishing of a Nation."

5. Lu Waihou, Zhao Jibi, and Du Guoxiang, *zongquo sixiang tongshi* [A General History of Chinese Thought], vol. 1 (Beijing: People's Press, 1957), 45–56, 144–50.

6. John King Fairbank, *China: A New History* (Cambridge, MA: Belknap Press of Harvard University Press, 1994), 51.

7. Li Zehou, *zhongguo gudai siziangshi lun* [Essays on the History of Ancient Chinese Thought] (Hefei, China: Anhui Arts and Literature Press, 1985), 13; A. C. Graham, *Disputers of the Tao: Philosophical Argument in Ancient China* (La Salle, IL: Open Court Publishing Company, 1989),19.

8. *Analects,* annotated by He Yan and Xing Bing, in *shisanjin zhu shu* [The Thirteen Classics Annotated and Interpreted] (Beijing: China Press, 1983), 12.1.

9. Ibid., 12.2.

10. Ibid., 15.18.

11. J. M. Roberts, *History of the World* (New York: Oxford University Press, 1993), 107.

12. *Analects,* 11.26.

13. Ibid., 5.5.

14. Ibid., 4.24.

15. Ibid., 15.27 and 15.11.

16. Ibid., 1.3.

17. Ibid., 12.3 and 13.27.

18. Ibid., 11.25.

19. Fung Yu-lan, *A Short History of Chinese Philosophy,* ed. Derk Bodde, (New York: Free Press, 1948), 32.

20. E.g., *Analects*, 1.7 and 1.14.

21. Yang Bojun, ed. and trans., *lunyu yi zhu* [Analects: Annotated and Translated into Modern Chinese], 2nd ed. (Beijing: China Press, 1980), 20.

22. Li Zehou, *gudai sixiangshi lun* [Ancient Chinese Thought], 30.

23. *Analects*, 17.18.

24. Li Zehou, *gudai sixiangshi lun* [Ancient Chinese Thought], 50.

25. *Mencius*, annotated by Jiao Xun, in *shisanjin shu shu* [The Thirteen Classics Annotated and Interpreted] (Bejing: China Press, 1983), IIIB.9.

26. Ibid., IIIB.2.

27. Ibid., IIIB.9.

28. Ibid., IVA.1 and IVA.10.

29. *Xunzi*, annotated by Yang Jing, in *zhuzi jicheng* [A Collection of the Works of Pre-Qin Schools of Thought] (Beijing: China Press, 1980), chapter on "Against the Twelve Philosophers."

30. Arthur Waley, *The Analects of Confucius: Translated and Annotated* (New York: Random House, 1938), 41; for a similar interpretation of *tian* as "Heaven that was the nature of the universe," see John K. Shyrock, *The Origin and Development of the State Cult of Confucius* (New York: Appleton-Century, 1932), 225.

31. *Analects*, 17.19.

32. *The Doctrine of the Mean*, edited and annotated by Zhu Xi, in *si shu* [The Four Books] (Beijing: China Press, 1981), section 33.

33. *Mencius*, VA.5.

34. *The Doctrine of the Mean*, section 33.

35. *Analects*, 12.19.

36. Ibid., 13.6.

37. Ibid., 15.17.

38. *Xunzi*, chapter on "Against Physiognomy."

39. *The Doctrine of the Mean*, section 33.

40. *Mencius*, VIB 6.9.

41. *Analects*, 6.16.

42. Ibid., 1.10.

43. Ibid., 7.1.

44. *Mencius,* IVB 28.

45. Kenneth Burke, *Language as Symbolic Action: Essays on Life, Literature, and Method* (Berkeley: University of California Press, 1966), 44.

46. *Xunzi,* chapter on "Against Physiognomy."

47. Bi Yuan, *xu zi zhi tong jian* [A Sequel to a Comprehensive Mirror in the Aid of Government] (Shanghai: Classics Press, 1987), vol. 66.

48. Xiong Xianguan, *zonghengjia yanjiu* [A Study of the Itinerary Political Strategists of the Warring States Period] (Chongqing, China: Chongqing Press, 1998), 288.

49. Guo Jieming, *sanzijin jingjie* [The Three-Character Classic Annotated] (Taibei: Hongye Press, 1971), 211, 179, 200.

Works Cited

Analects. Annotated by He Yan and Xing Bing. In *shisanjin zhu shu* [The Thirteen Classics Annotated and Interpreted]. Beijing: China Press, 1983.

Bi, Yuan. *xu zi zhi tong jian* [A Sequel to a Comprehensive Mirror in the Aid of Government]. Shanghai: Classics Press, 1987.

Burke, Kenneth. *Language as Symbolic Action: Essays on Life, Literature, and Method.* Berkeley: University of California Press, 1966.

Doctrine of the Mean. Edited and annotated by Zhu Xi. In *si shu* [The Four Books]. Beijing: China Press, 1981.

Fairbank, John King. *China: A New History.* Cambridge, MA: Belknap Press of Harvard University Press, 1994.

Fung, Yu-lan. *A Short History of Chinese Philosophy.* Ed. Derk Bodde. New York: Free Press, 1948.

Graham, A. C. *Disputers of the Tao: Philosophical Argument in Ancient China.* La Salle, IL: Open Court, 1989.

Guo, Jieming. *sanzijin jingjie* [The Three-Character Classic Annotated]. Taibei: Hongye Press, 1971.

Hanfeizi. Annotated by Wang Xianshen. In *zhuzi jicheng [A Collection of the Works of Pre-Qin Schools of Thought].* Beijing: China Press, 1980.

Jaspers, Karl. *The Origin and Goal of History.* New Haven, CT: Yale University Press, 1953.

Laozi. Annotated by Wei Yuan. In *zhuzi jicheng* [A Collection of the Works of Pre-Qin Schools of Thought]. Beijing: China Press, 1980.

Li, Zehou. *zhongguo gudai sixiangshi lun* [Essays on the History of Ancient Chinese Thought]. Hefei, China: Anhui Arts and Literature Press, 1985.

Lu, Waihou, Zhao Jibin, and Du Guoxiang. *zhongguo sixiang tongshi* [A General History of Chinese Thought]. Vol. 1. Beijing: People's Press, 1957.

Mencius. Annotated by Jiao Xun. In *shisanjin zhu shu* [The Thirteen Classics Annotated and Interpreted]. Beijing: China Press, 1983.

Mozi. Annotated by Sun Yirang. In *zhuzi jicheng* [A Collection of the Works of Pre-Qin Schools of Thought]. Beijing: China Press, 1980.

Roberts, J. M. *History of the World.* New York: Oxford University Press, 1993.

Waley, Arthur. *The Analects of Confucius: Translated and Annotated.* New York: Random House, 1938.

Xiong, Xianguan. *zonghengjia yanjiu* [A Study of the Itinerant Political Strategists of the Warring States Period]. Chongqing, China: Chongqing Press, 1998.

Xunzi. Annotated by Yang Jing. In *zhuzi jicheng* [A Collection of the Works of Pre-Qin Schools of Thought]. Beijing: China Press, 1980.

Yang, Bojun, ed. and trans. *lunyu yi zhu* [Analects: Annotated and Translated into Modern Chinese]. Second ed. Beijing: China Press, 1980.

Confucian Silence and Remonstration: A Basis for Deliberation?

Arabella Lyon

"Confucian democracy is clearly a contradiction in terms."
Samuel P. Huntington *The Third Wave*

Kongzi or Confucius[1] (traditionally 551–479 B.C.) has been cursed as an idealist, a misogynist, a proponent of slavery, an idolater of inherited aristocracy and wisdom, and the cause of rigid traditions that handicap a society's development.[2] He also has been praised as the "most influential thinker in human history," the proponent of harmonious and egalitarian society, and the hope of democracy in China and human rights throughout Asia.[3] For more than 2,500 years, his works—fragmented, edited, even written by disciples—have been used to make a cacophony of claims about the nature of humanity, government, education, and the East. Even now, his philosophy is held to the lens of contempt and admiration, embroiled in debates about human rights and the future of democracy in China. Undeniably Confucius is a major figure in world history, a figure of great controversy, but a figure who, with rare exception, has been ignored within the discipline of rhetoric.

Rhetoricians, by and large Western, have avoided noncanonical texts for all the usual disciplinary reasons, but as well, in the case of Confucius, they may be put off by the large task of engaging both Chinese culture through the millenniums and copious Confucian writings on government, citizenship, and rhetoric. As a first step toward controlling copious possibility in this paper, I will focus on deliberative rhetoric, the forward-looking process of reaching consensus and coming to action. Deliberative rhetoric with its historical connections to democracy will be a lens for understanding Confucian rhetoric and its relationship to current democratic and civil rights movements in Asia. In looking through this glass, I risk distortion, but my purpose is to place

Confucius within a defined rhetorical tradition and to place Confucius in twenty-first-century rhetoric. I will show the rhetorical within the Confucian tradition by looking closely at the early text *Lunyu* or *The Analects,* exploring its presentation of remonstration and silence, and what they imply about deliberation and democracy. While later interpretations of Confucian teachings, such as those of Mencius and Xunzi, are necessary to a full view of classical and Confucian China, to include them here would increase the heteroglossia that already overwhelms an introduction to Confucius. For this reason, I stay focused on *The Analects.*

Rhetoric and Deliberation

The concept of rhetoric has had many permutations throughout its history in the West, though the most basic formulations circle around the work of Plato and Aristotle. It is fair to say that Aristotle's definition, finding the available means of persuasion in any given case, dominates the tradition. True, definitions of rhetoric can vary dramatically, but they all involve a metalinguistic awareness of language, awareness of language as a system or complex to be manipulated in the service of identity, communication, persuasion, or artifice. Rhetorical theory describes how metaphors, repetition, questions, and so on affect an audience with an assumption that the rhetor can put this theoretical information into practice and achieve some end.

The Chinese, especially the ancient Chinese, do not share many western assumptions about language, communication, and the individual.[4] As a consequence, if one goes to early texts looking for an explicit, systemic, theoretical approach to language or even a critical metalinguistic awareness, she will not find it in a form easily recognized.[5] In ancient China there was virtually no systemic grammar, linguistics, rhetoric, poetics, or literary theory *as Westerners after Plato conceive them.* Sophistry (as glibness) was and is greatly disdained, and so there is great skepticism about persuasion as an ethical undertaking and even about language as revealing knowledge, action, or character. Furthermore, in the Confucian tradition, much of the training in effective language consists of memorizing great texts; knowledge is gained through indwelling, imbibing, and conserving great accomplishment, not through acquiring rules and explicit strategies nor through creating and innovating in any individualistic or romantic sense. In contrast to democratic Athens, the individual act of persuasion here is difficult to imagine, especially to imagine as an ethical undertaking. I do not wish to overstate the differences, but the differences are valuable, because they offer opportunities to study a different conception of language and knowledge.

These cultural differences also create a significant problem for writing about rhetorical theory in China. While obviously there are rhetorical activities in China, how do you define rhetoric in a culture without a homologous word? If you simply import rhetoric as a concept, what are the implications of bringing western concepts to Chinese culture? For while Confucius was clearly a masterful practitioner of rhetoric, committed to verbal transmission from the past to the present, and while the dialogues written by his disciples are strategically drawn, there is no reason to believe that rhetorical theory was part of their concern. In bringing the concepts of rhetoric and rhetorical theory to Confucian texts, are we colonizing China, or are we disrespecting rhetorical theory, a cultural perspective of the West? We may be doing violence to both traditions if we are not consciously and continuously aware of the value of unique resources and the necessity of their conservation. I can force a rhetorical theory upon Confucius, but what am I missing? Can I read ethically when I am reading from a historically privileged position? If I use the lens of rhetoric, do I fully know how it was ground? What was ground out?

China has a profound intellectual tradition and a dynamic future: it must be engaged. This pragmatic need, the need to understand alternative strategies for language use, forces a conceptual form—the concepts available in the discipline of rhetoric—upon a different conceptual system, one that values relationship over individual, conservation over experiment, and spirituality and self-cultivation over material accomplishment. It creates a private/public distinction within a culture that has little. China's philosophical concern with process, cycle, and movement over Being, creation, and permanence is more congenial with rhetoric, but our prior understandings of what is rhetoric may focus us on the wrong aspects of Chinese culture and filter out what is significant. One may obscure what is uniquely there by foregrounding western assumptions and so distort and colonize. It is the dilemma and tragedy of translation.

Even in an equitable model of cross-cultural exchange, conversation, and translation, loss is inevitable. In translation, it is key to identify words, grammars, concepts that allow one to move between locations, to traverse the divide. A translator and a reader may have to redefine or simply appropriate the word as received in its original culture, but clearly one must engage the original language as well as the original context. This task has begun in the scholarship on Chinese rhetoric and has moved to the point of honest disagreement about translation. Xing Lu and David Frank suggest that *bian* (argue, debate) is the term that most closely approximates "rhetoric" between 500–200 B.C.E.. They write that its frequency, history, and specificity make it the best stand-in for rhetoric.[6] Longing for a one-to-one correspondence, however, will not allow us to understand the rich differences that Chinese offers. Such a simple term, one existing without a formal system of action, cannot provide nuance for communicative action. Mary Garrett, in her discussions of translation, expands the list to include *shuo* (explain, make clear) and *shui* (persuade), and Lu has recently added to her list.[7] In seeking rhetorical theory in classical writing, especially Confucian texts, one must as well consider other words, such as *quan* (urge), *jian* (remonstrate), *ming* (naming, dialectics), *yue* (speaking), *ci* (speech), and *yan* (say, language).[8] These terms together allow one to glimpse both the breadth and nonconfrontational nature of Chinese rhetoric. One gives up the specificity of a disciplined concept of rhetoric, but one has the possibility of seeing new aspects and understanding the resources of language more complexly.

Given the problem of identifying activities analogous to rhetorical theorizing in ancient China, I approach the Confucian tradition through a defined process of looking for strategies of deliberation. Because Confucianism is often held up as a source of democratic possibility in China and because democracy is based on deliberative processes, it makes some sense to focus on this legislative term despite its Aristotelian origins. In the *Rhetoric,* Aristotle himself defines deliberation as political speech urging us to do or not to do something either in private counsel or in public (1358, 8–10), but this perhaps is underdeveloped for discussing our contemporary understanding of deliberation. In defining deliberation, I slightly adapt Lani Guinier's definition by adding rhetorical elements (my additions in parenthesis). Deliberation is "the process of (articulating and) framing issues to be resolved, proposing alternative solutions, examining the reasons for and against the proposed solutions, (advocating specific solutions, recognizing and responding to the concerns of others,) and settling on an alternative (action)."[9] This definition opens up what might be the agonistic nature of an Aristotelian deliberation, giving us a lens bigger than *bian* (argument) with which to examine deliberation within Confucian texts.

Who Is He?

Living at a time of political schism and social disorder, Confucius—as portrayed in the texts and commentaries assembled after his life—sought to reestablish order with moral teachings. He lived in the period of the late Zhou dynasty, when feudal princes controlled much of the country and the dynasty was collapsing. While the Zhou king claimed to rule all under Heaven, he did not actually control most small city-states, headed by nobles and populated mostly by commoners. There, ruling was based on relationships, mostly among the nobility, but with an eye towards the people. Their support was essential for governance.[10] As Confucius wrote, arguing against the primacy of food and defensive arms, "Give up food . . . Death has been with us from ancient times, but if the common people do not have confidence in their leaders, community will not endure" (*Analects* 12.7). Primary to governing is the ruler's competence and the resulting harmonious relationship between ruler and ruled. There is hierarchy here, but one modified by a profound need for mutual respect. The community is not an ideal, but a necessity of order and life.

Confucius himself came from an impoverished aristocratic family, and many speculate that the difficulties of his youth made him sensitive to needs and views of commoners. Certainly he would have had daily contact with people of all classes. Somewhat like Plato, Confucius aspired to governing, but his periods of political work were not as significant as his life as a scholar and teacher. While Chinese culture is now perceived as valuing education highly, this was not true during his chaotic lifetime. Confucius, thwarted from a career in politics, demonstrated that scholarly life could have importance, that teaching had significance beyond that of ruling and waging war.

Like Socrates' and Jesus' words, Confucian sayings were assembled after his death and are more the interpretations of his disciples than the authorial word. The textual focus of this essay, *The Analects,* reflects over three hundred years of accumulation and editing. It is the text most closely associated with Confucius, but other early texts, such as the *Mencius,* and the *Spring and Autumn Annuals,* are followed by a commentary tradition that further elaborates the fragments, syntax, and issues of the classical texts. Together they form the basis of understanding culture (*wen*) that would unify the huge land mass and various peoples included in what came to be called China.

Called the founder and creator of Chinese culture, obviously Confucius himself was formed and created by Chinese culture. He writes, "The Zhou dynasty looked back to the Xia and Shang dynasties. Such a wealth of culture! I follow the Zhou" (3.14). Confucius valued tradition too much to rewrite it overtly. He himself obeyed the ethical principle of filial piety, a principle that extended beyond the nuclear family to elders, men of high moral character, and the state. This placing of family relationships and obligation, what the West usually sees as private, at the center of all forms of Chinese life is a key strategy in Confucian thought. In its most basic articulation, Confucian thought offers a valuing of ethical, internal principles and traditions (ritual propriety or *li*) as a counterbalance to the external rule of law (*fa*). In bringing to cultural consciousness this tension, Confucius did not offer simple submission, but rather offered a sense of morality and nobility within the thinking person, qualities available to all, extending beyond birth, nurtured by instruction and fortified by self-cultivation.[11]

Within the Confucian tradition, moral action is greater than political action: the moral character of the emperor sets the tone of the empire and an example for his subjects, and the moral obligations of the subjects are greater than their legal obligations. Citizenship is determined more by the subjects' moral sensibility than their political allegiance. Exemplary people (*zunzi*) must take the high road and must speak out even to those above them (14.23). Peoples' political duties in social obligations and relationships are more important than their legal privileges; their rites are greater than their rights. The nature of their response and responsibility historically has been qualitatively and quantitatively different from that of citizens in the public spheres of the West, because harmonious human relationships have been more important than strict adherence to rules. While rules and laws may be the product of intersubjective agreement and disciplinary apparatus, within the Confucian text the family is the prime model of relationship, and so relationship ideally is intimate, face to face, hierarchical (but mutually respectful), and ritualized.

To understand how these differences effect deliberation, I look at two themes in *The Analects,* silence and remonstration, themes in keeping with the antisophistic orientation of the book. From start to finish, Confucius makes statements such as, "It is a rare thing for glib speech and insinuating appearance to accompany authoritative conduct (*ren*)" (1.3) and "Exemplary persons would feel shame if their words were better than their deeds" (14.27). Sophistry is shameful, and *The Analects* repeatedly advises against glib speech and words not tied to deed (see also 5.5, 14.22, 14.5, 15.22, 15.41). Instead it values speech as communication and understanding, as connection among people (13.3). Consequently, if on the first page it suspects glib speech, the last line of *The Analects* admonishes, "A person who does not understand words has no way of knowing others" (20.3). Not entertainment or power in speaking, but the person's relationship to others is his source of human knowledge, self-cultivation, a society based on care ethics, and a healthy government. For Confucius, becoming human is a lifelong process (2.4). We all have potential as human beings, but being human is an accomplishment of self-cultivation within society. Very differently than "I think, therefore I am," one might say, "we relate, therefore we are."[12] To make clear the implications of this point for the process of deliberation, let's look at two recurring and interacting themes in the *Analects,* silence and remonstration.

Silence

Just as we use words for many different purposes, we use silences for many different purposes. We must not make King Lear's mistake of equating silence with disengagement and disregard, but rather identify chosen silence with the ineffable and unnamable, that which exceeds speech. Silence is more than absence or quiet; it is a constitutive part of interactions, communication, and even making of fulfillment, knowledge, choice, and commitment. Silence can indicate questions, promises, denial, warning, threats, insult, requests, command, deference, and intimacy.[13]

Within *The Analects,* silence is valued as a tool, a positive tool, for building relationships; it works through emphasizing the worth of action, the character of the silent one, and the wisdom of not engaging what cannot be changed. Inherent in the elevating of silence is a distrust of speech and a fairly clear distinction between speaking and acting, between saying nonsense and showing what is important. Silence here is not a rhetorical silence in the senses we are most familiar with (for example, communicating empathy, censor, impartiality). Rather Confucian silence repudiates glibness and puts an emphasis on material action. Human character is revealed in our worldly acts, not in the articulation of ideas and plans, not in senseless shouting, pontificating, or manipulating of others. Deeds exceed speeches.

Postmoderns tend to believe that the dichotomy between words and deeds is false or overdetermined, but this useful theoretical distinction need not be an absolute divide. As parts of the larger concept of human-making, words and deeds can be seen as different sorts of action. The implications are telling. Emphasizing the value of one's acts over the effect of one's words stresses that the rhetor is a human-in-process and in relationship to others and a natural world, rather than a solitary Cartesian thinker or speaker in control. The value of the acts becomes a guide to self-worth and social responsibility; their value displaces *poesis,* artistic discourse, or solipsistic sophistry. To put this in the plain style, "The master said, 'The ancients were loath to speak because they would be ashamed if they personally did not live up to what they said'" (4.22, see also 4.24). This desire for a speech true to the life and character of the speaker results in a careful reticence. Silence here is in service of ethos, but it also works to foreground action and the ethical relationship between speech and act. The lived character of the rhetor is more important than his speech (4.22, 4.24, 5.5, 5.8, 12.3, 14.3). Because of this distinction between speaking and acting, Confucius teaches, "When something is difficult to accomplish, how can one but be slow to speak," and asks "what need is there for eloquence?" (5.5).

Confucius would not be a proponent of speech act theory, and this is sign of a deep cultural difference in the understanding of language. Much of speech act theory arose from examples with rules and laws: saying "I do" in marriage (Austin), conditions of satisfaction (Searle), playing a game (Wittgenstein). Speech act theory is based on speaking in highly codified situations, often ones with written rules. In ancient and contemporary China, the rule of law is not embedded in cultural practices. Situations are negotiated as they arise through the lens of tradition and relationship. Since the Confucian world sees relationships and rites as more important than laws and rules, speech as enacting laws ("I sentence you to death") are not part of the conscious culture.

Confucian silences go beyond a reticence to speak, a willingness to act, and a refusal of eloquence. In addition, silence works by not saying what should be obvious, what should be self-discovered, and that which alienates. When Confucius leaves off speaking, his disciple Zigong protests, "How will we your followers find the proper way?" He responds that *tian* (heaven/nature) doesn't speak, but the seasons turn and things are born and grow (17.19). Silence in this context serves several functions. First it privileges the *dao*, the Way, over the speech of the teacher by implying that language is not necessary to finding the way. Rather the student must have relationships with the world; the speech of the teacher is less important than the experiential action of the student. Confucius's silence also obliges students to find their own way. Confucianism is often criticized as hierarchical, but here the teacher cultivates student autonomy and cognition. This silence is somewhat like an enthymeme. For both, there is a missing term, or piece of the logic. Unlike the enthymeme though, the missing term is not readily known. Hence, its apprehension requires effort. Silence calls the student to action.

Like other nonverbal forms of communication, the meaning of silence is contingent and contextual. So, *The Analects* lays out the use of silence within certain rhetorical situations. The situation may call for silence instead of speech, because there is no value in speaking on what is finished or already has immutable direction. Confucius says, "You don't discuss what is finished and done with; you don't remonstrate over what happens as a matter of course; you don't level blame against what is long gone" (3.21). If what matters is action, then speech that cannot affect action is not simply redundant; it also uses energy best placed elsewhere and potentially diminishes relationships by creating tensions (4.26, 12.24, 15.8).

Perhaps most significant is the danger of speech that alienates and damages relationships. At the close of Book Four, Confucius has said that it is hard to go wrong by personal restraint (be slow to speak) and that excellent people are not solitary, but "have neighbors" (4.23, 4.24, 4.25). The quality of daily social engagements is a significant part of one's worth, and they should be cultivated with care. A disciple Ziyou states: "If in serving your lord you are unrelenting, you will bring on disgrace; if in your friendships you are unrelenting, you will find yourself ostracized" (4.26). Ziyou emphasizes the differences in consequences in similar acts of engagement, disgrace, or ostracism, depending on the hierarchy. In all cases, unrelenting behavior results in a breakdown of relationship. If one is unrelenting, unable to be silent, unable to respect neighbors and their actions, one will lose them, and in doing so, one loses the chance to speak again and even the opportunity to be human.

Remonstrate

I persuade you. . .I remonstrate that

In Confucian thinking, there is a clear discomfort with persuasion and argumentation. Instead one is to remonstrate (*jian*). In *The Analects,* one should be slow to speak and be relenting in attempts to engage or convince another (see 4.24, 4.26,12.23, 12.3). With such a diminished place for speaking and persuasion, Confucian rhetoric has a very different speaker-audience relationship than Aristotelian rhetoric. Despite the intimacy and importance of harmony implied in self-in-relationship, there is little sense that one must reach a consensus; "people who have chosen different ways cannot make plans together" (15.40). While one's consciousness and subject-position are defined in relationship, one follows one's own path without direct responsibility for or control over the actions of others. One does not fashion the way, but follows the Way, perhaps enlarges the Way. Order is aesthetic rather than legal, and so social order is modeled on an interrelationship of human and nature/heaven (*tian*), not on autonomous human construction. Furthermore, as part of self-cultivation, one must preserve values and care enough for others that they can cultivate their own way, that they can "realize it." (8.9)

If there is less argumentative force to Confucian rhetoric, there is instead an emphasis on remonstration within a relationship of trust (19.10). Differences of opinion can be acknowledged through a more respectful process of modeling or demonstration. In persuading, there is an audience to be induced or moved. Per and *suadere* together imply a bringing *through by speech.* Movement to a different place and speaking are significant here. *Monstrare,* however, emphasizes the act of showing or demonstrating. Persuasion may be an effect of demonstration, but it need not be, and so the audience's logical and interpretative skills are more prominent. They see the action or demonstration, and based on its value, they respond. The effect of the remonstration, the action of the interlocuter (not a rhetor per se), is left open.

One can push this difference further with some basic tools of ordinary language philosophy. Building on insights in Aristotle's *Metaphysics,* Gilbert Ryle discusses the difference between verbs of terminus and process verbs.[14] Process verbs, like "seek," describe on-going action. On the other hand, terminus verbs, like "find," declare an end. "Remonstrate" is a process verb." "Persuade" is a terminus verb. If I say, "I persuade him that. . . ," there has been an end. The act of persuasion rarely occurs in the present tense, as an ongoing process. It is unusual to say "I am persuading him,"—one can imagine the context for this, but it is unusual. Almost always when one speaks of persuading, there has been a change in him, and the act of persuading is finished. In fact, if we think of this in temporal terms, the future and the past are the realms of persuasion: "I will persuade him" or "I persuaded him." This is all less true of remonstrate. If I say, "I remonstrate that . . . ," it is less clear that there has been an end or what would constitute an end. The ending of an act of remonstration is very different from the ending of an act of persuasion. In remonstrating, one can run out of time, energy, or materials, but otherwise one can continue the process. In persuading, there is an end, a change in the audience: the speaker may do most of the action, but the end is in changing an audience. With remonstration, the effect is less clear and unnecessary to judging the act: the speaker will have done all the identified action; the end is in the finishing of the demonstration. While an audience is implied in remonstration, there is no defined relationship. The remonstrator shows something. Those who see it are free to interpret it, heed it, repeat it, or ignore it. The action of remonstration is finished with end of the show, when the demonstration stops.

Consequently, if we think of persuasion as a terminus verb and remonstration as a process verb, remonstration places the outcome of the situation in the hands of the participants. Each decides how to proceed. There is no opportunity for Gorgias to acquit Helen because of the force of persuasion. The relationship defined in Confucius is not one of force. We can also highlight this difference by using the concepts of showing and telling. In the acts of telling or persuading, the rhetor has desires and knowledge, and she *knows that* her view might or should be acceptable to others: the listener should accept her expression. Showing or remonstration assumes that there may be a shaky foundation under language, that knowing and communication are contingent and incomplete and unstable. Mastery of language or the situation is more a questionable enterprise, not controlled by anyone of us. In the act of showing or remonstrating, the rhetor also has desire or knowledge, but she refuses to define the response to that desire or knowledge. Like showing, remonstration focuses more on the responsibility of representing well, while persuasion or telling focuses on the acts of saying and swaying (the effect on the audience).

Still there is more implied in remonstration. Confucius is quite clear on the limits on telling others and on judging others. Propriety exceeds *almost all,* not for the sake of preserving existing conditions, but to avoid damage to proper relationships. In a conversation about ethics and morality with the Governor of She, a proponent of the law, Confucius discusses a son's relationship with his father. While the Governor of She praises the son who turns in the dishonest father, Confucius says, "Those who are true in my village conduct themselves differently. A father covers for his son, and a son covers for his father. And being true lies in this." (13.18) Here is revealed a major difference between the thinking of those concerned with law and governing and Confucian concern with relationships. In positing that the true son chooses his father over the law (*fa*), Confucius places relationships and propriety (*li*)—granted in the narrow, hierarchical model of family—as the most significant of human qualities. This passage, while at first glance is removed from issues of remonstration and persuasion, shows us how Confucius sees familial relationships as truer than what can be thrust on another by the wily speaker or external laws. If the family is the basic model of relationship, the model of engagement is one of intimate contact, where one might remonstrate (4.18), but cannot manipulate, judge, or force.

Remonstration together with silence works to create a respectful society, one where the continuation of hierarchy is perhaps too enabled, but also one where connections among people are more important than a single individual's will or judgment. Using the family as a model of interaction, Confucius advises, "In serving your father and mother, remonstrate with them gently. On seeing that they do not heed your suggestions, remain respectful and do not act contrary. Although concerned, voice no resentment." (4.18) The child who remonstrates with the parent allows the errant parent to find his potential while preserving the relationship between parent and child. Furthermore, the child is spared the acts of anger, aggression, and disrespect. If she cannot move the parents, at least her own actions and moral worth are preserved. Like the example of the outlaw father and the loyal son, it is not the hierarchy that is being respected here, but rather the relationship.

Within *The Analects,* there is—instead of a controlling persuasion—an open-ended possibility of change in keeping with the harmony of human relationships. This has significant implications for deliberative rhetoric. This rhetorical practice does not distinguish a public sphere as a particular social space; in fact, it has little sense of public sphere, only a space of human connection. Within a rhetoric of relationship, persuasion is sophistic and a perverse distortion of respect, and analyzing silence and its significance is as an important theoretical activity as understanding the role of logos.

Confucian Democracy and Deliberation

None of this would prevent a process of decision-making and coming to action. Deliberation from a Confucian perspective would proceed more slowly; it might even be more subject to breakdown, because resistance is less engaged and more tolerated. In practice it might look more like the ritualized coming to consensus practiced by Quakers, a deliberation where one does not move to the next step until all agree. This is difficult to imagine as a governing process; while Confucianism has informed Chinese governance for 2,500 years, it has not functioned in a democracy much to the detriment of Confucian deliberation.

Due to the Confucian emphasis on human potential, it is often held up as a populist, if not democratic, force within Chinese culture. In opposition to the view voiced by Samuel Huntington at the beginning of this essay, some see New Confucianism in China as a cultural basis for democracy.[15] As well, there are moderate voices. Li Chenyang, for instance, sees democratic values as different from Confucian values, but demonstrates the value of both, ultimately arguing that they can coexist in tension. Among my purposes in positing a Confucian rhetoric has been a desire to understand its potential for democratic deliberations. I must say that initially I was inclined against the possibility, but after this analysis of two key concepts, I find the question open and in need of continued work.

To envision a democratic government and rhetoric based in the Confucian tradition, we need to have full and constant cognizance that China is not western and that what would constitute a more democratic government in China would not be western. What will constitute a healthy rhetoric in China will not resemble Aristotle's; even using the concept rhetoric distracts from what is the Chinese tradition. Confucius did not discuss the individual, he did not recognize all as created equal, nor did he see the people as a subjective force in society. On the other hand, he believed that even elites could and must learn from commoners, the least of men could not be deprived of their will, and that government must demonstrate virtue to win its population and bring order to society. Furthermore, even if his purposes were not those of a deliberating democrat, within his writing is an implicit model of deliberation, one which may not be forceful enough to promote rapid changes and responses, but one that respects interlocutors and honors their way of going in the world.

Notes

This essay was written with the help of many people. Most particularly I want to thank Roger Ames, Lan Haixia, and Newton Garver for pointing me in the right directions. Roger DesForges's careful reading of a draft helped keep me on track. It's not their fault if I got lost along the way. I am also grateful for my Fulbright year in Sichuan and my NEH Institute on Chinese religion and politics at the East-West Center.

1. Also known as Kong Fu-cu (Kung the Teacher), his full name was Kong Qiu.

2. See Kam Louie, *Critiques of Confucius in Contemporary China* (New York: St. Martin's, 1980), and Vitaly A. Rubin, Individual and the State in Ancient China, trans. Steven I. Levine (New York: Columbia University Press, 1976), xxiv–xxv. See also Wm. Theodore de Bary and Tu Weiming, eds., *Confucianism and Human Rights* (New York: Columbia University Press, 1998).

3. Confucius, *The Analects of Confucius: A Philosophical Translation,* trans.

Roger T. Ames and Henry Rosemont, Jr. (New York: Ballantine, 1998), 1. Among the many positive readers of Confucius are Tu Weiming, "Human Rights as Confucian Moral Discourse," in *Confucianism and Human Rights,* (New York: Columbia University Press, 1998) 299–302; Ann Kent, *Between Freedom and Subsistence: China and Human Rights* (New York: Oxford University Press, 1993); and David L. Hall and Roger T. Ames., either *The Democracy of the Dead: Dewey, Confucius, and the Hope for Democracy in China.* (Chicago: Open Court, 1999) or *Thinking Through Confucius.* (Albany: State University of New York Press, 1987).

4. In *Demystifying Mentalities* (New York: Cambridge University Press, 1990), G. E. R. Lloyd provides an excellent overview of the similarities and differences between classical Greece and China. His most telling point is to remind us that cultures are never monolithic and broad claims are troublesome.

5. The average undergraduate can paraphrase their theories of language in Plato or Aristotle. Theories of language in Chinese classics are much harder to extrapolate. For exceptions to this claim, one must work in later periods. See, for instance, Zong-qi Cai, *A Chinese Literary Mind: Culture, Creativity, and Rhetoric in Wenxin diaolong* (Stanford University Press, 2001) or Zhuangzi's *Qi Wu Lun* or "Seeing Things as Equal" (369–286?B.C.E.). J. I. Crump translated *Intrigues of the Warring States: Studies of the Chan-Kuo Ts'e* (Ann Arbor: University of Michigan Press, 1996) and in his work on *Intrigues* has written some excellent commentaries arguing that it is a set of sophistic models.

6. Xing Lu and David A. Frank, "On the Study of Ancient Chinese Rhetoric/*Bian,*" *Western Journal of Communication* 57 (1993): 445–63.

7. Mary Garrett, "Classical Chinese Conceptions of Argumentation and Persuasion," *Argumentation and Advocacy* 29 (1993): 105–15. In *Rhetoric in Ancient China: Fifth to Third Century B.C.E.* (Columbia: University of South Carolina Press, 1998), Xing Lu discusses definitions further.

8. I was dependent on Lan Haixia for developing this list.

9. Lani Guinier, *The Tyranny of the Majority: Fundamental Fairness in Representative Democracy* (New York: Free Press, 1994), 256.

10. Rubin, *Individual and the State,* 1–3

11. See David L. Hall and Roger T. Ames, *Thinking Through Confucius* (Albany: State University of New York Press, 1987) and Rubin, Individual and the State, 20–28;

12. I owe Roger des Forges the wonderful "we" extension of Descartes.

13. Muriel Saville-Troike, "The Place of Silence in an Integrated Theory of Communication," *Perspectives on Silence,* eds. Deborah Tannen and Muriel Saville-Troike (Norwood, NJ: Ablex, 1985), 6, 16.

14. Gilbert Ryle, *Dilemmas* (New York: Cambridge University Press, 1954), 102–109. Thanks to Newton Garver for this reference.

15. See Hall and Ames, *The Democracy of the Dead,* 87; He Baogang, *The Democratic Implications of Civil Society in China* (New York: St. Martin's, 1997), 50–52; Tu, "Human Rights," 299–302.

Works Cited

Chan-Kuo Ts'e. Trans. J. I. Crump. Ann Arbor: University of Michigan Press, 1996.

Chen, Li-Fu. *Why Confucius Has Been Reverenced as the Model Teacher of all Time.* New York: St. John's University Press, 1976.

Confucius. *The Analects of Confucius: A Philosophical Translation.* Trans. Roger T.Ames and Henry Rosemont, Jr. New York: Ballantine, 1998.

Crump, J. I. *Intrigues of the Warring States: Studies of the Chan-Kuo Ts'e.* Ann Arbor: University of Michigan Press,1964.

Crump, J. I., ed. *Legends of the Warring States: Persuasions, Romances, and Stories from the Chan-Kuo Ts'e.* Ann Arbor: University of Michigan Press,1998.

De Bary, William Theodore, and Tu Weiming. *Confucianism and Human Rights.* New York: Columbia University Press, 1998.

Garrett, Mary M. "Classical Chinese Conceptions of Argumentation and Persuasion." *Argumentation and Advocacy* 29 (1993): 105–15.

Guinier, Lani. *The Tyranny of the Majority: Fundamental Fairness in Representative Democracy.* New York: Free Press, 1994.

Hall, David L., and Roger T. Ames. *The Democracy of the Dead: Dewey, Confucius, and the Hope for Democracy in China.* Chicago: Open Court, 1999.

———. Thinking Through Confucius. Albany: State University of New York Press, 1987.

He, Baogang. *The Democratic Implications of Civil Society in China.* New York: St. Martin's, 1997.

Huntington, Samuel P. *The Third Wave: Democratization in the Late Twentieth Century.* Norman: University of Oklahoma, 1991.

Kam, Louie. *Critiques of Confucius in Contemporary China.* New York: St. Martin's, 1980.

Kent, Ann. *Between Freedom and Subsistence; China and Human Rights.* New York: Oxford University Press, 1993.

Li, Chenyang. *The Tao Encouters the West: Explorations in Comparative Philosophy.* Albany: State University of New York Press, 1999.

Lloyd, G. E. R. *Demystifying Mentalities*. New York: Cambridge University Press, 1990.

Lu Xing. *Rhetoric in Ancient China: Fifth to Third Century B.C.E.* Columbia: University of South Carolina, 1998.

Lu, Xing, and David A. Frank. "On the Study of Ancient Chinese Rhetoric/Bian." *Western Journal of Communications* 57 (1993): 445–63.

Rubin, Vitaly A. *Individual and the State in Ancient China*. Trans. Steven I. Levine. New York: Columbia University Press, 1976.

Ryle, Gilbert. *Dilemmas*. New York: Cambridge University Press, 1954.

Saville-Troike, Muriel. "The Place of Silence in an Integrated Theory of Communication." *Perspectives on Silence*. Deborah Tannen and Muriel Saville-Troike, eds. Norwood, N.J.: Ablex, 1985. 3–18.

Tu, Weiming. "Human Rights as Confucian Moral Discourse." In *Confucianism and Human Rights*, William Theodore de Bary and Tu Weiming, eds. New York: Columbia University Press, 1998. 299–302.

"Nothing Can Be Accomplished If the Speech Does Not Sound Agreeable": Rhetoric and the Invention of Classical Chinese Discourse

Yameng Liu

If we stop fretting about the ever-baffling notion of a Chinese rhetoric "in its own terms," and assume instead that the general understanding of rhetoric as dealing with effective use of symbolic resources in discursive and sociocultural practices is applicable cross-culturally, then an abundance of available textual evidence would certainly lead us to the conclusion that the Chinese had early reached an impressive level of sophistication in what is readily recognizable as *rhetorical* thinking. In *Shi Jing* [*Classic of Poetry* 诗经], an anthology of poems dating mostly to the Western Zhou period (c. 1045–771 B.C.E.), many versified aphorisms attest to a heightened rhetorical awareness among the general populace. "Only plain speech [*er yan* 迩言] is listened to," one poem goes, "only plain speech to strive for." Another observes that "[when] the discourse [*ci* 辞] is consonant, the people are harmonious/When the discourse is uplifting, people feel reassured."[1] Such popularly held assumptions about a close interrelationship among rhetoric, discourse, the public-cum-audience and social order were further codified in canonized classical texts such as *The Analects,* where Confucius (551–479 B.C.E.) famously argues, for instance, that

> if names [名] are not properly defined and used, the speech [yan 言] can never sound agreeable. If the speech jars, nothing can be accomplished. This means that there would be no proper observance of ritual and ceremonial activities, the legal system would collapse, and people would no longer know how correctly to behave themselves.[2]

Chained together in this sorites-like argument is a heterogeneous set of domains and practices, from semantics, speech, rituals, ceremonies, the legal system, to human dispositions and behaviors, with those constitutive of rhetoric placed at the very foundation of the resultant discourse/power network.

Within an overall conceptual framework made up of penetrating insights like these, it is little wonder that a vigorous development in both rhetorical thought and its application should have been able to sustain itself throughout the entire preimperial period of Chinese history (c. the eleventh to the third century B.C.E.), culminating in the emergence, toward the end of this axial age, of great rhetorical practitioners/theorists such as Xunzi (c. 313–238 B.C.E.) and *Han Feizi* (c. 280–233 B.C.E.). A cursory look at *nan* [难 rebuttal], Han Feizi's favorite genre of writing, offers a vivid illustration of the way rhetoric was conceptualized and practiced in China around the third century B.C.E. Typically starting out with a concise representation of what must have been a widely circulated commonplace at that time, a *nan* features in the middle section either a subversive analysis or a critical reinterpretation of the commonplace concerned. With prima facie validity of the conventional truth now called into serious question, an alternative perspective, already implied in the critical interrogation, is then offered in a sharply worded statement with which to wrap up the "rebuttal." The concluding remark at once deals a coup de grace to the piece of conventional wisdom being questioned and completes what in effect is a process of invention aimed at the formulation of a new, counterconventional point of view.

In one piece of *nan* from *Han Feizi,* we find the following passage:

> Master Li [Li Ke 李克] has defined as *tiao yan* 窕言] eloquent speech that pleases the audience but does not conform to reason. And yet "eloquence" is a quality of the speaker. Being "pleased" is a state of the listener. Since speech and he who listens to it are two entirely different entities, "not conforming to reason" applies only to the speech and has nothing directly to do with the listener. The listener is either a man of quality [*junzi* 君子] or a vulgar person. Should the listener be a vulgar person, he would know nothing about reason therefore would not be in a position to pass judgment on the extent to which the speech conforms to reason. If, on the other hand, the listener happened to be a man of quality, how could he be "pleased" with a speech not conforming to reason? Li's definition is therefore utterly invalid.[3]

Apart from the high analytical level on which it operates, this critique impresses us with a number of notable features. It talks about what we now call enabling principles of a symbolic action (i.e., addresser, audience, message) with an easy familiarity. The quasi-logical approach it adopts is so sophisticated that it reminds us of, for example, the famous "Pascal's Wager." And underneath what appears to be a purely technical analysis of a definition, one detects an ideological struggle between an entrenched Confucian doctrine to "rectify names" and fight "glib-tongued speakers" as the way to restore social order, and attempts by the Legalists, another major ancient Chinese school of thought of which *Han Feizi* was a leading proponent, to undermine the ideological domination by the Confucians so as to open up space for their own program. Rhetoric, it appears, did not just help to give shape to the diverse and contending opinions and perspectives. It became *in itself* a major terrain on which the conflicting interests battled one another.

Technically and conceptually striking as this example is, the kind of analysis and critique it offers is by no means an exception to Han Feizi's writings in general. Neither is it found only in his works. The anthology bearing his name counts among its selections three fully developed treatises dealing with topics from the origin of argumentation to the difficulties in addressing an audience. One of the trio, titled *"Wen bian"* [问辩 "Whence Comes Argumentation: A Reply"], elaborates on two central theses about the subject: that a "lack of clarity" on the part of the "highest authorities" gives rise to all contentions and arguments, and that "utility should be the *telos* and the standard with which to judge all words and deeds." The first of the twin claims easily lends itself to a diachronic "translation"—into the modern understanding that rhetorical invention is contingent on a primordial ambiguity or indeterminacy, and is enabled only by the *absence* of an ultimate "arbitrator." In *"Shui nan"* ["On the Difficulty of Persuasion" 说难], another of his major treatises, Han Feizi goes beyond a mere emphasis on the rhetor's need to adapt to the audience, focusing instead on the difficulty of accurately capturing deep-lying motives. What the audience *professes* to believe, feel, like, etc., he cautions, does not often constitute a reliable basis for designing persuasive efforts.[4]

Han Feizi, moreover, was not the first to adopt the strategy of technically deconstructing the rhetoric of an opponent so as to discredit his ideology. The approach had become popular long before his time, and with virtually all the leading discursive practitioners or 'masters' of the preimperial China. The work of Mencius (c. 382–300 B.C.E.), for example, shows "a methodological pattern of zeroing in on the structuring metaphor or analogy of his opponent and refuting the opponent's point by problematizing and invalidating this very metaphor," either "through *reductio ad absurdum* or by otherwise showing that the metaphor is irrelevant or inappropriate."[5] And if we could not but call such practice *rhetorical criticism,* there is nothing surprising about that realization. For the only self-identification Mencius offers throughout his corpus is that he was someone who "[knew] *yan*," which he further elaborates as being able "to detect what a concealing speech tries to cover up, what a high-flown speech attempts to make up for, from which position a deviant speech has strayed, and what an evasive speech really aims at."[6]

Even without being further contextualized and supported, these telltale bits and pieces of information alone are enough to offer us glimpses into the kind of depth, scope and complexity that classical Chinese rhetoric had managed to achieve. The achievement has started to receive a belated, and in many cases still grudging, recognition from established scholars of ancient China. Summarizing his findings about "language and writing" prior to the Qin (221–207 B.C.E.) or the Han (206 B.C.E.–220 A.D.) dynasty, sinologist William G. Boltz calls attention to "an ill-defined but wide-ranging concern with words: with their meanings, their logical usage, and their relation to one another and to the outside world of real things." Even though he sounds as if he was talking here about some purely linguistic interests (e.g., the relationship between signs and referents), Boltz actually points to a much larger backdrop, when he singles out this "wide-ranging concern" with *yan* [whose meaning in classical Chinese language is much closer to "speech"/"discourse" than "language"] as the defining feature of extant classical Chinese texts and goes on to conclude that formal manifestations of this concern "reveal an intellectually sophisticated sense of the nature of words and language and of the relation of these to the world of real objects."[7]

Similarly, David L. Hall and Roger T. Ames have become the first leading western sinologists to pay serious attention to rhetoric as a proper topic in conceptualizing classical Chinese thought. Whereas in sinological studies the dominant trend has been toward showing that "most of the ancient Chinese thinkers are very much more rational than they used to look" and that logic or "rational demonstration" plays a much larger role in the preimperial debate over *dao* (the Way) than was believed previously,[8] in a section of their *Thinking From the Han* titled "Logic and Rhetoric," Hall and Ames maintain instead that "it was not logic, but rhetoric . . . that was the privileged mode of communication" in ancient China. In support of this claim, they offer four observations: 1. "throughout their history the Chinese have been more apt to argue along *pathos*- and *ethos*-based lines than to employ objective *logos*-style argumentation"; 2. "the rhetorical uses of language found in classical Chinese texts . . . involve 'analogical reasoning'" which, as "employed by the majority of Chinese philosophers . . . [appeals] to the authority of tradition and to the exemplars (of the sages and cultural heroes) of that tradition"; 3. "in China an idea is a proposal for feeling and action"—it is "*dispositional*," in the strict sense that it "disposes individuals to implement it," and "there is no reflection of a thinking/acting dichotomy in the Chinese formulation"; and 4. "Chinese modes of expression may be thought to function imagistically and metaphorically," and "what we call metaphors, images, and concepts are more on a par in classical China."[9]

Whether in Boltz's identification of a preoccupation with *yan* as the defining feature of classical Chinese texts, or in Hall and Ames's more direct observation that rhetoric was the "privileged mode of communication" throughout the preimperial China, one senses a deepening realization that the body of existing textual evidence about ancient Chinese discourse lends itself more readily to a *rhetorical,* as opposed to, for instance, a philosophical or a literary, reconstruction. The entrenched old paradigm of sinology as a subfield of philosophical, linguistic, and literary studies, however, dies hard. Boltz's background in linguistics asserts itself by turning an interest in *yan* into an obsession with the "meaning of words" and their relationship with "objects" in the real world. Similarly, the terministic screen Hall and Ames employ could not but impose *a* philosophical point of view. For all they say about the rhetorical character of the discursive practices of ancient China, the Chinese masters remain for them "philosophers." And their understanding of what rhetoric is about betrays both a commitment to maintaining a "logic/rhetoric" distinction at the latter's expense—and a seriously flawed notion of "rhetoric." Whether from classical or modern western rhetorical theories, one can find no support for their definition of rhetoric in terms of "*pathos*- and *ethos*-based lines" rather than "objective *logos*-style argumentation," or their association of rhetoric with "analogical" or "imagistical" modes of expression only.

The domination of what has long been set up as the normative framework for thematizing pre-Qin (i.e., prior to 221 B.C.E.) Chinese discourse is so thorough that even professional students of rhetoric could not but feel—and in many cases yield to—the conceptual and methodological constraints it imposes on their own investigations. Such investigations typically undertake to examine the "rhetorical perspectives" of ancient Chinese "thinkers" or "philosophers." They are frequently guided by the kind of questions philosophers-cum-sinologists are most interested in raising, such as "how did the ancient Chinese perceive and conceptualize language and speech" and "how was [sic] such theories [i.e., the ancient Chinese masters' "rhetorical perspectives"] related to their philosophical views."[10] Their reports, moreover, are often structured as a review of how the various established "schools of thought" articulated widely differing views on rhetoric. And to account for the divergence of these perspectives, obvious sociopolitical factors, such as the breakdown of traditional social order during the Spring and Autumn period (770–476 B.C.E.) and the ensuing politicodiplomatic maneuverings for hegemony during the Warring States period (475–221 B.C.E.), are often cited as the only causal factors. "[Classical] Chinese rhetorical theories and practices," it is popularly assumed, are "*reflections of,* and functional *responses to,* cultural patterns and crises of ancient China."[11]

Even though it is still capable of producing useful accounts on many of the individual topics and areas covered, this approach is flawed in three by no means negligible aspects. If, as Hall and Ames tell us, "there is no reflection of a thinking/acting dichotomy in the Chinese formulation" and ideas in ancient China are better understood as "[proposals] for feeling and action" or for "[disposing] individuals to act," it is unwarranted, at least for a historical reconstruction purportedly from a *rhetorical* point of view, to continue identifying originators of classical Chinese discourse as primarily "philosophers" or "thinkers" who happened to take an *incidental* interest in rhetoric. The classical Chinese discourse was never differentiated on a disciplinary basis in the first place. If Mencius's self-identification is any indication, most of the ancient masters were more likely to have thought of themselves as "rhetorical critics" or "discursive practitioners" than as "thinkers" in modern terms. The use of the label of "thinker" or "philosopher" in referring to the masters, moreover, automatically assigns a subordinate status to the oratory they practiced, necessarily resulting in a restricted and distorted vision of the scope, complexity, and significance of rhetorical activities in ancient China.

Secondly, it fosters the unwarranted presumption that because the "various schools" held conflicting "philosophical views," their perspectives on oratory must necessarily diverge also. In fact, the projected "differences" among the masters' rhetorical perspectives often point only to varying foci and emphases of a shared understanding. The "three tests" [*biao* 表] of an argument [i.e., assessing an argument through an examination of its origin, validity, and applicability] codified in the Mohist corpus[12] are regarded in standard accounts as a unique component of a *Mohist* theory of rhetoric. And yet the trio of standards was tacitly accepted by virtually all schools of thought: no other preceding or subsequent master is known to have taken exception to the criteria. Similarly, because the key distinction between *zhi* [质 substance] and *wen* [文 style] and the need for a proper balance between them were first articulated in the Confucian *Analects,* they have often been associated exclusively with a *Confucian* theory of rhetoric. Other masters are, accordingly, each assigned either a pro-*wen* or pro-*zhi* stance in order to differentiate their respective perspectives on rhetoric from Confucius's. In reality, the various views on the *wen/zhi dichotomy differ from each other only "relatively." A theorist "may be promoting* zhi, but that does not necessarily mean that he attaches no importance to wen"*: the same commentator often "sounds pro-wen on some occasions and pro-*zhi* on others."[13]

A school-by-school account of rhetorical thinking in ancient China that emphasizes the divergence of views is further undermined by recently discovered textual evidence. The earliest known versions of many canonized classical texts, inscribed on the Warring-States-period bamboo strips excavated in the 1990s in China's Hubei Province, have consistently displayed a significant mix of what are now recognized as Confucian, Daoist, or Mohist doctrines in one and the same text, so much so that scholars are prompted to talk about a "Confucianization of the Daoist literature" or vice versa as a common phenomenon in classical Chinese discourse. The possibility that Chinese discourse "had remained undifferentiated prior to Zhuangzi [ca. 369–280 B.C.E.]" is being entertained with increasing seriousness by sinologists worldwide.[14]

Equally problematic, finally, is the assumption that the growth of classical Chinese rhetoric was a mere "reflection" of or "response" to preexisting "cultural patterns and crises of ancient China."The unilinear explanation is unjustified both theoretically and pragmatically. It treats "existing social or cultural conditions" as a given and a prior order ontologically separated from discourse. It denies discourse's role in creating social and cultural meanings that shape the perceptions, desires, feelings, and hence behaviors of individual or institutional actors. It stresses, in New Historicist terms, the "historicity of texts" to the complete neglect of the "textuality of history." In the specific case of reconstructing classical Chinese rhetoric, the one-directional account deflects attention from the more persuasive belief that as a special form/mode of discourse, rhetoric must necessarily have interacted with, impacted on, conditioned and in turn been conditioned by other discursive and institutional practices of ancient China. It fails to properly acknowledge the extent to which "cultural patterns and crises of ancient China," as historian Mark Edward Lewis argues in his recent study of the "uses of writing to command assent and obedience in early China," were themselves products of discursive practices at that time.

Lewis calls attention to the fact that "types of writing" were employed in ancient China as "forms of control" in "state and society to generate and exercise power."[15] He argues that while writing was instrumental in such areas as the creation of diverse "new groups," its "ultimate importance . . . to the Chinese empire and imperial civilization" lies in a writing-enabled "imaginary realm" on which the empire was based. A "shared commitment" to the "texts" within which such an imaginary realm was produced "created the links between the imperial system and localities, links far more numerous and penetrating than those provided by a bureaucratic administration."[16] Drawing inspiration from the Foucaultian admonition that "the formation of discourses and the genealogy of knowledge" should be analyzed "not in terms of types of consciousness, modes of perception and forms of ideology, but in terms of tactics and strategies of power,"[17] and from Benedict Anderson's definition of the nation as "an imagined political community,"[18] Lewis sees "writing" more as an enabling, generative, and determining factor than something having its development and functioning completely shaped by the prevailing material conditions. His argument amounts thus to a reversal of the kind of unilinear historical interpretation mentioned above.

Even though for Lewis, writing is no more than a technique of power or a means of imagining, with his emphasis on "[commanding] assent and obedience" as its modus operandi and its vital role in the creation of "new groups," including the various "schools" and ideology-specific communities named metonymically after the various "masters" of classical Chinese discourse, his treatment of the subject shades into a discussion on rhetoric and rhetorical invention. Perhaps unintentionally, it highlights the need to conceptualize anew classical Chinese oratory along a similar line, as an enabling and generative factor in the production of canonized ancient texts, the invention of classical Chinese discourse, and, ultimately, the creation of the "imaginary realm" that was classical China.

There is nothing new in seeing rhetoric as a productive art. Richard McKeon called upon us decades ago to think of it as "an art of structuring all principles and products of knowing, doing, and making."[19] The same understanding has been reaffirmed from time to time by rhetoricians committed to seeing communication as no less than a key enabling factor for all discourses and practices. And yet the perspective remains largely ignored in efforts to retell the story of either classical Chinese rhetoric or classical Chinese discourse as a whole. As a result, interpretative inadequacies continue to mar most of the accounts of the intellectual development in ancient China, one recent example being that offered by sociologist Randall Collins.

Collins uses the formal concept of "opposition" to anchor his story of how an intellectual network took shape in ancient China:

> Chinese philosophy begins in . . . conflict. Confucius and his followers sprang up around 500 B.C.E. in conscious opposition to existing political and religious practices. The Mohists emerged two generations later with doctrines explicitly contradicting many Confucian points. Both schools of moralistic activism were soon challenged by Yang Chu, with his anti-moralistic and anti-activist alternative . . . Mencius in turn counterattacked the Yang Chu movement with an explicit defense of the goodness of human nature; this opened up yet another slot in intellectual space which Hsun Tzu filled with the opposing doctrine that human nature is evil and requires the imposition of social and ritual restraints. . . .[20]

The narrative is not off the mark in stressing, as the mode of intellectual production in classical China, a contra-stance toward dominant discourses and a contentious interaction among the various "schools." Yet Collins is unable to shake himself free from the unilinear way of thinking, continuing to maintain that the "existing political and religious practices" in Confucius's time set off the entire chained opposition he narrates. And he bases his approach on the ultimately simplistic assumption that "intellectual creativity is driven by op-position" and that "[philosophical] positions develop by taking one another as foils,"[21] failing to offer any genuine insight into the functioning of debate and argumentation (i.e., rhetoric) as the agency for the kind of development he talks about. This prevents him from raising what ought to be the central ques-tion in the context of his discussion, that is, why is it that the oppositional confrontation he describes should have resulted in an outburst of seminal ideas, diverse and significant perspectives and culture-shaping ideologies in-stead of degenerating into fruitless bickerings, contentious exchange among the deaf, in short, mere sound and fury?

Both the lively contention of the so-called "one hundred schools" of dis-course active during the preimperial China and the amazing productivity of their interaction point to a number of simple but often neglected facts: that the discursive practitioners of this period communicated with one another well rather than talked at cross-purposes; that they were capable of critically en-gaging one another's ideas rather than being trapped in their own ideological soliloquies; and that their contentious interactions were oriented toward the invention of new ideas and perspectives rather than a mere vindication or re-jection of existing ones. These facts in turn entail, as their conditions of possi-bility, that the discursive practitioners of this period, regardless of their ideo-logical affiliations, must have *shared* a body of terministic and conceptual resources, subscribed to the same set of basic problematics, assumptions, and norms, and functioned within the same rhetorical framework.

To identify these resources, assumptions, and norms embodied in the corpus of canonized ancient Chinese texts as a whole thus offers a way of si-multaneously representing classical Chinese rhetoric anew as what McKeon calls "an architectonic productive art"[22] and establishing the key role rhetoric played in the invention of the classical Chinese discourse. For the kind of dis-course that came into being under specific historical circumstances, as Pierre Bourdieu argues from the opposite side of the case, ultimately depends on the kind of discursive resources available for that particular moment:

> in what is unthinkable at a given time, there is not only everything that cannot be thought for lack of the ethical or political dispositions which tend to bring it into consideration, but also everything that cannot be thought for lack of instruments of thought such as prob-lematics, concepts, methods and techniques."[23]

While it would take a book-length study to identify and catalogue all the "in-struments" of thought and discourse available in preimperial China, a brief look at classical Chinese texts[24] would suffice to reveal rhetoric's role as the supplier of these shared assumptions, concepts, techniques, etc., those whose employment accounts for what Collins terms "innovation through opposition."

No matter what discursive community one belonged to, a practitioner in ancient China was likely to subscribe to a body of basic assumptions about the nature and function of rhetoric. Shared by all is the sense that *ci* or *yan* is a practice whose sociopolitical importance can never be overestimated. Confucius, as has been pointed out, believed nothing could be accomplished without first 'smoothing out' one's *yan*. Mozi sees argumentation (*bian*) as that which makes it possible "to distinguish between the right and wrong, to tell the true from the false, to determine what leads to order and what would give rise to chaos, to identify similarities and differences, to see whether a name fits what it signifies, to locate the advantages and disadvantages, and to decide what to do whenever one is in doubt."[25] Summarizing the classical masters' comments on this topic, Liu Xiang (77–6 B.C.E.) observes that for all of them, "the authority of the monarch and the personal worth of the subject, the security of the state and the safety of the individual all hinges on ci. Therefore, one cannot but strive to cultivate one's speech and perfect one's persuasive skills."[26]

Just as universally acknowledged by the various schools is rhetoric's role as a fundamental means for the pursuit of self-cultivation and self-advancement. Nowhere is this rhetoric/self nexus more authoritatively affirmed than in the earliest pronouncement about xiuci, the closest Chinese equivalent for *rhetoric:* "To cultivate [*xiu*] *ci* so as to establish one's sincerity."[27] The curtness of the dictum opens up possibilities in its construal. Yet whether "sincerity" here is meant to be taken as a textual effect, as the projected *ethos* of the speaker, or as the quality of the rhetor's character in real life, regulated and refined through the proper use of speech, it is clear that a close link between *yan* and the personal or the ethical is no less firmly presupposed than that between *yan* and the social or the political. "All pre-Qin schools of thought stress without exception that the only purpose of cultivating speech is to advance politico-ethical interests."[28]

With so much importance being attached to *yan,* the stakes became too high for anyone to take it lightly. As a manifestation of the high seriousness with which practitioners during the period treated the diverse discourses in circulation, the need for conflicting viewpoints to engage and check against one another was taken for granted. Between the true and the false *yan,* it is commonly assumed across schools, there can be no compromise, and it is the rhetor's duty to refute the latter in order to promote the former. Mencius best exemplifies this commitment. He justifies his perceived eagerness for disputation on the ground that unless all popular yet pernicious discourses be put to rest, "the Confucian way can never ascend to a position of prominence."[29] The same attitude was adopted by all masters involved in the contentious discursive interaction that was classical Chinese discourse, and was reiterated as late as the first century A.D., when Wang Cong articulates a position virtually identical with Mencius's:

> Without exposing and banishing such [untruthful and absurd] words, we can never put an end to the flashy and yet specious discourses [now in vogue]. The continued and unrestrained circulation of these discourses would make it impossible for true and grounded ideas to be adopted.

Or as he states more philosophically, "[just] as only through a clash of two blades can we find out which one is the sharper, so it is by letting two theories check against each other that we can determine which one is correct and which one wrong."[30]

Such a "clash of two blades" would never be meaningful without reference to some general criteria and norms. A keen awareness of this situation must have led to a general consensus about the need to subject an argument to a "test" or "validation" (*yan* 验), as well as to a *copia* of terms and pronouncements serving evaluative purposes. Yang Xiong (53 B.C.E.–18 A.D.) speaks for all classical authors when he dismisses untestable kinds of speech as "nonsense" and goes on to lay down the methodological principle for tackling the difficult cases. One should attempt, he advises, to test "the shady with the well-lit, the distant and remote with what is close to hand, the over-scaled with the ordinarily sized, and the subtle with the clearly marked."[31] In addition to Mozi's "three tests" mentioned above (i.e., origin, validity, and applicability), a whole range of standards had been proposed from different interested positions and yet managed to remain noncontroversial. From a moral-ideological point of view, Mencius defines the ultimate end of *yan* as to "set people's understanding right, put illicit discourses to rest, oppose devious actions, and banish excessive speech."[32] Mozi, on the other hand, chooses to stress a fit between the rhetor's talk and the specific rhetorical situation he faces, or "selecting the right topic for one's address," as the single most important criterion. He dictates,

> If a state is suffering from corruption and chaos, promoting personal integrity and valuing unity would be the right thing to do. If a state is mired in poverty, one should address its people instead on the need to be frugal . . . If a state indulges in aggressive acts against its neighbors, the appropriate theme should be the upholding of universal brotherhood and renunciation of attacking one another.[33]

A more general interest in determining what it means to be "good at persuading" led to the formulation and circulation of a whole range of technically based criteria. In surprisingly modern terms, one observer equates being good at persuading with "describing the situation in such a way that what the [rhetor's] *yan* proposes would appear to be the way to take care of what the circumstances urgently demand to be addressed" [善说者, 陈其事, 言其方人之急也].[34] And embedded in the following discussion are standards with which to evaluate not just the persuasive process, but each of the major steps making up this process:

> If one's persuasion does not work . . . , it is because the case has not been clearly presented. If the case has been clearly presented and the speech still fails to persuade, it is because no conviction on the part of the audience has been achieved. If the audience has indeed been convinced of the validity of the thesis and still refuses to act accordingly, it is because the conviction does not fit in with the audience's deep-seated values. To argue in a manner that is readily comprehensible to the audience, to succeed in convincing them of the justification of the point being made, and to appeal to their cherished values . . . this is what we mean by "being good at persuasion."[35]

The above discussion straddles both the evaluative and the technical realm, bearing witness to a careful and sophisticated conceptualization in both. Just as well-defined criteria were amply supplied to rhetorical critics of the time, so techniques of argumentation were meticulously identified and classified to facilitate their application in discursive production. Mozi famously identifies seven techniques of arguing: arguing from probability (*huo* 或), from supposition (*jia* 假), from exemplification (*xiao* 效), from comparison (*pi* 辟), from analogy (*mou* 侔), from reciprocity (*yuan* 援), from inference (*tui* 推).[36] Xunzi broadens the scope of inquiry a bit by articulating what must have been a normative perspective on what he calls "the technique of speaking and persuasion" (*tan shui zhi shu* 谈说之术): "present your thesis in a dignified manner; treat the issue with sincerity; persist in arguing for your case; clarify by making distinctions; illustrate with figures and tropes; work up emotion and enthusiasm as you conclude; endow your speech with a high relevancy and a magical charm—if you address an audience this way, your speech will always be accepted."[37]

Elaborating on the Confucian dictum of "Watch for the right time to deliver your speech," Xunzi also offers what amounts to a minitreatise on *kairos* as a technical consideration:

> One can never begin talking about the principle of the Way with anyone until the addressee is in a respectable and receptive mood. Nor

can one start addressing the reason of the Way before the initial verbal exchange becomes relaxed and smooth; nor can one bring up the topic of the Way's reach before the addressee appears humble and submissive. It is presumptuous to start talking with someone before he is in a mood to be addressed. It is excessively reserved [of the rhetor] to remain silent when the audience becomes addressable. And it is blind [of the rhetor] to speak out without first checking the appearance and manners of the addressee."[38]

Woven into this essay on timing are ideas about the need to put the audience in the right frame of mind, to manage the dynamic rhetor/audience interaction in view of the specific task at hand, and to adapt one's persuasive efforts to the audience's changing attitude.

A close look into Xunzi's discussion also reveals the fact that he frames his thesis by building up on two key distinctions. First made by Confucius, these are the distinction between the "addressable" and the "unaddressable" audience and that between the "loss of [otherwise persuadable] people" and the "waste of speech." For Confucius, "failing to address the addressable [*ke yü yan* 可与言] amounts to a loss of people [otherwise capable of being won over](*shi ren* 失人), whereas venturing to address the un-addressable would amount to a waste of *yan* [*shi yan* 失言]." A "wise person," for Confucius, "would suffer neither losses."[39] The role played by these two previously formulated pairs of concepts in the invention of Xunzi's treatise draws our attention to still another major category of resources. This is the category of the terms, concepts, and distinctions, the very access to which rendered possible a wide range of speech acts and discursive activities that practitioners of this period are found to have committed.

From the early appearance of specialized terms such as *chen ci* (忱辞 sincere speech), *li kou* (利口 artful speech; glib tongue), *ti yao* (体要 , of documents, complete in principle and compendious in expression) and especially *dan ci/liang ci* (单辞/两辞 one-sided/two-sided presentation) in the *Book of Documents*,[40] through Mohist authors' designation of *gu* (固 cause), *li* (理 reason) and, *lei* (类 kind) as the three enabling principles responsible for the invention of *ci*,[41] to Han Feizi's coinage of *shui zhe* (说者 the addresser) and *suo shui* (所说 the addressee), an ever expanding vocabulary of rhetorical concepts and terms opened up ever more new opportunities and possibilities for thinking of, talking about, and indeed doing rhetoric and discourse in general. Confucius's distinction between *zhi* (质 substance) and *wen* (文 style), for example, went well beyond enriching the way people thought and talked about composing and textualization. In fact, the distinction added to the shaping of the normative style of the elites (*junzi* 君子) of his time and thus to the regulation of their behaviors. Xunzi distinguished among

the sage's, the *junzi*'s, and the petty/inferior person's (*xiao ren* 小人) eloquence,[42] which allowed him to contrast the sage's unplanned, spontaneous
eloquence with the *junzi*'s deliberative persuasiveness, and the *junzi*'s adherence to the right Way with the petty person's deviation from it, in their respective modes of discourse. The distinction helped bring about a hierarchization
of different kinds of rhetoric, on both technical and political grounds. And
this in turn contributed to the institutionalization of a hierarchized social
order.

Just as exemplary of this category of shared resources in general is the
way problematic modes of *yan* (or its synonym *ci* or *yu* 语) were minutely
differentiated, meticulously identified and carefully named. This resulted in
ready availability of technical terms with which to refer to and critique almost
any imaginable deformity of speech. Notable among the names of flawed *yan*
(*ci* or *yu*) found in classical Chinese texts are *yi yan* (逸言 insincere speech),
pian yan (諞言 artful speech); *qiao yan* (巧言 *clever/glib-tongued speech*);
mei yan (美言 flashy speech); *you yan* (游言 ungrounded and flighty
speech); *tiao yan* (佻言 alluring but morally suspect speech); *bi ci* (詖辞 bi-
ased speech); *yin ci* (淫辞 excessive speech); *xie ci* (邪辞 deviant speech);
dun ci (遁辞 evasive speech); *pian ci* (偏辞 unbalanced speech); *hua yan*
(华言 floral yet unsubstantial speech); *xie shuo* (邪说 heretical speech); *jian
yan* (奸言 immoral and unjust speech); *guai shuo* (怪说 outlandish speech);
qi ci (奇辞 sensational speech); *kong yan* (空言 empty speech); *xüwang zhi
yan* (虚妄之言 fanciful speech); *bu yan zhi yu* (拙而不伦 untested/unsub-
stantiated speech). In addition, Han Feizi also provided a list of twelve accusations that people of his time commonly leveled against forms of speech they
found disagreeable: "colorful and florid yet devoid of substance" [华而不实];
"too clumsily structured to be coherent" [拙而不伦]; "too fanciful to be of
any real relevancy" [夸而无用]; "too simple and plain to be eloquent"
[劌而不辩]; "too aggressively pushing one's case to leave room for necessary give-and-take" [僭而不让]; "too overblown and overstated to be applicable" [夸而无用]; "shallow and trivial to the point of insignificance" [谀];
"fawningly conformist and conventional" [谀]; "bizarre and absurd" [诞];
"excessively eloquent and fluent" [史]; "coarse and uncouth" [鄙]; "bookish
and unoriginal" [诵].[43]

Axiologically and ideologically loaded, these terms and phrases served
both to enable and to regulate. While their mastery would greatly facilitate
critical interactions and add significantly to what was thinkable and what was
sayable about the diverse discourses one was confronted with, the rhetorical
values and acceptable modes of textual production inscribed and embodied in
these lexical items also tended to condition the practitioners' own discursive
practices, alerting them to all the stylistic or structural pitfalls to which they
themselves were susceptible. This in turn must have contributed to the con-

struction and maintenance of a normative discursive order during classical China and helps explain why it was an amazing outburst of intellectual creativity, rather than a noisy and unproductive verbal melee, that resulted from the fierce contentions among discursive practitioners of ancient China.

In conclusion, while it goes without saying that classical Chinese rhetoric is capable of being reconstructed in different yet equally legitimate ways, the traditionally received approach to mapping this topic area remains trapped in its own conceptual, theoretical, and interpretive myopia. My intention in undertaking this chapter is to introduce a new way of thinking and writing about the subject. Two major discoveries from a close examination of textual evidence in the original undergird my discussion: 1. instead of a mere by-product of philosophical inquiries, classical Chinese rhetoric was a discipline/practice in its own right and what the originators of traditional Chinese discourse were busy doing can better be described as *rhetorical criticism;* and 2. despite their differing politicoideological commitments and the fierce contention among heterogeneous 'Ways' that resulted, the various "schools" or discourse communities actually shared much in their rhetorical thinking and their modes of rhetorical practice. By raising and seeking to answer the question, "Why is it that the contending ideological-discursive communities concerned here were able to *engage* one another in a critical and yet surprisingly *inventive* and *productive* manner?" my study identifies a reservoir of shared rhetorical resources, ranging from noncontroversial assumptions about the telos and the methodology of discursive practices, agreed-upon values and criteria, to commonly employed concepts, genres, criteria, techniques, strategies. This reservoir offers a basis for redefining classical Chinese rhetoric as an "architectonic productive art," one that contributed vitally to the cultural and ideological production of the time by rendering possible meaningful interactions among divergent thoughts and ideologies.

Notes

1. Zheng & Tan (1980): 2–3.

2. *Zhu Zi Ji Cheng* (henceforth abbreviated as *"ZZJC"*) (1954): Vol. I, *The Analects*, p. 283 (henceforth abbreviated as "I/Analects 283"). Unless otherwise noted, English translations of cited source materials in Chinese in this chapter are mine.

3. *ZZJC* (1954): V/*Han Feizi* 279.

4. *ZZJC* (1954): V/*Han Feizi* 301–302; 60–66.

5. Liu (1996): 41.

6. *ZZJC* (1954): I/*Mencius* 123.

7. Loewe & Shaughnessy (1999): 95–96.

8. Graham (1989): 7.

9. Hall & Ames (1998): 135–139.

10. Lu (1998): 127.

11. Lu (1998): 5. Emphasis added.

12. *ZZJC* (1954): IV/Mozi 164.

13. Wang (1992): 93.

14. Qi (2000).

15. Lewis (1999): 1.

16. Lewis (1999): 4.

17. Foucault (1980): 77.

18. Anderson (1991): 6.

19. McKeon (1987): 2.

20. Collins (1998): 137–138.

21. Collins (1998): 137.

22. McKeon (1987): 11.

23. Bourdieu (1990): 5.

24. Unlike many other scholars, I find it arbitrary and simplistic to use 221 B.C.E., the year the Qin dynasty was formally founded, as the cut-off point for THE "classical period." The practice of what remained recognizable as classical discourse extended well into the Han Dynasty. And in the subject area of rhetoric, both Huan Kuan's *The Great Policy Debate Concerning Salt and Iron* [*Yan Tie Lun*], of the first century B.C.E., and Wang Cong's *Discourses Assessed* [*Lun Heng*], of the first century A.D., show such unmistakable and strong affinity with the classical rhetorical spirit and points of view that no discussion of the first flowering of Chinese rhetoric is complete without including both texts.

25. *ZZJC* (1954): IV/*Mozi* 250–51.

26. Zheng & Tan (1980): 34.

27. Zheng & Tan (1980): 1.

28. Zheng, Zong, et al. (1998): Vol. I, 4

29. *ZZJC* (1954): I/*Mencius* 269.

30. *ZZJC* (1954): VII/*Lun Heng* 279–280.

31. Zheng & Tan (1980): 35.

32. *ZZJC* (1954): I/*Mencius* 272.

33. *ZZJC* (1954): IV/*Mozi* 288.

34. Zheng & Tan (1980): 10.

35. Zheng & Tan (1980): 34.

36. *ZZJC*(1954): IV/*Mozi* 251.

37. *ZZJC* (1954): II/*Xunzi* 54–55.

38. *ZZJC* (1954): II/*Xunzi* 10.

39. *ZZJC* (1954): I/*Analects* 336.

40. Legge (1960): 370; 532; 609.

41. *ZZJC* (1954): IV/*Mozi* 249.

42. *ZZJC* (1954): II/*Xunzi* 56.

43. *ZZJC* (1954): V/*Han Feizi* 14.

Works Cited

Anderson, Benedict (1991). *Imagined Communities. Revised Edition.* London: Verso.

Bourdieu, Pierre (1990). *The Logic of Practice.* Stanford, Calif: Stanford University Press.

Collins, Randall (1998). *The Sociology of Philosophies: A Global Theory of Intellectual Change.* Cambridge: Harvard University Press.

Foucault, Michel (1980). *Power/Knowledge: Selected Interviews and Other Writings, 1972–1977.* New York: Pantheon.

Graham, A.C. (1989). *Disputers of the Tao.* Chicago: Open Court.

Hall, David L., and Roger T. Ames (1998). *Thinking from the Han.* Albany: State University of New York Press.

Legge, James (trans.) (1960). *The Chinese Classics, Vol. III.* Hong Kong: Hong Kong University Press.

Lewis, Mark Edward (1999). *Writing and Authority in Early China.* Albany: State University of New York Press.

Liu, Yameng (1996). "Three Issues in the Argumentative Conception of Early Chinese Discourse." *Philosophy East and West* 46.1: 33–58.

Loewe, Michael, and Edward L. Shaughnessy (eds) (1999). *The Cambridge History of Ancient China: From the Origins of Civilization to 221 B.C.E..* Cambridge: Cambridge University Press.

Lu, Xing (1998). *Rhetoric in Ancient China, Fifth to Third Century B.C.E.*: A Comparison with Classical Greek Rhetoric. Columbia: University of South Carolina Press.

McKeon, Richard (1987). *Rhetoric: Essays in Invention and Discovery.* Ed. Mark Backman. Woodbridge, Conn.: Ox Bow Press.

Qi, Yong (2000). *"Zhuanjia Hua Chu Jian* [专家话楚简 Scholars on the Warring States Period Inscribed Bamboo Strips Recently Excavated in Hubei]." *Guangming* Daily (on-line). Beijing: *Guangming* Daily [cited on 21 Jan., 2000, from www.guangmingdaily.com.cn].

Wang, Kaifu, et al. (eds.) (1992). *Zhongguo Gudai Xiezuo Xue* [古汉语修辞学 Classical Chinese Theories of Composition]. Beijing: People's University Press.

Zheng, Dian, and Tan Quanji (eds.) (1980). *Gu Hanyu Xiuci Xue Ziliao Huibian* [*Classical Chinese Rhetoric: A Sourcebook*]. Beijing: Shangwu Press.

Zheng, Ziyu, Zong Tinghu, et al. (eds.) (1998). *Zhongguo Xiuci Xue Tongshi* [中国修辞学通史 *A General History of Chinese Rhetoric*]. 5 vols. Changchun, China: *Jilin Jiaoyu Chubanshe* [Jilin Education Press].

Pentateuchal Rhetoric and the Voice of the Aaronides

David Metzger

Moses said to the L/rd, "Please, O L/rd, I have never been a man of
words.. . . . I am slow of speech and slow of tongue. . . . Please make
someone else your agent." The L/rd became angry with Moses, and
He said, "There is your brother Aaron the Levite. He, I know, speaks
readily."

Exodus 4:10–14[1]

How are we to begin a study of the rhetoric of the Pentateuch (the first
five books of the Hebrew Bible)? We do not have the opportunity to examine
"the original stone tablets." In fact, not until the discovery of the Dead Sea
Scrolls in 1947 did we have examples of biblical texts earlier than 10 C.E..
What is more, given the difficulties in establishing a chronology for the composition of the Pentateuch, we are on less solid ground when speaking of the
"cultural background" or the "political agenda" of the Pentateuch than our
colleagues who have chosen to focus their work on "Prophetic Rhetoric."[2] It
may very well seem to scholars of rhetoric that the Pentateuch is better left
alone, since answers to basic questions regarding the Pentateuch are so hotly
contested by biblical scholars: who wrote, it and when was it written/redacted/
compiled?

It may even come as a surprise to some readers that biblical scholars
have argued that the Pentateuch preserves a variety of narrative traditions or
sources. Two of these traditions are identified by the letters J and E: J for the
group of stories that identifies the deity as Jehovah (the name formed by putting together four Hebrew consonants: yud, hey, vav, hey); E for the group of
stories that identifies the deity as *El* or *Elokim* (I follow, here, the traditional
substitution of "k" for "h" in secular texts). Within the E-group, scholars fur-

165

ther observed that there seemed to be two versions ("doublets") of a number of stories. These doublets also exhibit differences in concerns, language, and style. Since one of these doublets addresses the concerns of priests (the deity's own concern for their well-being as well as stories of a people's sacrificial obligation and ritual), this group of stories came to be called P, the priestly source. And scholars found that these three sources account for the first four books of the Pentateuch. But Deuteronomy was seen to preserve a narrative tradition different than we find in J, E, and P: there are differences in vocabulary, details, and a general retelling of the first four books. So, scholars posited a fourth source for the pentateuchal narrative called D for Deuteronomy or for the Deuteronomist. This is not to say that D gets the final word, however. The P-strand does make a brief but important appearance at the end of Deuteronomy—telling us that Moses was a prophet and that he was unique among the prophets (the only prophet to talk to G/d face to face). What is more, given the length of the P-narrative and the fact that the P-narrative mirrors (comments on) much of the material presented in the J and E strands, the Pentateuch seems to be stretched on a priestly mounting. Scholars, then, posit the existence of a redactor (called R), an editor, who exploited the length of the P-strand to shape J, E, P, and D as the Five Books of Moses, the Pentateuch. This assertion of four narrative traditions in five books is called the "documentary hypothesis."

A more detailed explanation of the documentary hypothesis will be presented in the first section of this essay, and we will see how a majority of biblical scholars have related the composition and preservation of various narrative strands in the Pentateuch to very particular social and political circumstances. The documentary hypothesis supports—is itself a variation of—a common definition of rhetoric: rhetoric is the use of language to communicate and authorize a particular social/political agenda. In the second section of this essay, we will focus on the P-strand: sections from Numbers, where the P narrative and priestly concerns dominate. These two examples will provide us with a different vision of pentateuchal rhetoric. Certainly, we will see that the concerns of one political entity are represented over and against the concerns of another political entity. In Numbers, the Aaronidic priesthood (members of the "House of Levi" but also the "Sons of Aaron") will assert its authority over Israel's ancestral houses as well as over the Levitical priesthood (members of the "House of Levi" who are not the "Sons of Aaron"). But we will also see that the rhetorical model has changed; in the hands of the Aaronides, the Pentateuch is more than four narrative traditions in five books. The Pentateuch is an orchestration of voices: the voice of the Aaronides, the Levites, the monarchs, the patriarchs, the prophets, the scribes, as well as the voice of Moses. Each of these voices will be authorized by its relation to the voice of the deity, each authorized over and against the legitimacy of the other. But we will see something else as well: that the cumulative effect of the Aaronidic project is to represent the deity as a form of consciousness rather than simply one voice among many. After our discussion of the documentary hypothesis and our examination of the voice of the Aaronides, we will elaborate the theoretical implications of this understanding of pentateuchal rhetoric.

Section I: The Documentary Hypothesis

With the documentary hypothesis, we have the starting point for a rhetorical analysis; that is, we have our texts (J,E, P, and D).[3] We simply need to find an author and an audience in order to fill out the rest of our "rhetorical triangle." This should not be too difficult since, from these texts (J, E, P, D), we can derive a coherent set of intentions and political concerns from which we can then infer an author and a social context.[4] For example, imagine that we ask, "Who would call the deity El?" Remembering "El" is used in the E-strand, we might respond, "The person who established a cultus at Beth-El (Hebrew for "The House of El")." Who was that? Jeroboam (the king of the newly created Northern Kingdom). We then ask, "Why would Jeroboam establish such a cultus?" And, again, there is an answer: "because he did not want worshippers living on the border between the newly formed Northern and Southern Kingdoms to take the wealth of the Northern Kingdom (called Israel) to the temple in Jerusalem, the capital city of the Southern Kingdom (called Judah)." "Why would Jeroboam use the name of an ancient Caananite god, El, to signify the deity?" Name recognition: the Northern Kingdom, called Israel, had a large Canaanite population. The writing of the E narrative could then be reasonably assigned to the period of the divided monarchy (around 928 to 728 B.C.E.)—a time after the death of Solomon when his son/successor, Rehoboam, unsuccessfully attempted to hold together the northern and southern regions of his kingdom. There had been a great deal of resentment on the part of the northern, non-Judahite constituency during the time of Solomon, and Solomon had, indeed, conflated the concerns of his southern borders (the concerns of Solomon's tribe, Judah) with the concerns of his "nation": spending more on the defense of his southern borders, even financing the erection of the Temple in Jerusalem from materials offered by the Phoenican King Hyram of Tyre in exchange for a piece of northern Israelite land.

Now that the political situation is clear, now that we have our author/speaker and text, we can begin to imagine there must have been competing stories coming from representatives of the Southern Kingdom (Judah) ruled by Rehoboam. Like contemporary media consultants, these representatives could choose to discredit the competing product/cultus as well as promoting their own. Do we find such an example? Yes, in the story of the golden calf. Insert historical detail: rather than the cherubs used in the temple at Jerusalem (the capital of the Southern Kingdom), the Beth-El cultus (in the Northern Kingdom) used the figure of a golden calf as the pedestal for the deity's throne. From the perspective of the southern cultus, the golden calf would be the abomination non pareil, and there is a narrative tradition (J) that represents the anger and the persuasive powers of Judah (the Southern Kingdom): the story colorized in DeMille's film "The Ten Commandments."

All of this having been said, we still need to account for the production of the P and D traditions, as well as the redaction of these four strands into the Pentateuch. As I've already indicated, one of the defining features of the P-strand is its focus on rites of sacrifice and the development of the Aaronidic priesthood over and against the claims of the Levitical priests. At what time would such a division in the priestly class be of importance? Whose interests would have been represented by such a division? One answer: after the fall of the Northern Kingdom to Assyria in 722 B.C.E., a number of Israelites sought exile in Judah, some of them members of the priestly class supported by Jeroboam and his successors. Although the Israelites and the Judeans shared a language and a religion, they understood that religion in terms of two different narratives. The Judeans (the Southern Kingdom) knew the stories preserved in J; the Israelites (the Northern Kingdom) knew the stories preserved in E. Since both of these narrative traditions shared stories about the patriarchs, the exodus from Egypt, and travels in the wilderness, these two traditions could be brought together as one narrative (identified as JE) thereby valorizing both traditions without putting into question the "authenticity" of one or the other.

We can now turn our attention to the two remaining narrative traditions: D and P. Both the D and P narratives can be understood as responses to the "unity" promised by the assimilation of the J and E strands: one response was very favorable (the D-strand, D for the Deuteronomist, who could take or leave the Aaronides); the other response asked that we appreciate a distinction between Levites, who assisted the priests, and the "sons of Aaron" who were the priests (the P-strand, P for priest). There are commonalities in the two responses: both D and P favored the centralization of religious practices; both supported the idea of an eternal covenant with the deity, and both met the challenge of asserting such a covenant when the nation suffered great political losses. How then can we account for the different responses to the synthesis of J and E? P will have nothing to do with a world if there are no Aaronides in it, and D has no use for the Aaronides. For the P narrative, the hope and promise of a troubled nation will be in the Aaronides' expiative powers and in any monarch/leader who will support Aaronidic initiatives; for the Deuteronomist, this hope rests on the king and the monarch's power to reform.

Why, then, in a discussion of pentateuchal rhetoric, should we focus our attention on the synthesizing of the P-strand and not the D? Because the Pentateuch is the vehicle for the priestly synthesis. Something else (what scholars have called the Deuteronomistic History) is the vehicle for the monarchic synthesis. That is, Deuteronomy is both the last "book" of the Pentateuch and the first "book" of a history that ends with the Book of Kings.

A discussion of D's function in the Pentateuch would merit its own essay. But we might note two points that will help us to suggest how the Pentateuch was used/read. Point One: Deuteronomy is the only book of the Pentateuch to speak of the "Sefer Torah," the book/scroll of the Torah ("teaching"); D then provides the redactor with a name for the work produced by his labors. If the Pentateuch is, in fact, a vehicle for the priestly synthesis, then would not R, the so-called redactor, have to be an Aaronid or someone closely associated with Aaronidic interests? Yes, and some scholars have argued as such.[5] We would also expect that the Redactor would need to disassociate Deuteronomy from its position in the Deuteronomistic History, so that it might function as the concluding "book" of the Pentateuch.[6] Point Two: Ezra (an Aaronid) is credited with instituting the reading of the Torah scroll at Temple services.[7] How does this "reading" disassociate Deuteronomy from the Deuteronomistic History? Those familiar with Jewish liturgy/study know that the Pentateuch is chanted/read according to either an annual or triannual cycle, so that, in some Jewish congregations, the Pentateuch is read/chanted in the service over the course of a year or over the course of three years. On the same day that the last verses of Deuteronomy are read, Jewish congregations read/hear the first chapter of Genesis. Like Moses, we do not cross over the Jordan with Joshua (so that at a later date we might appoint a king, see Deuteronomy 17: 15–17); we return to creation/the beginning (Genesis/Bereshit). The public reading/chanting of the Pentateuch, an Aaronidic invention, makes Deuteronomy the last book of the Pentateuch![8] We will now turn to a discussion of the relationship of the P-narrative and what we have already identified as "the voice of the Aaronides." Our discussion will focus on a section attributed to the P-narrative from the Book of Numbers (the fourth book of the Pentateuch), where the Aaronidic voice is placed in opposition to the voice of the *beit avot,* the ancestral houses of Israel, and where the priestly narrative places its legitimacy claims squarely in the hands of Aaron as the "father" of a hereditary priesthood.[9] We will not have the occasion to speak any more about the relationship of the Aaronidic voice to the voice of the monarchs and the D-strand; our attention will be directed to the relationship of the Aaronidic voice to the voice of the *beit avot,* the ancestral houses of Ancient Israel, and we will see how an analysis of voices can help us to account for the particularities, the wording, of the Hebrew text.

Section II: P and The Voice of the Aaronides

IIA: The Voice of the Aaronides and the Voice of the Ancestral Houses

Although the P-strand appears throughout the Pentateuch (in fact, it provides the frame for the work), Numbers provides us with the clearest presentation of the Aaronidic voice, as it sets the stage for legitimizing the voice of the Aaronides over and against the voice of the *beit avot,* the ancestral houses of Ancient Israel, and the other members of the tribe of Levi (remember both Aaron and Moses are members of the tribe of Levi). Numbers begins with the voice of G/d, a divine command: a census must be taken of the clans and ancestral houses, listing the name of every male who is capable of bearing arms. While both Aaron and Moses shall record (put into writing) these names, a man (the head of each ancestral house [*rosh l'veit avotaiv*]) from each tribe (*matteh*) will accompany them; these men are important enough to have their names recorded in verses 5–15. The subsequent count of men is organized according to the names of the twelve tribes (the descendants of Reuben, Simeon, Gad, and the other sons of the patriarch, Jacob). The process of legitimization at work here seems to be straightforward: Aaron and Moses are leaders of the community because the deity speaks to them; they are the instruments by which the deity's instructions will be passed on to Israel. But what authorizes the actions and decisions of the *beit avot*? The occasion of this census (literally, this record of those who lift their heads [*nasa rosh*]) introduces us to an organization of peoples around familial relations and allegiances to households authorized in the name of the patriarchs. What is more, we are shown that this organization of Israel (Yisrael appears in this text) according to ancestral house (*beit avot*) and clan is Israel's means of coordinating military actions. But how could a census be understood as a threat to the *beit avot*?

Only one ancestral house (*beit avot*) is not recorded in this military census: the house of Levi. "[For] the Lord had spoken to Moses, saying 'Do not on any account enroll the tribe of Levi or take a census of them with the Israelites'" (1:49). In Numbers, the deity speaks to Moses telling him to "advance the tribe of Levi" by "plac[ing] them in attendance upon Aaron the priest to serve him" (3:5). The House of Levi is promised that it will not be called into battle unless the sanctuary itself is threatened. In exchange, the Levites are to be henceforth the servants of the Aaronides. We could see evidence of a bargain, here, or we could see how, in order to assert their claims, the Aaronides (who, like Moses, are members of the House of Levi) must separate the other Levites from the military organization (family-clan-ancestral house) written into the census. Only after the "other Levites" (the non-Aaronides) have been separated from the tribal/organization is there a deliberate accounting of the various clans subsumed under the House of Levi, each Levitical clan being assigned the portion of the Tent of Meeting for which it is responsible:

> [For example,] The clans of Merar were to camp along the north side of the Tabernacle. The assigned duties of the Merarites comprised: the plans of the Tabernacle, its bars, posts, and sockets, and all its furnishings—all the service connected with these; also the posts around the enclosures and their sockets, pegs and cords. (3:35–37)

We do not find another house treated in such a fashion. The deity takes the Levites as its special portion, as recompense for the deity's redemption of the first-born of Israel in Egypt (3:12). The census is not a pledge, assuredly, but it is a form of social contract with the chief signatories being the House of Levi. But their contract is not with the Aaronides or the other clans; it is with the deity. The deity speaks (*dabar*) and instigates this contract. We find, here, the deliberate construction of a community of servants (*avodim*) around a moveable sanctuary, whose authority is guaranteed by the promise of land and, when the land is possessed by others, by the promise of sanctity (our relation to the sanctuary).

This last point is crucial. If we suppose that the ascension of the Aaronides occurs when there are questions about how a nation lost possession of a land (the Northern Kingdom to the Assyrians) and might lose possession of what remains (Judah to the Babylonians), then their authority could not rest on the possession of the land but on the land's being possessed by others. What is more, the promise of the land being possessed by Israel would need to be placed in perpetual deferment in order to protect the Temple against the suspicions of the occupying force.

Earlier, I had suggested that we might be able to identify the power base for the *beit avot*, and we are now in a position to do so. The *beit avot*, loosely organized around the patriarchal delineation of tribes, gains its authority from a relationship to the land: each tribe is assigned its particular portion; each tribe is responsible for defending or working (with the help of the other tribes) to acquire that land. The priests (both the Levitical and the Aaronidic) are set aside as G/d's own portion; they maintain the tent of meeting where the deity itself resides, and they are themselves G/d's claim on the people of Israel (the price for the deliverance from Israel).

We can clearly see in Numbers that Israel does not occupy the land. Bad reports are given by a reconnaissance group sent into Canaan. But not just any group of people is sent into Canaan. Numbers identifies these individuals as *nasi,* chieftains from the ancestral tribes (13:2), and we are given their names (see 13:4–16) as if in the form of a census (a *naso et-rosh,* a lifting up of the head, in the language of Numbers 4:22). It makes sense that, before beginning a military campaign, members of the military organization should send scouts to survey the territory. The scouts give their report: "the people of the land are powerful, and the cities are fortified and very large. . . . We cannot attack that people, for it is stronger than we" (13:28,30). There is great distress among the Israelites; there is even a suggestion of the threat facing a communal order grounded on the system of ancestral houses: "And they said each to his brother, 'Let us appoint a head (*nitnah rosh*) and return to Egypt'" (lit.trans. 14:4). If the *beit avot's* power, its obligation to the deity, is the acquisition and defense of the promised land, then that power is subject to changes in fortune, and—understandably—the *beit avot's* decisions will be based on exigency. In this context, however, the strength of the *beit avot* is shown to be a weakness. Their statements/suggestions/actions cannot represent what the deity wants for, has given (*natan*) to, Israel. The Hebrew is provided, here, so that you might see the contrast between "nitnah rosh" (the heads of *beit avot* who want to return to Egypt) and *natan* (the deity's gift of land to Israel). We may hear in the homophony of the two phrases what Charles Bazerman has called an "embedded voice," the use of a word or phrase to evoke an entire matrix of legitimation: the deity is not circumscribed by exigency, and the *beit avot's* power (land, military force) is related to Pharoah, who was defeated by the ten plagues on Egypt. With a remarkable twist, those who enjoy the fruits of the land are those whose actions jeopardize the fulfillment of the land covenant. That is, without the land, the contract with the deity is finished; rather than be the servants/worshipers (*avodim,* same word for both) of the deity, Israel can return to Egypt to be the servants/slaves (*avodim,* same word for both) of Pharoah. Or, living in any land—even Canaan—when it is not possessed by Israel makes Israel a servant of someone other than the deity.

The P-narrative assumes this matrix of legitimation by transferring the obligations of the land-covenant to a Temple-covenant, but to do so, the Temple (and its predecessor, "The Tent of Meeting" in the wilderness) must be rendered as the fulfillment of the promise of the land (wealth, produce, the effects of labor) if not the promise of the land itself. In order to accomplish this, the tribal structure represented in the census must be reoriented, since "the tribe" is also a system for transmitting land as inheritance. This would explain why the authority of the Aaronidic voice is asserted over the voice of the *beit avot.* Moses and Aaron then respond to the revolt prompted by the scouts' bad report by falling on their faces (14:5). If the nasi (the ones who literally put their heads above the rest in the census) declare their social contract with the deity null and void, then, Moses and Aaron will lie down; they will not be counted. That is, not being counted as one of the *beit avot* can serve as the beginning of a contractual relation with the deity. And Hosea, a scout from the House of Ephraim, whose allegiance to Moses-Aaron rather than his allegiance to the *beit avot* is demonstrated by the gift of a new name by Moses (the new name: Joshua), this freshly minted Joshua repeats the terms of this new (Temple) covenant before the whole community: "If the Lord is pleased with us, he will give us that land." But this new covenant is not well received; indeed, "the whole community threat[ens] to pelt them [Moses and Aaron] with stones" (14:9). The presence of the Lord then appears in the Tent of Meeting, and Moses intercedes on behalf of Israel. The promise of the land is not revoked, but the deity tells Moses and Aaron that, of the scouts who gave such a discouraging report regarding Israel's ability to acquire the land by force, only Calev (Heb. for "dog," i.e., "faithful") and Joshua (Hebrew for "the one who saves") will reside in the promised land—while "all of you who were recorded in your various lists from the age of twenty years up...not one shall enter the land in which I swore to settle you" (14:29).

The continuity of the patriarchal covenant is not broken, here, but those who would make claims in light of that covenant—that is, in terms of their own relation to the patriarchs without the mediation of Moses and Aaron—they (the *beit avot*) are doomed to die in the wilderness (the Hebrew name for Numbers is, in fact, *Bamidbar,* "in the wilderness"). Given the choice to die in the wilderness or on the battlefield, the *beit avot* move into Canaan, despite the deity's new instructions (Do not enter; wander in the wilderness!), and they are slaughtered (14:45).

But not all of the *beit avot* were slaughtered, so the authority of the (remaining) *beit avot* must be diminished further when, in Chapter 15, the terms of the new compact are introduced by the phrase "when you enter the land" (*ki tavovu el aretz*)—that is, not when "you [land owners] possess it." What is more, the rights associated with covenant are extended beyond the *beit avot* as potential signatories of a pledge with the deity. The new covenant includes the resident stranger: "There shall be one law for you ('all the native-born' [*kol-ezrach*] 15:13) and for the resident stranger (*ger*); it shall be a law (*chukat*) for all time (*l'olam*) throughout the ages" (*l'dodoteycem,* 15:15). It is easy to approve of this expansive gesture if one does not have anything to lose by it. What do the *beit avot* lose? In terms of the law, they (as descendants of Abraham, Isaac, and Jacob) are comparable to the *gerim* (the resident strangers who were more than likely servants, immigrant workers, or the children of immigrant workers). What do the Aaronides gain? Authority over Israelites and non-Israelites alike. Note. This is not simply a covenant "for all generations" (a way of understanding "eternity" as the movement from father to son) but a covenant "for all time" (*l'olam*). Indeed , this is a covenant whose perpetuity is not guaranteed by the prosperity/continuance of the *beit avot* or the promise of land. The terms of this covenant may obtain for the *beit avot,* but it is not limited to a single signatory instance. In fact, this contract is binding not because it was signed by our "forefathers," but because it is performed/recalled in the ritual of cultic expiation.

IIB: The Priestly Covenant

Compare the following descriptions of Abram/Abraham (attributed to the J-narrative) and Aaron (attributed to the P-narrative):

> **Abram:** Then He said to him [Abram], "I am the Lord who brought you out from Ur of the Chaldeans to assign this land to you as a possession." And he said, "O L/rd G/d, how shall I know that I am to possess it?" He answered, "Bring Me a three-year-old heifer, a three-year-old she-goat, a three-year-old ram, a turtle dove, and a young bird." He brought Him all these and cut them in two, placing each half opposite the other, but he did not cut up the bird....When the sun set and it was very dark, there appeared a smoking oven, and a flaming torch which passed between those pieces. On that day the L/rd made a covenant [lit. "cut a covenant"] with Abram, saying, "To your offspring I assign this land, from the river of Egypt to the great river, the river Euphrates. . . . "(Genesis 15:7–18)

> **Aaron:** Then Moses said to Aaron, "Take the fire pan, and put on it fire from the altar. Add incense and take it quickly to the community and make expiation for them. For wrath has gone forth from the L/rd: the plague has begun." Aaron took it, as Moses had ordered, and ran to the midst of the congregation, where the plague had begun among the people. He put on the incense and made expiation [*kaper*] for the people; he stood [*yaamod*] between the dead [*ha-metiym*] and the living [*ha-chayim*] until the plague was checked. (Numbers 17:11–13)

Literature on the requirements/formulae for a covenant is vast—academic discussions being driven by comparisons of biblical rituals and examples of early Near Eastern vassal treaties.[10] In the story of Abram above, we see that an animal is cut into two halves and the contracted party must pass between the two halves of the animal. Some scholars have suggested that the two halves of the animal symbolize what will happen to the party that breaks the covenant: that the offending party will be split in two. If this is the case, then how is it possible for a human being to "cut a covenant" with the deity? In a dream, the flaming torch (the deity who will later illuminate the path of the freed Israelites) passes between the two halves. In the description from Numbers, the problem is slightly different. Israel has become numerous. How can a whole people cut a covenant, pass between two pieces of the animal? Aaron can stand in for all of Israel, and Israel can stand in the place of the animal (the living and the dead being the two halves of Israel). And where is the deity? In Genesis, the deity is a smoking torch; in Numbers, the deity is somewhere in the smoke cloud of incense. This is not to say that Aaron stands in the place of G/d; rather, the Temple rite—the burning of incense—is a sign of G/d's presence among the Israelites (like the Temple when Israel occupies the promised land, like the Tent of Meeting when Israel wanders in the desert).[11] Those who are not accustomed to accepting the validity of visual arguments will, no doubt, point out that in the example from Numbers, Moses (not the deity) tells Aaron to burn the incense. But the authority for this transference of power, the authorization for the "equations" assumed by this discussion, has already been established. In Exodus 7:1, Moses suggests to the deity that he (Moses) is not prepared to speak to Pharoah; the deity replies: "See, I place you in the role of G/d (*elokim*) to Pharoah, with your brother Aaron as your prophet (*neviecha*)." However, this image of Aaron walking between the two halves of the people is not our only evidence for the construction of a priestly covenant. In Numbers, we also have a special name assigned to this covenant, and we see the establishment of this covenant for the descendants of Aaron, as well.

In Chapter 17, twelve staves are placed in the Tent of Meeting—each with the name of one of the twelve leaders (*nasi*) of an ancestral house (*beit av*) written (*tiktov*) on it; Aaron's name is inscribed (written: *tiktov*) on the staff of the House of Levi (17:18).[12] The deity speaks to Moses and tells him that the staff of the man G/d chooses shall grow. We are not told specifically for what purpose this man will be chosen, but we may presume that he is to be chosen for leadership. As one might expect, the staff of Aaron, which is also the staff of the House of Levi, sprouts and bears fruit. And the deity says to Moses, "Put Aaron's staff (*matteh*) back before the Pact, to be kept as a lesson to rebels, so that their mutterings against Me may cease, lest they die" (17:25). The Hebrew word for staff, matteh, is also used by extension to mean "tribe." So, we have here a contest of tribes with Aaron's staff/tribe being the one that will bear fruit. To participate in the Aaronidic cultus is to live; to work against the cultus (as a member of the *beit avot*) is to sin and die. Before this trial, Aaron was given a position of prominence; after the trial, he is the founder of a dynastic priesthood: "The L/rd said to Aaron: You with your sons and the ancestral house under your charge shall bear any guilt connected with the sanctuary; you and your sons and the ancestral house under your charge shall bear any guilt connected with the sanctuary; you and your sons alone shall bear any guilt connected with the priesthood" (Numbers 18:1). The priesthood, then, becomes like one's membership in the ancestral houses, something that is passed from father to son. And this covenant between G/d and Aaron is even given a name; it is a covenant of salt (*brit melach*)—perhaps referring to the salt used in the sacrifices. Later in Numbers, again in a portion attributed to P, the L/rd tells Moses of the deity's covenant with Aaron's grandson—Phinehas: The L/rd spoke to Moses, saying, "Phinehas, son of Eleazar son of Aaron the priest, has turned back My wrath from the Israelites by displaying among them his passion for Me, so that I did not wipe out the Israelite people in My passion. Say, therefore, 'I grant him My pact (*brit,* covenant) of friendship. It shall be for his and his descendants after him a pact (*brit,* covenant) of priesthood for all time, because he took impassioned action for his G/d, thus making expiation (*caper,* like Aaron before him) for the Israelites" (Numbers 25:10).

In the example of Phinehas, we have an explicit association of the covenant and the Aaronides' power to expiate; after the test of staves, we see that Aaron is given authority over the ancestral house (*beit avot*) in his charge. One might well have wondered why the Aaronides would need to associate and disassociate themselves with/from the *beit avot*. The political answer may be that the Aaronides needed to establish the legitimacy of a hereditary priesthood and not simply the "authority" of Aaron. The *beit avot* served as the model for the formation of a hereditary priesthood inasmuch as the *beit avot*'s claims on land and resources are supported by the language of the patriarchal covenant: "to your [Abram's] offspring, I assign this land" in the example above.

Section III: How The Aaronides Make a Rhetoric

Thus far, we have accounted for certain particularities in phrasing. It is possible to imagine that students of rhetoric would ask for something more than such a "rhetorical reading" of a biblical text. We have come to expect more of rhetoric than a general accounting of specific word choices in light of purpose and social circumstance. And the P-narrative that we have examined does have more to offer. We observe, here, nothing less than the creation of a new voice: the voice of the Aaronides. We have seen how the Aaronidic voice is created: (1) by associating itself with and disassociating itself from the house of Levi and (2) associating with and disassociating itself from the voice of the *beit avot,* and finally (3) by being associated with the voice of the deity through the priestly covenant.

The Jewish historian, Ellis Rivkin, has suggested that without the Aaronides there would be no Pentateuch. I would suggest that without the emergence of the Aaronidic voice, there would be no such thing as a pentateuchal rhetoric. As members of the house of Levi, the Aaronides could emerge only as a voice and, in doing so, create the rhetorical landscape (the writing) of the Pentateuch, a landscape populated by the voice of Moses, the voice of the *beit avot,* the prophets, and so on. After all, a voice must be addressed to some other, and—in the process of enunciation—the addressee projected by a particular voice becomes itself a voice. The Aaronides address the *beit avot,* and the *beit avot* can be identified as a voice; they address the monarchs, and they become a voice. What is more, for the Aaronides to legitimize their claims over and against their addressee (the *beit avot* in the discussion above), the authority of the addressee must be reoriented as a superaddressee—in this instance, the deity.[13] We see this process quite clearly in the test of staves/tribes discussed above. In the scene where Aaron makes expiation for the people, standing between the living and the dead (what I have suggested is the cutting of an Aaronidic covenant), we can see something else: we can see the Aaronides constructing for themselves the position of a superaddressor (a neologism we will not find in Bakhtin, who chose not to situate the Pentateuch in his genealogy of genre formation). In Genesis, there is the covenant (*brit*) cut between G/d and Israel through the patriarch Abraham; now the vehicle for the transmission of the terms of that covenant is Aaron as Israel's agent of expiation. Of course, if the Pentateuch were a novel, we would not need the term "superaddressor"; we would simply say, following Bakhtin, that the Aaronidic voice becomes the "consciousness" of the work. But the Aaronides could not become the consciousness of the Pentateuch. If they had, then we might simply dismiss the Pentateuch as an example of one interest group's bald-faced grasping after power, a press release, and the Aaronides' "rhetorical project" would have failed.

What is that rhetorical project? In our previous discussion of the documentary hypothesis, we observed that the P-strand dominates both the content and the structure of the Pentateuch. Some biblical scholars have even suggested that Ezra (an Aaronid) was the final redactor of the individual narrative strands. Even if this is not the case, it makes good sense rhetorically. In order for the Aaronidic voice to dominate the other voices of the text, the Aaronidic voice must be aligned with the deity without subsuming the authority of the deity. To accomplish this, the deity, not the Aaronides, must be the consciousness of the text, if the Aaronidic voice is to be supported by G/d, who is understood as the authority non pareil. G/d is and must be more than the "superaddressee" of this text; as the superaddressee, the deity could not itself emerge as a voice; the deity's will could be voiced by any interest group with whom the Aaronides might be required to speak; the deity would be a common ground, an ultimate value informing how to speak and how not to speak, when to speak and when not to speak. The Aaronidic rhetorical project is then twofold: 1) dominate the other voices; 2) make the deity a form of consciousness (not a voice among many, not a voice at all, but "I am that I am"). And the Pentateuch might be understood as the accomplishment of this twofold project. The Pentateuch establishes the following:

> (1) An agreement between humanity and G/d at the beginning of time, a time before the construction of ancestral ties and kinship relations when everyone might be understood as having a relation (beyond family, beyond tribe) with the deity and everyone else (the Garden of Eden, Noah, the patriarchs). This move establishes the possibility of creating a centralized cultus, the Aaronidic vision, unhampered by the customs and claims of the *beit avot*.[14] (2) The inscription of the deity's obligation in a middle-time (Numbers, in the wilderness) where the land-covenant is transformed into a Temple-covenant. This move shields the cultus from criticism, when the "promise of land" is fulfilled and the continued necessity for a hereditary priesthood is questioned. (3) An end-time that is incipient but unrealized (Moses dies, and Joshua prepares to cross the Jordan). This move shields the cultus from criticism, when the "promise of land" (divided among the *beit avot*) is not fulfilled and the continued obligation to a land-covenant is put into question.

We have only elaborated the first half of this project, here; the second half will need to be treated at length elsewhere. But we can see the beginnings of such an elaboration in Jack Mile's *God: A Biography,* where the author shows, by way of his "novelization" of the Hebrew Bible, how G/d became "a virtual member of the Western family. . . . To the eyes of faith, the Bible is not just words about God but also the World of God; He is its author as well as its protagonist"[15]. And we also have Margaret Zulick's magisterial essay, "The Active Force of Hearing: The Ancient Hebrew Language of Persuasion," where she contrasts Hebraic rhetoric with the Hellenic elaboration of rhetoric as a theoretical model accounting for the effects of "active persuasion." If G/d is a voice, Zulick tells us, the deity is the voice of the heart: "Words carry weight; they convince because they are the right words, the authoritative words, and not because of the persuasive art of the orator. . . . [This] effect is particularly true in divine speech. Perhaps it owes something to the Hebrew concept of the heart as the seat of the human mind and will, a secret place inaccessible to any but God and the self."[16] We might link our elaboration of the "artful speech" of the Aaronides to Zulick's work—and thereby begin to see the relation of the two parts of the Aarondic project—by observing that, if these are the attributes of divine speech, then the deity is not a voice but a consciousness, leading us to chart, in a more theoretical fashion, the relationship between "superaddressee" and "consciousness."

Notes

1. This and all subsequent translations, except when otherwise noted, as well as the Hebrew text are from the *JPS Hebrew/English Tanakh* (1999).

2. Yehoshua Gitay's careful attention to prophetic language and his familiarity with rhetorical theory makes his work essential reading for those interested in biblical rhetoric. Samuel Raphael Hirsch provides a suggestive discussion of "prophetic pathos" in his *The Prophets*. In their short article on biblical rhetoric in Garland's *Encyclopedia of Rhetoric and Composition*, Metzger and Sexson argue that Hebraic rhetoric is fundamentally prophetic.

3. For an accessible discussion of the development of the "documentary hypothesis," see Friedman (1987). Niditch (1996) provides a socio-historically informed discussion of the Hebrew Bible as "orature" or as "oral-traditional literature."

4. All of these examples (questions and answers) and the subsequent analysis provided in this section of the essay have been drawn from Friedman's *Who Wrote The Bible?* See also McNutt (1998) for a helpful summary of modern attempts to reconstruct the social and political life of Ancient Israel.

5. See, for example, chapter 13 of Friedman (1987).

6. Wurthwein (1995) provides an introduction to biblical textual scholarship and the material culture of writing in Early Israel.

7. Watts (1999) provides an extended discussion of the rhetorical effect of the public reading of the Torah.

8. Deuteronomy also helped the Aaronides to restrict the authority of the "unauthorized" prophetic voice; only prophecy that agrees with the words of the "Sefer Torah" is to be heeded (Deut. 34:10). For a discussion of the "prophetic threat to centralization" (whether Aaronidic or monarchic), see Rivkin (1971), chapter 2.

9. For further discussion of the social/historical environment of the priesthood, see Bleckinsopp (1995), Grabbe (1995), and Haran (1985).

10. Samples of Near Eastern legal texts can be found in Pritchard (1969), 159–322.

11. We might contrast this Aaronidic expression of the covenant with Deuteronomy 11:26–30, where we find another way of solving the problem of how to cut a covenant with the whole of a people. As we would expect given what we have briefly said about Deuteronomy earlier, this covenant is intimately linked to the acquisition of land: the company of Israel must walk between two mountains to enter the promised land; on one mountain, the blessings of the covenant are to be spoken, on the other mountain, the curses. So, the basic formula for a covenant is, again, two parties (hence the "cut" in "cutting a covenant"), identifying the expectations for fulfilling the covenant (the priests and the monarchs add the curses to the formula), and the passage of the one who is contracted into the "cut."

12. See Nurmela (1999) for a discussion of the political relationship of the Levites and the Aaronides.

13. For further discussion of this basic rhetorical move, see Bakhtin (1987), 126.

14. Olyan (2000) provides a convincing argument for seeing the P-narrative's version of creation in Chapter 1 of Genesis as a synecdoche for the Pentateuch's subsequent formation of a hierarchic and binary value system.

15. Miles (1995), 5.

16. Zulick (1992), 379.

Works Cited

Bakhtin, Mikhail. *Speech Genres and Other Essays.* Eds. Caryl Emerson and Michael Holquist. Trans. Vern McGee. Austin: University of Texas Press, 1987.

Blenkinsopp, Joseph, and Douglas A. Knight (eds). *Sage, Priest, Prophet: Religious and Intellectual Leadership in Ancient Israel.* Louisville, KY: Westminster/ John Knox Press, 1995.

Friedman, Richard Elliott. *Who Wrote The Bible?* New York: Summit Books, 1987.

_____. "Prophecy and Persuasion." *Forum Theologiae Linguistica* 14. Bonn: Linguistica Biblica, 1981.

Gitay, Yehoshua. *Isaiah and His Audience.* Assen, Netherlands: Van Gorcum, 1991.

Grabbe, Lester. *Priests, Prophets, Diviners, Sages: A Socio-Historical Study of Religious Specialists in Ancient Israel.* Harrisburg, Pennsylvania: Trinity Press International, 1995.

Haran, Menachem. *Temples and Temple-Service in Ancient Israel: An Inquiry into Biblical Cult Phenomena and the Historical Setting of the Priestly School.* Oxford: Clarendon University Press, 1985.

JPS Hebrew-English Tanakh. Philadelphia: Jewish Publication Society, 1999.

McNutt, Paula M. *Reconstructing the Society of Ancient Israel.* Louisville, KY: Westminster/John Knox, 1998.

Metzger, David, and Lynda Sexson. "Biblical Rhetoric." *Encyclopedia of Rhetoric and Composition.* Ed. Theresa Enos. New York: Garland Publishing Co., 1996, 74–75.

Miles, Jack. *God: A Biography.* New York: Vintage Books, 1995.

Niditch, Susan. *Oral World and Written Word: Orality and Literacy in Ancient Israel.* Louisville, KY: Westminster/John Knox Press, 1996,

Nurmela, Risto. *The Levites: Their Emergence as a Second-Class Priesthood. Atlanta:* Scholars Press/Studies in the History of Judaism, 1999.

Olyan, Saul. *Rites and Rank: Hierarchy in Biblical Representations of Cult.* Princeton: Princeton University Press, 2000.

Pritchard, James. *Ancient Near Eastern Texts Relating to the Old Testament.* 3rd ed. Princeton, NJ: Princeton University Press, 1969.

Rivkin, Ellis. *The Shaping of Jewish History.* New York: Scribner's, 1971.

Watts, James. *Reading Law: The Rhetorical Shaping of the Pentateuch.* Sheffield, England: Sheffield Academic Press, 1999.

Wurthwein, Ernst. *The Text of the Old Testament.* Trans. Erroll F. Rhodes. 2nd ed. Grand Rapids, MI: Eerdmans Publishing Co., 1995.

Zulick, Margaret D. "The Active Force of Hearing: The Ancient Hebrew Language of Persuasion." *Rhetorica* 10.4 (Autumn 1992): 367–380.

The Art of Rhetoric at Rhodes:
An Eastern Rival to the Athenian Representation
of Classical Rhetoric

Richard Leo Enos

Introduction

Much of our knowledge about ancient Greek rhetoric comes from Athens. The impressive and dominant development of Athenian rhetoric encourages us to think that this system is representative of rhetoric throughout Greece. At the same time, however, ancient sources allude to other manifestations of rhetoric, such as the Asiatic and the Rhodian style. Of particular interest is the art of rhetoric that developed on the island of Rhodes, for its differences are striking and its impact enduring. In fact, Rhodian rhetoric sustained popularity through the Roman Republic and into the Empire and can be considered the first true Greco-Roman rhetoric. Despite its differences and longevity, the features of Rhodian rhetoric are known only generally, its history is not developed, and (consequently) its impact is not understood. This study explains the nature, development, and longevity of Rhodian rhetoric by comparing its features with the dominant paradigm, Athenian rhetoric. The results of this study also help to explain why our characterizations of Greek rhetoric must now be qualified when we make interpretations based solely on Athenian representations. Lastly and indirectly, presenting a version of Greek rhetoric different from its Athenian counterpart encourages rhetoricians to engage more in basic research and historiography that emphasize further investigation of primary material.

There are several reasons for historians of rhetoric to examine the art of rhetoric on the island of Rhodes. First, as mentioned above, our history of Greek rhetoric is inordinately disproportional. Much of what we take to mean as "Greek" rhetoric is actually Athenian rhetoric. There is evidence to show not only that rhetoric thrived and prospered throughout Greece in variant forms, but also that these representations of rhetoric were so different from Athenian classical rhetoric that our understanding of Hellenic rhetoric must be qualified. This work seeks to show that Rhodes is just such a center. The nature and impact of Rhodian rhetoric was different than its Athenian counterpart and an in-depth study is intended to make those differences apparent. This study contrasts conditions on Rhodes with Athens in order to establish how this variant and dominant form of rhetoric emerged and prospered in Antiquity.

Second, there is another association of classical rhetoric with Athens that also must be qualified. All rhetoric is functional; that is, rhetoric thrives in social situations because it serves that society's needs. In Athens, a democratic environment, the functions of rhetoric served the democracy and concentrated on internal, civic affairs. The operations of courts, political deliberations, and ceremonial settings all dictated the orientation of rhetoric toward forensic, deliberative, and epideictic modes important to the normative and regulative operations of that community. So endemic was the democratic-based rhetoric in Athens that we have come to associate Greek rhetoric with democratic functions. The orientation of rhetoric at Rhodes was not internal but external. That is, the emphasis on rhetoric at Rhodes was directed toward facilitating communication with other peoples.

Third, and as a corollary to the second point, the possibility that such humanistic arts as rhetoric flourished in societies that were less or even nondemocratic may be surprising. While Rhodes had representative governments throughout her history, the extreme democratic practices of Athens were different from the political practices of Rhodes. The functions of rhetoric in the civic affairs of democratic Athens would tempt us to think that rhetoric thrives best and only in such an egalitarian environment. We will see, however, that rhetoric also flourished on Rhodes but manifested itself in a far different way than the practices at Athens. From our own, more recent experiences of the last century, we know that arts can flourish in nondemocratic societies and under political conditions that we may even find to be repulsive. For example, some of the great gains in Roman archaeology came under the Fascist reign of Benito Mussolini. Similarly, certain features of higher education, art, and culture deemed by the Nazi Party of Germany to be "appropriate" flourished under the dictatorship of Adolph Hitler. All this is to say that to gain a sensitive understanding of how Greek rhetoric operated in the Hellenic world, we need to expand our notion and tolerance of what rhetoric is when it occurs in non-Athenian cultures and capture those features as accurately as our historical research permits.

Understanding the history of Rhodian rhetoric provides insights into the pervasiveness of Greek rhetoric and, indirectly, an inducement to continue such research, so that we may have a more representative picture of classical rhetoric throughout ancient Greece than currently exists. Furthermore, inquiry into non-Athenian Greek rhetoric requires nontraditional methods for retrieving nontraditional primary sources. The sources for this history of classical Rhodian rhetoric are inclusive; not only were extant literary and rhetorical sources examined, but archaeological, epigraphical, and architectural artifacts as well. The results of this study are intended to help explain the nature and development of Rhodian rhetoric, and why its influence endured and transcended Greek to Roman culture. In summary, our attention to Rhodes has the potential to produce a number of benefits. Such research provides us with a more sensitive understanding of an important and enduring manifestation of Greek rhetoric. This knowledge will provide us with a basis from which we can compare and contrast Rhodian rhetoric with Attic rhetoric and a paradigm for the further study of other manifestations of rhetoric. Lastly and indirectly, presenting a version of Greek rhetoric different from its Athenian counterpart encourages rhetoricians to engage more in basic research and historiography that emphasize the investigation of primary material.

The Hegemony of Athenian Rhetoric

Werner Jaeger's *Paideia: The Ideals of Greek Culture* is a unique and monumental contribution to scholarship. At the same time, however, it is also common and representative of the way historians generalize from the Athenian mentality to the remainder of the Greek world. Jaeger uses the "Greek" concept of *paideia,* or the virtue of intellectual excellence, as the touchstone for understanding both Hellenic mentality and its manifestations in politics, art, literature, and (of special interest to us) rhetoric. Through his exegesis of the thoughts of individuals such as Plato, Aristotle, and Isocrates, we come to grips with the issues that concerned some of the best minds about the practice of rhetoric at Athens in the classical period. In many ways, the contributions and criticism of rhetoric at Athens by such individuals, and their presentation by Jaeger, has encouraged us to generalize this representation of rhetoric from Athens and apply it to Greece at that moment and place in time. That is, we have tended to "freeze" rhetoric to Athens and the late fifth and early fourth centuries B.C.; this moment for us has come to stand in for classical Greek rhetoric.

The dominance of Athenian rhetoric, however, has made such a strong impression that it has distorted our historical accounting and, consequently, our historical accuracy. The amount of primary material recorded about Athenian rhetoric in terms of treatises, orations, and histories is enormous; there is a wealth of evidence to be weighed and sifted. In fact, the preoccupation of Victorian scholars was to explicate this material in the forms of translations, commentaries, and histories. For the historian of rhetoric, these literary artifacts constituted the "evidence" that warranted scholarly interpretations; the topic of conversation about Greek rhetoric was synonymous always with the adjective, "Athenian." Any other mention of the forms of teaching and practice of Greek rhetoric are often characterized as anecdotally curious derivatives from the Athenian standard. Yet, if we are willing to dilate our notion of evidence to include such artifacts as epigraphy and archaeological remains—much of which has become available only during the last century—then we can extend our sources of knowledge beyond literary texts to include other resources for understanding rhetoric in Greece.

While the inclination to define Athenian rhetoric as Greek rhetoric has made it difficult to consider other forms of rhetoric, ancient sources allude to other forms of rhetoric. The thought that Aristotle's *Rhetoric* may have been an accounting of rhetoric that was not meant as a universal explanation but rather as a study of rhetoric indigenous to Athens is so out of harmony with our assumptions that it is not given serious consideration. It is possible, however, that Aristotle's treatment of rhetoric was based on rhetoric as practiced in Athens, that his accounting of rhetoric would be based on observations of civic functions at Athens and an explanation of the system based on Athenian praxis. Aristotle, as was his inclination with other subjects, often collected every form of a species and then made observations by citing differences and similarities. His *Synagoge technon*—a collection of early manuals of rhetoric that is now lost—was purported to have been done for this very process (Erickson). Regardless of whether or not Aristotle wrote his *Rhetoric* as an Athenian rhetoric or more generally as an Hellenic rhetoric, it is obvious that we have taken it to be the latter. We have accepted the Aristotelian accounting of Athenian rhetoric as synonymous with classical Greek rhetoric, despite our awareness that other representations of rhetoric existed in ancient Greece and, as will be discussed, were often far different versions than Aristotle's (Athenian) rhetoric.

We have thus come upon a problem for historians of rhetoric. On the one hand, we have represented and generalized the Aristotelian version of Athenian rhetoric as Greek rhetoric. On the other hand, we have knowledge of other manifestations of Greek rhetoric that do not match the Aristotelian rhetoric of Athens. Our ways of resolving this incompatibility have not been helpful nor historically accurate, particularly when discussing rhetoric at Rhodes. We have sought to resolve (or reduce) this incompatibility by just mentioning that other types of rhetoric existed in the Greek world—Asiatic and Rhodian rhetoric are the two versions most frequently listed. We mention these two forms of rhetoric, however, making them appear to be derivative or inferior versions of the one true rhetoric: Athenian rhetoric.

Rhodes: A Rival to the Athenian Rhetoric

Rhodian rhetoric sustained popularity through the Roman Republic and into the Empire. In order to understand the emergence and development of rhetoric at Rhodes we must first understand the cultural and political conditions that existed, since these forces did as much to shape the art of rhetoric at Rhodes as did the intellectual insights of its teachers and practitioners. There are several factors that contributed to the development of rhetoric on Rhodes. Rhodes is an island off the southwest coast of Asia Minor, separated by the strait of Marmara for a distance of about seven miles. Rhodes's need for proficiency in shipping and her strategic commercial location made the island attractive to the earliest colonizers, and there is some evidence of such activity dating back to Bronze Age Cretan and Mycenean settlements. In fact, Rhodes had been colonized as early as the eleventh century B.C. (Pindar, *Olympionikos VII*). This settlement was directed by Tiryns and clearly establishes the ethnic heritage of Rhodes as Dorian. The three most ancient cities of Rhodes (Lindos, Ialysos, and Kamiros) united in 408/7 B.C. to create the new capital city of Rhodes. The willingness of these three powerful cities to cooperate to the extent that they would create a new, united community (the synoecism) was a sign of Rhodes's political temperament. Throughout her history, Rhodes was famous for moderate republicanism and tempered democracy (Berthold 22ff.). Demonstrating this cooperative temperament off the island, Rhodes united with the neighboring Dorian cities of the area (Kos, Kindos, and Halicarnassos) to form the Dorian Hexapolis (Homer 2. 656; Herodotus 1. 144). Located along the trade route between Greece and the East, Rhodes was in a strategically geographic position to be exposed to a number of cultures. Rhodes's early contact with the seafaring Phoenicians meant that she was one of the first to apply the Greek alphabet and to provide some of the earliest evidence of Greek writing (Jeffery 346–7). There is a strong argument to be made, with the Phoenicians and the evolution of their alphabet, that people who have active seafaring, commercial interests develop systems that enable them to be proficient in communicating with people in other language groups. Because of their commercial wealth and long-recognized interest in the arts, Rhodes became an attractive and diverse cultural center—a natural site for developing effective strategies for communicating with peoples of other cultures.

The Dorian identity of Rhodes is also an important factor in understanding not only their heritage, but also how they contrasted ethnically with other prominent Greeks, especially Athenians. Ancient Greece is distinguished by five dialect groups: Arcado-Cyprian, Aeolic, Attic-Ionic, North West Greek, and Doric. These dialect distinctions are also cultural distinctions; that is, the dialect is much more than the language, it is the register of cultural and kinship ties. The Doric dialect dominated the Peloponnese and Western Greece in the classical period (Palmer 58). These dialect groupings are determinants of social identification and kinship bonding, for by the dialect of Greek people we have a sign for tracing cultural expansion, colonization, and identification (Cook 10). Rhodes clearly identified with kindred Dorian cities such as Corinth and Sparta and, conversely, formed no cultural identity with the Attic-Ionic Athenians (Diodorus Siculus 12. 54 1–7; Livy 24. 35; Thucydides 2. 73). The Dorian heritage of the ancient cities of Rhodes is important in three areas: their commercial proficiency, their aggressive colonization, and their political practices.

Rhodes also had an active and widespread interest in colonization, establishing settlements in Gela (Thucydides 6. 4. 3–4), and possibly Rhegium (Southern Italy) and Phaselis (east coast of Lycia). In Rhodes's interaction with various cities, particularly those that were colonized by citizens, it would be reasonable to expect that the oral, literary, and fine arts would flourish. We know that, akin to commercial trading, many western cities such as Syracuse were active patrons of the arts. The most striking evidence of this interaction and patronage is during festivals such as the Olympic Games. Pindar (518–438 B.C.), the lyric poet from Doric-speaking Boeotia, provides us with the earliest literary accounts of Rhodes's history. A much sought-after artist famous for his *encomia,* Pindar was frequently offered patronage by admirers from several Dorian-speaking centers including Corinth, Syracuse, and Rhodes. Diagoras of Rhodes was crowned victor at the boxing competition at Olympia in 464 B.C., and Pindar was commissioned to compose an epideictic poem in honor of the champion.

Long-established legends and myths of Rhodes's earliest history are woven within and throughout Pindar's *Olympionikos VII.* Buried within these accounts, however, is important information on the prehistory of Rhodes and, of equal value, its peoples' belief about their origins. Pindar's epideictic rhapsody reinforces a long-standing legend on the founding of Rhodes. Helios selected the island and had three sons by the nymph Rhodos: Lindos, Ialysos, and Kamiros. These three sons became eponyms of the three ancient cities of Rhodes that bear their names. The Dorian ancestry is reinforced by the legend that Tlepolemus, a hero from Dorian Tiryns and descendent of Heracles (20–25, 75–80), founded the city of Ialysos, which, along with Lindos and Kamiros, formed the three earliest cities on the island of Rhodes. These cities annually held a festival honoring Helios called the Halieia. As was the Greek custom with many such festivals, they offered a much larger version quadrennially that became well known throughout the Hellenic world. To this day, the archaeological remains of the stadium and theater bear testimony to Rhodes's commitment to her festivals.

Pindar's praise of Diagoras presents another illustration of a well-established honor befitting Rhodes. Pindar's ode explains that Rhodes's long history of games in reverence to the gods is a fitting homage, since Rhodes is a site where immortals such as Athena have given them every art (50–55). Pindar sings of Rhodes's glory with the assumption that all auditors share a common knowledge of Rhodes's passion for and excellence in the arts and athletics, and their history of contests that celebrate and nurture such excellence. "Rhodes," wrote William V. Harris, "may for some time have been the city with the nearest thing to universal public education for boys ever seen in antiquity" (131). By the first century B.C. Rhodes was, in the words of H. I. Marrou, "a great university city" (160). Later, Rhodes would become the intellectual retreat for such Roman Emperors as Tiberius and Hadrian (Bowersock, *Augustus* 77, 134; Bowersock, *Greek Sophists* 121). What we have, then, with Rhodes, is a people linguistically and culturally tied with other Dorians but constantly exploring and being placed in contact with other people. Such interaction is not only indicative of pan-Hellenic commercial interaction but also provides an insight to the sources for her cultural riches. Rhodes was recognized as an artistic center for Greece, and her widespread interaction and influence could well be a source that explains how the arts came to flourish early in the Dorian cities of the West. Moreover, it is also indicative, as we will also discuss later, of how cities other than Athens were active and lively centers for arts such as rhetoric.

Many Greek cities were not democratic but rather ruled by kings, tyrants, and oligarchs. We know, for example, that rhetoric was practiced in Syracuse before her relatively brief period of democracy. Under the rule of autocrats many cities, such as Syracuse, prospered, and patronage of the arts generally and literature specifically is well documented by both ancient and modern sources (Enos). That form of rhetoric, however, not only employed civic functions so important for a democracy—forensic and deliberative rhetoric—but also artistic and epideictic rhetoric. When the reign of the Syracusian tyrant Thrasybulus was overthrown in 467/66 B.C., the city was ruled by a democracy. It is easy to see, however, how such aesthetic functions of rhetoric could be adapted to more pragmatic and expedient civic and political functions when such Dorian cities as Syracuse revolted from tyranny to democracy. That is, artistic proficiency in ceremonial rhetoric could be the basis for effective training when presbyters or representatives were sent to Greek cities for political purposes. Epigraphical recordings of the activities of presbyters survive and are available for study (e. g. Enos 52–6).

While rhetoric formally "began" as a discipline in a democratic system, the training for eloquence originated in nondemocratic societies. From this perspective, rhetoric's origin is more accurately represented not as a beginning but as a transformation and redefinition. That is, the functions of eloquent expression changed from an art form driven by autocratic patrons to the system of effective expression, where "eloquence" was adjudicated by needs and desires of common listeners. Rhetoric as an "art" emphasized pragmatic functions that ensured its popularity and preservation in a democracy, where the eloquence of persuasive discourse served the normative and regulatory functions of an egalitarian society. Rhetoric in less egalitarian environments of ancient Greece existed as an art and service supported by influential patrons, many of whom were tyrants. In such situations, the invention of rhetoric was directed toward creating discourse that was epideictic and ambassadorial, where lines of argument were often articulated in terms of reinforcing values internally or presenting views to other cities. There is certainly later evidence of such uses of rhetoric, specifically when Romans made a transition from Republic to Empire, and when court orators flourished in Renaissance Italy. In such instances, rhetoric's emphasis on invention shifted from those functions that were important in a Republic (forensic and deliberative) to educational, artistic, and politically ceremonial. We may even go so far to say that under the Augustan Principate literary works created by Horace, Livy, and Vergil were manifestations of a type of rhetoric that was artistic but also suasory in its persuasive appeal to values in harmony with Augustus's rule.

In some respects, Rhodes is an eastern counterpart to the phenomenon of rhetoric that took place among Sicily, Athens, and later, Rome. Also like Syracuse, rhetoric did have a transition to a democracy on Rhodes, exhibiting an open and flexible disposition that was necessary for interaction with a variety of foreign cultures that her intense commercial activities required. Yet, Rhodes's evolution of rhetoric was different than Athens'. Athens disseminated rhetoric throughout the Greek world as she established her Empire. Rhodian rhetoric evolved into its own very effective system but essentially remained on the island of Rhodes and became its epicenter. Rhodes's early and well-developed artistic heritage, and her long history of balanced republican and democratic rule, would make her a likely source for such a form of rhetoric. Our efforts, now, will be directed toward a more specific understanding of Rhodian rhetoric through an examination of these political and artistic forces and, eventually, how this manifestation of Rhodian rhetoric survived and prospered, not only in ancient Greece but also through the Roman Empire.

Aeschines and the Transplantation and Adaptation of Athenian Rhetoric to Rhodes

The climate for a type of rhetoric was present on Rhodes. Ironically, the evolution of Rhodian rhetoric, a rhetoric clearly different from Athenian rhetoric, was started in Rhodes by an Athenian named Aeschines, one of the ten Attic orators of classical Athens. Just as Gorgias of Leontini left Sicily and introduced rhetoric to Athens, so also did Aeschines leave Athens to develop rhetoric on Rhodes. Known to historians of rhetoric chiefly as a respected actor who became an eloquent spokesperson for Athenian civic policy, Aeschines often was chosen to be one of Athens's ambassadors as an official rhetor or spokesman for the city. On such embassies, Aeschines would accompany other prominent rhetors, such as Demosthenes, and articulate his and the city's political position to figures of no less power than Philip of Macedonia. Such deliberations were extremely important, for Philip's ever-increasing power in Greece was obvious to Athenians, many of whom viewed him as an enemy. Similar to Isocrates, Aeschines often pled for peace; unlike Isocrates, Aeschines argued for a peace that would not de facto subordinate Athens to Macedonia. Aeschines' primary opposition came from Demosthenes, who viewed Philip as an untrusted enemy who could only be stopped by war. Ultimately, Demosthenes' persuasion unwisely convinced Athens and her allies to battle Philip (and Alexander) at Chaeronia in 338 B.C. Philip's crushing defeat of the Athenians not only ended that city's hegemony but also opened the way for Alexander's well-documented conquests. There is little doubt that such events were both tumultuous and important; there is also little doubt that rhetorical discourse played an important role in determining such events.

Much of how scholars such as Edward M. Harris explain and analyze Athenian policy during this critical time is through the extant orations of Aeschines and his rhetorical adversary, Demosthenes, who was taught delivery by the actor Andronicus of Rhodes (Quintilian, *Institutio Oratoria* 11.3.7). In fact, Demosthenes' speech "On the Crown," often regarded as the finest example of classical oratory, was a response to Aeschines' prosecution of Ctesiphon's "illegal" proposal to reward Demosthenes public honors for his civic service. Plutarch provides one of the earliest accounts of the Rhodian patronage of rhetoric. After losing his argument to Demosthenes, the Attic orator and politician Aeschines left his home in Athens and established a school of rhetoric on Rhodes (Plutarch, *Vitae Demosthenes* 840D). We treat Aeschines' loss to Demosthenes as the last phase in his important career as a rhetor but ignore the event as the beginning of his career as the founder of Rhodian rhetoric. Aeschines' departure from Athens and his establishment of a school of rhetoric on Rhodes is comparable to Gorgias's famous trip to Athens several decades earlier. That is, just as Gorgias went to Athens to represent the interests of his city, Leontini, as a presbyter, and introduced the formal study of rhetoric to Attica, so also did Aeschines, a former rhetor, leave Athens and introduce the formal study of rhetoric in Rhodes. To this day, Rhodini Park is credited as the site of Aeschines' school of rhetoric. Unfortunately, no physical evidence remains at Rhodini Park to enrich our knowledge of his school.

Our limited scholarship on Aeschines—particularly when contrasted with studies on Demosthenes—restricts an understanding of the forces that shaped his school of rhetoric when he left Athens for Rhodes. Given Aeschines' fame and obvious ability in rhetoric, we should ask what sort of school of rhetoric would Aeschines have in Rhodes, a city that did not follow the political or social manifestations of rhetoric that were enacted in a democratic polis such as Athens. Aeschines' orientation toward rhetoric stressed the ability to negotiate and communicate with those who did not share political orientation or cultural ties. We know from Plutarch, for example, that when Aeschines wished to illustrate his ability in rhetoric to the Rhodians, he declaimed the argument that he had made against Demosthenes as his model (*Moralia: Vitae Decem Oratorum* 840 C.E.). The diversity and adaptability that Aeschines manifested as an ambassadorial rhetor was compatible with the Rhodian culture that required effective communication across cultures and political orientations. Indirectly, this may tell us much about Aeschines' school of rhetoric: the formal role of rhetors, the important tasks of ambassadors who articulated policy, and the ethical standards and techniques that are so different from our values. Athenian rhetoric was developed to expedite the civic functions internal to that city. Rhodian rhetoric was orientated toward effective external communication, that is, across different cultural and political perspectives (Marrou 195).

Later schools of rhetoric at Rhodes are known to us by the fame of their educators. Apollonius (fl. 222–181 B.C.) was not a native of Rhodes, but like his predecessor, Aeschines, was attracted to the island and left Alexandria to establish a school of rhetoric (Marrou 144). So popular was Apollonius among the native Rhodians that they "adopted" him with the cognomen, "the Rhodian." Similarly, the grammatical scholarship of Aristodemus of Nysa and Dionysius of Thrax added to Rhodes's history of developing and attracting scholars of rhetoric (Marrou 160, 170 [Strabo 14. 650], 252). Epigraphical evidence attests to the esteem that Rhodians held for educators. In one instance, an educator was honored by the inhabitants of Rhodes for having taught for fifty-two years (Marrou 147 [*IG* 12.1.141]).

Long recognized as a center for artistic expression, Rhodes attained her greatest fame in rhetoric under Roman rule. Romans such as Cicero and Quintilian clearly admired the moderate, balanced style of rhetoric that was so compatible with their open and diverse temperament (Cicero, *Brutus* 316; Quintilian, *Institutio Oratoria* 12. 10. 18). Rhodian rhetoric so facilitated cultural diversity that it became the first Greco-Roman rhetoric. In fact, Harry Caplan argues that it was the Rhodian model that first introduced the study of rhetoric to Rome and that the *Rhetorica ad Herrenium* may well be little more than a Roman version of a Rhodian manual of rhetoric ("Decay" 162; see also, Calboli). There is little doubt of heightened attention to declamation in the city after Apollonius Molo left Rhodes and visited Rome (possibly) in 87

B.C. and in 81 B.C. (Caplan, "Introduction" xv; Cicero, *Brutus* 307, 312; Marrou 412). Molo experienced great fame in Rome, thus continuing the reputation of Rhodes as a center for the study of rhetoric (Cicero, *De Oratore* 1. 17. 75; 2. 1. 2–3; 2. 54. 217). In turn, many famous Romans were exposed to, and even attended, these schools of rhetoric, including Cato, Cicero, Titus Torquatus, Julius Caesar, Scaevola, and Lucretius. In fact, Cicero believed that one of his most beneficial experiences in rhetoric came from his education in Rhodes, principally because Molo's skill as a pleader, logographer, and teacher helped to temper Cicero's youthful, flamboyant style (*Brutus* 316).

The merits of Greek education in rhetoric and literature were begrudgingly recognized by many Romans. Even such a staunch defender of Roman culture as Cato the Censor was impressed with the benefits of Greek rhetoric and even became an advocate for Rhodes (Quintilian, *Institutio Oratoria* 12. 11. 23; Berthold 197–8). A thorough critique of Cato's support for the people of Rhodes is offered by Aulus Gellius (*Noctes Atticae* 6. 3. 1–55; Kennedy, *A New History* 106–11). Cato's argument for the support of Rhodes gives us a revealing picture of both his admiration for the commercial and artistic prosperity of the island and the benefits that a strong alliance with Rome would offer. Cato noted the ability of the envoys (*legati*) that Rhodes sent to Rome to discuss their relationship. In fact, Cato made a special point of mentioning how well the Rhodian *legati* expressed their views to a Roman Senate that was prone to be skeptical of their allegiance and their faithfulness as an ally (Aulus Gellius, *Noctes Atticae* 6. 3. 5–7).

Many Romans had strong reservations about Greek models for Roman eloquence but even the most stringent of these critics, the members of the Scipionic Circle, recognized that Greek education offered a paradigm for eloquence in their own language. Members of the Scipionic Circle advocated the most simple and direct style of Greek rhetoric, the Attic style (e.g. Cicero, *Brutus* 274, 283). These "Roman Atticists" were especially critical of a Greek style of rhetoric that originated in Asia Minor called Asianism or Asiatic rhetoric (Quintilian, *Institutio Oratoria* 12. 10. 16–22). Asianism, which they considered to be excessively bombastic, was seen by Roman Atticists as inappropriate and even anti-Roman in character (Cicero, *Orator* 8. 24–27).

The more moderate alternative to the Asiatic rhetoric was the Rhodian style (Quintilian, *Institutio Oratoria* 12. 10. 16–19). Although Roman Atticists even criticized the moderation of Rhodian rhetoric, it nonetheless became popular in Rome, primarily through the support of Marcus Tullius Cicero, who, as mentioned above, had studied rhetoric at Rhodes while in Greece from 79–77 B.C. Roman exposure to Rhodian rhetoric did not, however, begin with Cicero, for in his *De Oratore* Cicero has Scaevola mention that he conversed with Apollonius while serving as a *praetor* in Rhodes (1. 17. 75). Throughout his distinguished career and throughout his many works on rhetoric, Cicero continued to acknowledge the influence of Rhodian rhetoric. In fact, Cicero claimed that his *De Optima Genera Oratorum* was really a preface to his Latin translation of the speeches of Demosthenes and Aeschines (17–18). Cicero advocated the study of all three styles—Attic, Rhodian, and Asiatic—but saw clear advantages in Rhodian rhetoric. The single greatest advantage of Rhodian rhetoric was that it was ideally suited for declamation. The tempered style of Rhodian rhetoric was a balanced alternative to the plain and direct Attic style and the histrionic Asiatic style.

The primary method of rhetorical instruction was by declamation. Greek sophists throughout the Roman Empire stressed both oral and written composition. Declamation became such a popular method of rhetorical instruction that it became synonymous with the highest level of education. In fact, Marrou argues that the public lecture was the typical literary form of Hellenistic culture (195). Declamation gained ever-increasing popularity, as Rome shifted from a Republic to an Empire, and the appeal of Rhodian rhetoric grew proportionally to the extent that it became a major center for the study of Greek declamation. In fact, the sustained influence of declamation explains in large part the reason why the art of rhetoric at Rhodes prospered and endured well into the Roman Empire.

Conclusion

There are five important observations that come from our study of the art of rhetoric at Rhodes. First, Rhodes offered a rival and enduring version of rhetoric from her Athenian counterpart. The disproportionate amount of readily available evidence about rhetoric in Athens when compared with other sites has distorted our perspective on the viability of other manifestations of classical rhetoric. Second, Rhodian rhetoric stressed a very special variant of epideictic rhetoric. The early emphasis on cross-cultural ties through commercial activity, coupled with the training of rhetors dating back to Aeschines, reveals a sort of rhetoric that is decidedly more pan-Hellenic than the internal, civic practices of Athenian rhetoric. Third, the moderate style of Rhodian rhetoric made it ideal for the study and practice of declamation. Famous Romans such as Cicero stressed the importance of the training in declamation that he received at Rhodes. The enduring popularity of Sophistic rhetoric, and the establishment of declamation into the practices of higher education, help to explain why Rhodes would remain an active center for the study of rhetoric well into the Roman Empire. Fourth, Rhodian rhetoric was inherently inclusive, and its popular reception by Romans established the first, true, Greco-Roman rhetoric. Fifth and finally, it is apparent that there are rhetorical riches yet to be discovered on the island of Rhodes. To find these riches, however, we need to develop new research methods in the history of rhetoric. We can no longer be content to limit our knowledge to literary texts. Conventional narrative materials are essential, but can no longer be seen as sufficient. Rhodes simply does not have the "literary" history of rhetoric that Athens enjoys. That is not to say, however, that the evidence for a history is nonexistent; rather, the evidence is nontraditional. The hope is that a thorough history of rhetoric at Rhodes will also, albeit indirectly, provide an illustration of composing a history at sites that share such constraints as limited literary evidence. To engage in this new challenge, we need nothing less than to enact our tool-building creativity and develop new research methods for an archaeology of rhetoric.

Works Cited

All references to classical sources in the text of this essay follow the universal citation format and hence do not include reference to specific editions unless explicitly stated. Standard, authoritative texts are offered in both the Teubner and Oxford University Press editions. Translations of these classical works, with the primary language included, can be found in the Loeb Classical Library Series of the Harvard University Press.

Aristotle. *Rhetoric.*

Aulus Gellius. *Noctes Atticae.*

Berthold, Richard M. *Rhodes in the Hellenistic Age.* Ithaca and London: Cornell University Press, 1984.

Bowersock, G. W. *Augustus and the Greek World.* Oxford: Clarendon Press, 1965.

———. *Greek Sophists of the Roman Empire.* Oxford: Clarendon Press, 1969.

Calboli, Gualtiero. "From Aristotelian λεξις to *elocution.*" *Rhetorica* 16.1 (1998): 47–80.

Caplan, Harry. "Introduction." [Cicero]. *Ad C. Herennium De Ratione Dicendi (Rhetorica Ad Herennium).* Trans. Harry Caplan. Loeb Classical Library Series. Cambridge, MA: Harvard University Press, 1964: vii–xl.

———. "The Decay of Eloquence at Rome in the First Century." *Of Eloquence: Studies in Ancient and Medieval Rhetoric.* Eds. Anne King and Helen North. Ithaca and New York: Cornell University Press, 1970: 160–95.

Cicero. *Brutus.*

———. *De Optima Genera Oratorum.*

———. *De Oratore.*

————. *Orator.*

Cook, B. F. *Greek Inscriptions.* Berkeley and Los Angeles, CA: University of California Press/British Museum, 1987.

Diodorus Siculus.

Enos, Richard Leo. *Greek Rhetoric Before Aristotle.* Prospect Heights, IL: Waveland Press, 1993.

Erickson, Keith. "The Lost Rhetorics of Aristotle." *Landmark Essays on Aristotelian Rhetoric.* Eds. Richard Leo Enos and Lois Peters Agnew. Mahwah, NJ: Lawrence Erlbaum Associates, Publishers, 1998: 3–13.

Harris, Edward M. Aeschines and Athenian Politics. New York and Oxford: Oxford University Press, 1995.

Harris, William V. *Ancient Literacy.* Cambridge, MA, and London: Harvard University Press, 1989.

Herodotus. *The Persian Wars.*

Homer. *Iliad.*

Jaeger, Werner. *Paideia: The Ideals of Greek Culture.* 3 vols. 2nd ed. Trans. Gilbert Highet. New York: Oxford University Press, 1945.

Jeffery, L. H. *The Local Scripts of Archaic Greece.* Oxford: Clarendon Press, 1961.

Kennedy, George A. *A New History of Classical Rhetoric.* Princeton, NJ: Princeton University Press, 1994.

Livy. *Ab Urbe Condita.*

Marrou, H. I. *A History of Education in Antiquity.* Trans. George Lamb. Reprint 1974, Madison, WI: The University of Wisconsin Press, 1956.

Palmer, Leonard R. *The Greek Language.* Atlantic Highlands, NJ: Humanities Press, Inc., 1980.

Pindar. *Olympionikos VII.*

Plutarch. *Moralia: Vitae Decem Oratorum.*

————. *Vitae Demosthenes.*

Quintilian. *Institutio Oratoria.*

Thucydides. *The Peloponnesian War.*

Story–List–Sanction:
A Cross-Cultural Strategy of Ancient Persuasion

James W. Watts

Persuasion has been a key topic in rhetorical theory from classical to modern times. Though the study of rhetoric has been largely confined to western culture and texts, persuasion is an overt feature of many oral practices and written texts worldwide. The persuasive intent behind speeches or texts is often obvious, despite cultural differences in form and genre. Persuasion can therefore provide a useful starting point for comparing the rhetorical practices of different cultures. For the purposes of comparative analysis of ancient Near Eastern rhetoric, I therefore define rhetoric as including any and all forms of persuasion (cf. Burke 1950, 49–55, 61–62).

Persuasion motivated the creation of many ancient Near Eastern texts. This is especially true of royal inscriptions, whose concerns range from preservation of the inscription itself to dynastic propaganda. Persuasive interests also appear in instructional and literary works that exhort their audience to conform to social norms or celebrate the glory of the national gods. Ancient texts display their persuasive intentions overtly in the militaristic boasts and threats of kings or the promises and warnings of sages or, most obviously, by invoking blessings and curses from the gods on their readers and hearers. Persuasion was not limited to particular genres of discourse and literature but was frequently a stimulus leading authors to combine genres to create more persuasive forms. In this process, the rhetorical capacities of many different kinds of literature were harnessed for overtly persuasive purposes. One such rhetorical strategy combined three kinds of materials—stories, lists and sanctions—to influence its audience's ideas and behaviors. It shaped the form and content of texts from a wide variety of periods and cultures in the ancient Near East and eastern Mediterranean, including the foundational scriptures of

197

Judaism and Christianity. Through them it has influenced the subsequent course of western religious, legal, and academic rhetoric.

Juxtaposing Genres for Persuasion

A short example of the story–list–sanction strategy can be found in an inscription of Kurigalzu, one of several Kassite kings of Babylon by that name who ruled in the mid-second millennium B.C.E.. The complete text runs as follows:

(i 1) Kurigalzu, great king, mighty king, king of the universe, favorite of Anu and Enlil, nominated (for kingship) by the gods am I! King who has no equal among all kings his ancestors, son of [Kadash]man-Harbe, unrivalled king, who completed the fortifications of . . . who [fin]ished the Ekur, who [prov]ides for Ur and Uruk, who [guar]antees the rites of Eridu, who constructed the temples of Anu and Ishtar, who [guarantees] the regular offerings of the great gods,

(i 16) I caused Anu, father of the great gods, to dwell in his exalted sanctuary. To Ishtar, the most great lady, who goes at my side, who maintains my army, shepherds my people, subdues those disobedient to me:

(i 24) From the town Adatti, on the bank of the Euphrates, as far as the town Mangissi, bordering on the field Duranki, beloved of Enlil. From the town of my lady, Bit-Gashan-ama-kalla, as far as the border of the city Girsu, an area of 216,000 kor using a ratio per surface unit of 30 quarts of seed barley, measured by the large cubit, to Ishtar I granted.

(ii 5) 3 kor of bread, 3 kor of fine wine, 2 (large measures) of date cakes, 30 quarts of imported dates, 30 quarts of fine(?) oil, 3 sheep per day did I establish as the regular offering for all time.

(ii 11) I set up boundary stones in all directions and guaranteed the borders. The towns, fields, watercourses, and unirrigated land, and their rural settlements did I grant to Ishtar, my lady.

(ii 16) Whosoever shall arise afterward and shall alter my deeds and change the command which I spoke, shall take out my boundary stones, shift my boundary lines, take away the towns, fields, watercourses, and unirrigated lands, or the rural settlements in the neighborhood of Uruk, or cause (another) to take (them) away, or who shall attempt to convert them to state lands, may Ishtar, the most great lady, not go at his side in battle and combat, but inflict defeat and heavy losses upon his army and scatter his forces! (Foster 1993, 278–79)

The structure of this text shows a clear progression. After Kurigalzu boasts about his status with humans and the gods, he presents a short narrative of his accomplishments in building or restoring city defenses, temples, and temple rites, and in securing income for those temples. Then follow lists of the king's donations to the Ishtar temple, consisting of specifically designated land grants (i 24ff.), regulations for the daily offerings (ii 5ff.), and further description of the temple's rights over the donated land, including the notice that the boundaries were clearly marked (ii 11ff.; this text was itself probably inscribed on these boundary stones, though only copies on clay tablets survive). The inscription concludes with curses on any future king who revokes Kurigalzu's donations and promises that the god Ishtar will avenge her losses herself (ii 16ff.).

Two purposes clearly motivated the writing of Kurigalzu's inscription: glorification of the king and preservation of the Ishtar Temple's legal prerogatives and religious rites. To achieve the first, the text characterizes Kurigalzu by describing his greatness and then by narrating his accomplishments. The building of temples ("finished the Ekur," "constructed the temples of Anu and Ishtar") receives prominent attention because it casts Kurigalzu as a cult founder who "guarantees the rites" and "the regular offerings." The narrative thus legitimates his right to mandate the donations and offerings contained in the following lists. These lists in turn specify the contents of his decrees and so make their application possible. The first list describes the boundaries of the land grant both by the towns on its borders and by its area (approximately 525 square kilometers). The second list mandates the quantities of daily offerings to the deity. After emphasizing Kurigalzu's attention to establishing the land boundaries by visible markers, the third list specifies the contents of the donated land. Thus the lists verify and illustrate Kurigalzu's claim that he "guaranteed the rites" and "the regular offerings of the great gods."

At the same time, these lists legitimize the temple's claim to this land and its produce on the basis of the royal cult founder's original donation. Defense of these prerogatives after Kurigalzu's death cannot, however, depend on royal patronage that might prove fickle, so the inscription concludes with curses on any later king who might appropriate the property for other uses. Thus the text defends the temple's claims by citing the royal land grant and by promising divine enforcement.

The inscription's rhetoric is clearly directed at future kings and their officials, for it explicitly aims to persuade them not to expropriate the lands and income of the Ishtar temple. Unlike the other lists, however, the list of daily offerings does not at first glance seem directed at the same audience. This list could be interpreted as instructions for the temple priests, but the focus on quantities of offerings and the lack of any other ritual directions suggests that lay people are being addressed. Because the offerings list appears between descriptions of the donated land's boundaries and contents, it seems best to interpret the list as justifying the size and nature of the land grant by specifying why it was needed: substantial properties are required to support the temple's schedule of daily offerings. This also explains the deity's interest in defending the temple's lands, as promised in the curses: Ishtar receives the offerings that are produced on these lands. Future kings and their officials thus seem to be the target audience for these provisions as well.

To summarize: Kurigalzu's inscription aims to discourage expropriation of temple lands by justifying them as granted by the cult founder and as necessary to sustain the rites initiated by him and expected by the deity. The text mixes stories of the cult-founder's acts with lists of properties and offerings and divine sanctions against those who might infringe on the temple's prerogatives in order to make these claims persuasive for the later rulers at whom they are directed. It unites story, list, and sanction for the sake of persuasion.

Other examples of the complete pattern

Neither the literary structure nor the rhetorical purpose of Kurigalzu's inscription are particularly distinctive. I chose it for its brevity in order to present a complete example of the widespread tendency to bring together diverse kinds of material in a single inscription to enhance its persuasive effect. The pattern of story–list–sanction does not appear so consistently as to suggest a recognizable literary or rhetorical genre. Instead, these elements appear all three together or any two without the third in texts of such different genres, cultures, and time periods that their combination seems to represent a rhetorical strategy adopted irregularly to enhance the persuasiveness of a text.

The complete story–list–sanction pattern appears most commonly in inscriptions like Kurigalzu's that commemorate royal achievements. Thus Naram-Sin of Akkad (23rd cent. B.C.E.) recounts his conquest of two cities, then lists the measurements of (apparently) the two cities' fortifications, and concludes with curses by "all the great gods" on those who might appropriate his inscription as their own (Foster 1993, 52–53). The "Apology" of the Hittite king Hattusili III (13th cent. B.C.E.) concludes a long account of his rise to kingship with a description of properties donated to the deity Ishtar and curses against those who would claim those properties by diverting his successors from the worship of Ishtar or who would oppose them directly (Hallo and Younger 1997, 199–204). The Karatepe inscription of Azatiwada, the Phoenician governor of Adana (8th cent. B.C.E.), recounts his governmental, architectural, and military accomplishments at length before presenting a short schedule of offerings: "a yearly sacrifice: an ox; and at the time (season) of plowing: a sheep; and at the time (season) of reaping/harvesting: a sheep." It then concludes with blessings on Azatiwada and the inhabitants of his city and curses on any future ruler who might obliterate this gate inscription (Hallo and Younger 2000, 149–50). A dedicatory inscription of Seti I (14th cent. B.C.E.) narrates this Egyptian king's achievement in digging a well and constructing a temple (and town?) on the desert road to some gold mines. Then Seti addresses the rulers of Egypt with commands setting aside a troop of gold-washers for the Abydos temple as a perpetual grant, and curses extensively any king or official who appropriates this troop for other purposes while blessing those who maintain his endowment (Lichtheim 1976, 52–57). The Famine Stela (3rd- 2nd cent. B.C.E.) narrates how an Egyptian king ended a famine by making offerings to Khnum of Elephantine, then donated extensive lands and a tithe of their produce to the Elephantine temple. Concluding instructions for inscribing two copies of this donation end with the single sanction, "He who spits (on it) deceitfully shall be given over to punishment" (Lichtheim 1980, 94–103). From Asia Minor in the Persian period (4th cent. B.C.E.), a stela from the Leto Temple at Xanthos briefly records the community's decision to establish this temple, then follows with a list of exemptions for its lands and schedules of offerings as authorized by the Persian satrap and concludes with divine sanctions to encourage observance of these provisions (Metzger 1979).

The story–list–sanction pattern, however, is not restricted to dedicatory inscriptions. It structures some ancient law codes, such as Hammurabi's Code from Babylon (17th cent. B.C.E.) and the earlier Sumerian law code of Lipit-Ishtar (Roth 1995, 71–142, 23–35). Hittite treaties between imperial overlords and vassal rulers (late 2nd millennium B.C.E.) recount the history of relations between the states before listing the stipulations to which the vassal is obligated. Then after describing how the treaty document itself must be preserved and reread periodically, the gods of both states are listed and called upon to witness the agreement and enforce the curses and blessings that conclude the documents (Beckman 1996, 2–3). Legal texts from the Hebrew Bible (7th–5th cents. B.C.E.) were also shaped by the story–list–sanction structure. It is clearest in Deuteronomy, whose review of Israel's exodus from Egypt (chaps. 1–11) leads through the Deuteronomic law collection (chaps. 12–26) to extensive blessings and curses (chaps. 27–30; Watts 1999). Even the conclusion to an Akkadian epic uses this three-part rhetoric for religious persuasion: Enuma Elish, the Babylonian creation epic (later 2nd millennium B.C.E.), supplements its narrative with a list of the god Marduk's fifty names that occupies the last one-and-a-half of its seven tablets. The concluding sanctions take the form not of blessings and curses but of exhortations promising prosperity to those who study the names and warning of the god's anger and judgment (Foster 1993, 400–401).

Examples with two of the three elements

Many more texts combine any two of the story–list–sanction elements. Juxtaposition of narratives with lists appears fairly often. Though some inscriptions, like a donation stela of the Egyptian king Ay (14th cent. B.C.E.) from Giza, use narrative as little more than an introductory framework, many others use much longer stories to authorize the following lists. A boundary stela from El-Amarna in Egypt tells of Pharaoh Akhenaton (14th cent. B.C.E.) arriving in the city and issuing a declaration, which it quotes, that establishes the boundaries of the city. The Buhen Stela from the same period narrates the story of a military campaign, follows it with a list enumerating captives and enemy dead, and concludes by celebrating Akhenaton's power over foreign countries (Murnane 1995, 225, 81–86, 101–102). Several documents claiming to stem from the reign of Nebuchadnezzar I of Babylon (12th cent. B.C.E.) narrate military campaigns or travels and then list exemptions granted for service in battle, or give orders to restore a temple, or list supplies being donated for offerings (Foster 1993, 297–98, 302, 304–306). In the legal sphere, Pharaoh Horemheb's edict from Karnak (Egyptian 14th cent. B.C.E.), after praising the king, gives a paragraph narrating the circumstances of the edict before listing a series of provisions reforming state taxation, appropriations, and the judicial system (Murnane 1995, 235–40). Several Hittite myths make clear that recitation of the story that they recount is one component of a ritual designed to prompt specific actions by one or more deities. Thus one text clearly describes how a (short) narrative of the sun-god's departure was used within a ritual to bring about the deity's return (Hoffner 1990, 22–23). Ritual texts that cite stories as part of magical incantations are known from other cultures besides the Hittites.[1] The persuasive force of these texts is directed towards the gods, not humans, so apparently deities were also thought to be influenced by the combination of story and list.

Ancient stories that do not introduce lists may nevertheless conclude with sanctions. The eighth century B.C.E. Akkadian Erra epic promises rewards and threatens punishments against gods and humans alike on the basis of the treatment the epic itself receives (Foster 1993, 804; Hallo and Younger 1997, 415–16). Commemorative inscriptions frequently curse anyone who might destroy the inscription or appropriate it as their own. This tendency also appears in religious texts from the Hellenistic and Roman periods. The Letter of Aristeas (2nd–1st cents. B.C.E.) invokes sanctions against anyone who might alter the Septuagint Greek translation of the Jewish Bible (Charlesworth 1983, 2:33). The Jewish apocalyptic work of 1 Enoch

(104:10–13) from the late first millennium B.C.E. and the New Testament book of Revelation (22:18–19) from the late first century C.E. threaten divine sanctions against later editors. In a similar way, nonnarrative legal texts often conclude with sanctions (e.g. Assyrian treaties). New Greek laws were inscribed on monuments near temples to relate them to divine authority and emphasize that point with divine curses on those who fail to observe them (Thomas 1992, 72, 145–46).

One could object that some of these texts are not obviously structured in the manner in which I have suggested. In Azatiwada's inscription, for example, the sacrificial calendar has been considered part of the narrative of his accomplishments, and is in any case much shorter than the list of titles that introduce the text (cf. Younger 1998, 22; Greenstein 1995, 2428–32). In other cases, such as Ay's donation stela, the introductory titles overshadow the very brief narrative, which serves simply to introduce the quotation of the grant. Sanctions are frequently so brief that they seem merely to be one of several concluding formulae, as in the Famine Stela, rather than a crucial part of the main composition.

Such criticisms do weigh against any notion that the story–list–sanction pattern describes an essential feature of some ancient genre of literature; it does not.[2] More often than not, commemorative inscriptions, law codes, treaties, and epics lack one or more of the three elements in this pattern. Even when they occur together, any one of the three may be far more prominent than the others, as may other elements (such as introductory titles) that I have not included in this analysis. My point then is not to describe structural features of ancient literature so much as to point out the rhetorical effect of their combination. Wherever it occurs, the combination in various patterns and proportions of stories, lists, and sanctions serves the same recognizable purpose: persuasion.

Persuasion in Time

Each of the three components in the story–list–sanction pattern serves a distinct rhetorical purpose that shapes its use. Different literary genres may serve the same rhetorical role within the persuasive structure. The consistent function of the "story" is to ground each text's contents and origin in the past actions of some authority, which in the commemorative inscriptions is usually a king but sometimes a governor (e.g. Azatiwada) or a community (the Letoon inscription), and is a deity in the myths and epics, as well as the Torah.

The category I have labeled "list" contains far more diverse kinds of material. These range from numbers of enemy dead and captured (Akhenaton's Buhen Stela) through descriptions of land grants, exemptions, and endowments (e.g. the inscriptions of Kurigalzu, Ay, and Seti I), lists of offerings (e.g. Kurigalzu, Azatiwada), direct commands (Seti I), casuistic rules and regulations (e.g. the Code of Hammurabi, Horemheb's rulings, Hittite treaties, the Torah) to catalogues of a deity's names (Enuma Elish, Anzu). They all fall under the broad category of lists that John O'Banion argued "underlies all modes of systematic expression."

> Rendered as tallies, recordings of the movements of the stars, word lists, dictionaries, or codified laws, the list is a powerful tool for arranging and disseminating isolated pieces of information. It also comes to arrange and, to a considerable degree, dictate the nature of the lives of those who are affected by lists (O'Banion 1992, xiv, 12).

In literary form, lists are sometimes indistinguishable from the narratives that introduce them. The rhetoric of these lists aims, however, for a different persuasive effect than do the stories. While the stories ground the inscription's authority in the past, the lists describe obligations that are imposed on readers in the present. In other words, whereas the stories serve to memorialize the founders and legitimize past actions, the lists aim to dictate present behavior. The descriptions of land borders and contents, quantities of offerings, and tax exemptions aim to discourage infringement of these prerogatives by officials who read the inscriptions. The stipulations of vassal treaties, Horemheb's administrative reform, and the biblical laws aim to encourage acts in accord with their regulations and discourage prohibited behaviors. Surprisingly, the law codes of Mesopotamia seem to have functioned less as judicial directives than as portrayals of ideal justice to reflect positively on the character of their sponsor. They remind us that memorializing the founding king or deity is a major rhetorical goal motivating all of these texts. That is clearly the case in the lists of the deity's names in certain epics that aim to shape not only opinion but also religious practice. The names, according to Enuma Elish, "must be grasped: the 'first one' should reveal (them), the wise and knowledgeable should ponder (them) together, the master should repeat, and make the pupil understand. The 'shepherd,' the 'herdsman' should pay attention" (Foster 1993, 400). In all these cases, the lists direct attention to the present in contrast to the stories' focus on the past, while reinforcing the stories' (and opening titles') celebration of the king or deity.[3]

   The sanctions that conclude many of these texts address a wide assortment of behaviors, from preservation of the text itself through reversals of the founder's donations/exemptions, to adherence to and promulgation of the text's political, legal, or religious instructions. Texts from every period and region frequently limit their sanctions to inveighing against destroying or ignoring the text itself. At stake are the reputation and interests of kings, empires, temple priesthoods, and property owners, each of whom has a considerable stake in the text's preservation because of the implications of its contents. Therefore, concluding sanctions encourage preservation of the unaltered texts as a central and sometimes sole emphasis.

Some texts' claims extend beyond exhortations against plagiarism or vandalism to exhortations in favor of certain kinds of behavior and against others. They claim influence over the reader's future for good or for ill, depending on the response. By describing the possible futures that depend on the readers' behavior, the sanctions complete the persuasive rhetoric begun by stories of the past that authorize the text and continued in lists describing conditions or applying obligations to the present. Thus the rhetoric of story, list, and sanction invokes the past, present, and future for purposes of persuasion.

The overtly persuasive goals of most of the texts mentioned above allow description of their rhetorical intentions and methods with some precision. It is much more difficult to judge their effectiveness at encouraging and discouraging certain behaviors in their readers. However, the extant record contains indications that this rhetoric was taken seriously by at least some people. Lichtheim provided one indication of its effectiveness by noting that Seti's son, Ramses II, completed the Abydos temple and established its endowment as specified in Seti's inscription (1976, 52). The grants and endowments of previous kings provided effective legal standing for temples long into the future: the Roman historian Tacitus reported that the people of Miles in the reign of the emperor Tiberius successfully defended the asylum rights of their temple on the basis of a five-hundred-year-old grant by the Persian emperor Darius (Tacitus, *Annals* 3.63). Of course, we cannot know whether the original inscription at Miles took the story–list–sanction form or any part of it, nor whether Ramses was influenced to fulfill his father's endowments by Seti's inscriptions or by other factors. Nevertheless, such references suggest that ancient sponsors and scribes could reasonably expect the rhetoric of their texts to wield influence over at least some readers.

Persuasion Across Cultures

The preceding survey shows that texts of various genres from diverse cultures, periods, and areas of ancient Near Eastern and Mediterranean societies employ the persuasive strategy of story–list–sanction. They include texts from third millennium B.C.E. Mesopotamia (Sumer and Akkad), second millennium Mesopotamia (Babylon, Assyria), Anatolia (Hittites), and Egypt, first millennium Mesopotamia (Babylon and Assyria), Egypt, Syro-Palestine (Phoenicia, Judea), and Anatolia (Greek/Lycian Xanthos under Persian rule). Yet the strategy is not typical of any particular textual genre in any of these cultures, but seems rather to have been adopted ad hoc to enhance the persua-siveness of particular texts.

How should the cross-cultural use of this strategy be explained? One can observe two common features of most, but not all, of the texts employing the complete pattern: most are inscriptions or copies of inscriptions, and most stem from royal circles. Those texts that do not presuppose public display in inscriptional form notably emphasize their public performance at regular in-tervals: treaties usually include among their stipulations regular readings of the treaty documents, epics emphasize the study and performance of their po-etic texts (see the lines from Enuma Elish quoted above; similarly Erra), and biblical Torah explicitly requires public readings and private study. Since al-most all reading in the ancient world took place aloud, and usually to an audi-ence, setting up an inscription presupposed its performance as well (cf. Judge 1997, 808). Thus all these texts presuppose the public presentation of their contents. Conversely, magical instructions that may have been intended for more private use employ only part of the story–list–sanction pattern. Neither do private letters use the strategy much, despite the fact that many letters have persuasion as their obvious motivation. The concluding sanctions in the pub-lic texts specify their audience more specifically as kings and state officials, though some expand it to include various other categories of people up to the general level of "anyone who ...." The prominence of state functionaries in the intended audience does not contradict the public orientation of this rhetoric. The sponsors of these texts aimed to persuade future rulers and their under-lings to particular courses of action or nonaction precisely by making their ar-guments publicly, so that their stories, lists, and sanctions would bring pres-sure to bear on those in power to accede to their demands.

That point brings us to the other common characteristic of the texts using the story–list–sanction strategy: their origins in royal circles. The state inter-ests expressed explicitly in the treaties, laws, and commemorative inscriptions also motivate the epic Enuma Elish that celebrates the ascendancy of Baby-lon's patron deity to "kingship" over the other deities. The notable exception to such royal patronage is biblical Torah that claims in its story of origins to be, not the consequence of, but rather the prior condition for Israel's constitu-tion as a people. Nevertheless, the effect of crediting biblical law to divine rather than royal origins is to cast God as Israel's king (Watts 1999, 91–109).

The story–list–sanction pattern thus represents a state rhetoric evoking past acts, present obligations, and future possibilities to persuade a public au-dience to conform to the ruler's wishes. I think the desire for a comprehensive rhetoric of persuasion best explains the sporadic appearance of the strategy in works of diverse genres, cultures, and time-periods. The attempt to cover past, present and future naturally leads to juxtaposing genres in some variant of the story–list–sanction form. This explanation need not rule out some role for cultural diffusion: the scribes that staffed royal bureaucracies often worked in multiple languages and scripts and were therefore familiar with the inscriptional and literary forms of cultures across the region. The possibility of the diffusion of literary forms between Mesopotamian, Hittite, Egyptian, Levantine, and Greek cultures increases the more such texts derive from scribal circles in royal courts.

Because the strategy employs a temporal structure that prefers, but does not require, particular genres to play particular roles (e.g. narratives of the past, curses for the future), it easily accommodates the various expressions demanded by a particular culture or situation. The wide diversity of materials labeled "list" in the above survey demonstrates this flexibility. Some of these texts hint at culturally distinct developments of the form. The most elaborate cultural adaptation of the story–list–sanction strategy appears in the Hebrew Bible, where the pattern welds together the Pentateuch's vast array of genres and materials into a single rhetoric encouraging loyalty to divine law and the Jerusalem priesthood (Watts 1999, 131–61). Since the Pentateuch was the first scripture of Judaism and remains its most important part, it became the model for the two parts of Christian scripture as well: an Old Testament of histories (story), anthologies (list), and prophecies (sanction), and a New Testament of Gospels (story), didactic letters (list), and an apocalypse (sanction). Christian emulation of the pattern was probably less the result of conscious analysis of its Pentateuchal form than of the desire to reproduce the Torah's persuasive force based in past divine acts, present obligations, and possible futures in the form of a larger structure that displaced the Torah's centrality as scripture. Thus the rhetoric of story–list–sanction shaped key collections of western scriptures (Torah, Christian Bible) and through them entered subsequent western rhetoric.

Story–List–Sanction in Western Rhetoric

The persuasive strategy behind the story–list–sanction pattern does not correspond to the rhetorical forms recommended by early Greek theorists. In fact, they deplored the persuasive use of stories and sanctions. Aristotle considered narration introductory and superfluous, necessary only for "weak" audiences incapable of grasping the logic of enthymemic proof (Rhetoric 3.13–14). O'Banion noted that for Aristotle, "Such concerns were unfortunate tasks preliminary to proceeding with what, at least to him, really mattered— the reasons and the evidence" (1992, 52). Though the Roman theorists Cicero and Quintilian later emphasized the importance of narrative, O'Banion argued that Aristotle's influence persisted in western academic tradition, so that narrative methods of argumentation became disassociated from the analytical methods of reason and proof, and isolated within the separate discipline of literary studies. Divine sanctions found even less place in the Greek theorist's repertoire of acceptable means of persuasion. They classified blessings and curses as "magic," with all the pejorative connotations that the term still evokes, and viewed them as techniques for manipulating an audience's emotions (Romilly 1975, 4–6, 16, 25–43, 82–85). Plato called for punishment of those who use such tactics: let "there be among us no working on the terrors of mankind—the most part of whom are as timorous as babes" (*Laws* XI 933a; cf. *Republic* II 364b–c). Thus they denounced persuasive uses of stories and sanctions as unethical manipulations of an audience that diverted rhetoric from its proper goal, namely the rational demonstration of truth.

These normative claims by the Greek theorists show the prevalence of components of the story–list–sanction strategy in the Greek culture familiar to them. The full pattern is suggested by Plato's sarcastic description of the religious literature of his day:

> They produce a bushel of books of Musaeus and Orpheus, the offspring of the Moon and of the Muses, as they affirm, and these books they use in their ritual, and make not only ordinary men but states believe that there really are remissions of sins and purifications for deeds of injustice, by means of sacrifice and pleasant sport for the living, and that there are also special rites for the defunct, which they call functions, that deliver us from evils in that other world, while terrible things await those who have neglected to sacrifice (*Republic* II 364e–365a, trans. P. Shorey).

Here the reference to divine origins suggests a story that authorizes the contents of the books, their use in ritual indicates that their contents include didactic lists, and the enumeration of their various consequences points to divine sanctions, though without the texts themselves we cannot be sure that the strategy structured this literature. Be that as it may, the Greek theorists' misgivings about the rhetorical uses of stories and sanctions point out the use of these means of persuasion in ancient Greek society, as in the other cultures of the Near East and Mediterranean.

Their reaction against such practices also explains the negative evaluations of such methods common in much rhetorical theory in later periods. Broadly speaking, Aristotle's elevation of reason over narration, to say nothing of threats and promises, emphasized an elitist ideal of rational education over a populist strategy for mass persuasion. While rational method became increasingly paramount in medieval and modern academic institutions, mass persuasion has remained a major emphasis of western religious and political discourse. Thus the Greek philosopher's attack on the Sophists laid the basis for the institutional separation of philosophy from religion in western cultures, as well as distinguishing more generally between academic and popular discourse.

Space does not permit a full demonstration of the use of the story–list–sanction strategy in later periods, so I will simply point out some examples of the ongoing influence of this strategy. The relationship between narratives and lists of laws has been and remains a concern in legal studies. Medieval European collections of law appeared in manuscripts surrounded by historical narratives, genealogies and episcopal lists, a combination motivated by their intended use for public presentation (Richards 1986, 187). Explicit narrative contexts have faded from more recent western legal collections along with the expectation of religious promulgation. Yet Robert Cover has argued that law necessarily still invokes an implicit narrative for its justification (1983, 4). As the stories change that are applied to laws, legal interpretation changes to match. Cover's argument suggests that the persuasive strategy of combining story with list remains a potent part of contemporary legal and political discourse.

Divine sanctions found a reflection in some medieval manuscripts of laws and historical narratives that include rites of exorcism and excommunication near their end (Richards 1986, 196). On the other hand, they seem to have disappeared from modern legal contexts, now fully replaced by the judicial sanctions warranted in the laws themselves. Divine sanctions do remain a staple of much modern religious commentary on political and social affairs, but like threats of judicial penalties, these discourses tend to inhabit their own distinct texts and institutions. However, a secular language of threat and promise does still appear in political discourse.

Political speeches often preserve the full story–list–sanction form through their evocation of the past and their use of promises and warnings to motivate particular courses of action in the present. To cite only a single famous example, Martin Luther King Jr.'s speech in 1963 to the crowds assembled for the March on Washington cited the Emancipation Proclamation of a century earlier to introduce a description of African-Americans' circumstances in the more recent past and present (story), then called for change with a series of phrases beginning "Now is the time to . . ." (list), before warning of social turmoil if change is not forthcoming (sanction). More exhortations and narratives intervened before the speech reaches its memorable climax in the positive sanctions of "I have a dream . . . ," followed by the repeated exhortation to "Let freedom ring" and the final promise of freedom for all. Modern political discourse frequently weaves together these formal components, if rarely so skillfully.

These few indications of the effects on western rhetorical practice of the story–list–sanction strategy suggest that the distinction between modern academic, religious, political, and legal discourse was not just produced by the dictates of the classical theorists, but also by the ancient modes of persuasion against which they reacted. Some ancient rhetorical forms have survived alongside the arguments of theorists who rejected them, thereby institutionalizing that conflict in the social structures that shape contemporary public discourse.

Notes

1. From Egypt, e.g. the Book of the Dead 175 (Hallo and Younger 1997, 27–30) and the Legend of Isis and the Name of Re (Hallo and Younger 1997, 33–34); from Ugarit, e.g. "El's Banquet" and other texts cited and translated by N. Wyatt (1998, 404–413); from the Hittites, see also Telipinu and the Daughter of the Sea (Hoffner 1990, 25–26, though a break between the myth and the ritual provisions obscures the nature of their connection) and the Disappearance of the Sun God which, according to its last lines, when it is used as a successful incantation requires specific thank offerings: ". . . may he give you nine (sacrificial animals). And may the poor man give you one sheep" (1990, 26–28).

2. George Mendenhall's discovery of this pattern in both biblical law and Hittite treaties advanced the analysis of the Pentateuch's rhetorical impact, but failed to equate convincingly the biblical genre only with treaties (cf. McCarthy 1981). Modifications of the pattern's elements and contents, rather than being simply internal developments of Israel's covenant traditions, are in fact characteristic of the pattern's appearance in ancient literatures.

3. A possible exception to this analysis appears in the Buhen stela, where the list simply enumerates the human "plunder" (dead and alive) gained in the campaign. The stela, however, was found not in the royal court but in the region where the war took place, and therefore was probably intended to dissuade further attacks on Egyptian territory.

Works Cited

Aristotle. *Rhetoric*. Tr. W. Rhys Roberts. 1954. In *The Rhetorics and Poetics of Aristotle*. New York: Random House.

Beckman, Gary. 1996. *Hittite Diplomatic Texts*. Atlanta: Scholars Press/Society of Biblical Literature.

Burke, Kenneth. 1950. *A Rhetoric of Motives*. Berkeley: University of California Press.

Charlesworth, James H., ed. 1983. *The Old Testament Pseudepigrapha*. 2 vols. Garden City, NY: Doubleday.

Cover, Robert M. 1983. "Forward: *Nomos* and Narrative." *Harvard Law Review* 97/1:4–68.

Foster, Benjamin. 1993. *Before the Muses: An Anthology of Akkadian Literature.* 2 vols. Bethesda, MD: CDL Press.

Greenstein, E. L. 1995. "Autobiographies in Ancient Western Asia." In vol. 4 of *Civilizations of the Ancient Near East.* Ed. J. L. Sasson. New York: Scribners.

Hallo, W. W., and K. L. Younger Jr., eds. 1997, 2000, 2002. *The Context of Scripture: Canonical Compositions, Monumental Inscriptions, and Archival Documents from the Biblical World.* 3 vols. Leiden: Brill.

Hoffner, Harry A. Jr. 1990. *Hittite Myths.* Atlanta: Scholars Press/SBL.

Judge, Edwin A. 1997. "The Rhetoric of Inscriptions." *Handbook of Classical Rhetoric in the Hellenistic Period, 330 B.C.–A.D. 400.* Ed. S. E. Porter. Leiden: Brill.

Lichtheim, Miriam. 1973, 1976, 1980. *Ancient Egyptian Literature.* 3 vols. Berkeley: University of California Press.

McCarthy, D. J. 1981. *Treaty and Covenant: A Study in Form in the Ancient Oriental Documents and in the Old Testament.* 2nd rev. ed. Rome: Pontifical Biblical Institute.

Mendenhall, G. E. 1970. "Covenant Forms in Israelite Tradition." *Biblical Archeologist Review 3.* Ed. E. F. Campbell Jr. & D. N. Freedman. Garden City, NY: Doubleday.

Metzger, Henri. 1979. *Fouilles de Xanthos, Tome VI: La stèle trilingue du Létôon.* Paris: Librairie C. Klincksieck.

Murnane, William J. 1995. *Texts from the Amarna Period in Egypt.* Atlanta: Scholars Press/Society of Biblical Literature.

O'Banion, John D. 1992. *Reorienting Rhetoric: the Dialectic of List and Story.* University Park, PA: Pennsylvania State University Press.

Plato. *Laws.* Trans. P. Shorey. 1961. In *The Collected Dialogues of Plato.* Ed. E. Hamilton and H. Cairns. Princeton, NJ: Princeton University Press.

Plato. *Republic.* Trans. P. Shorey. 1961. In *The Collected Dialogues of Plato.* Ed. E. Hamilton and H. Cairns. Princeton, NJ: Princeton University Press.

Richards, Mary P. 1986. "The Manuscript Contexts of the Old English Laws: Tradition and Innovation." In *Studies in Earlier Old English Prose.* Ed. P. E. Szarmach. Albany, NY: State University of New York Press.

Romilly, J. de. 1975. *Magic and Rhetoric in Ancient Greece.* Cambridge, MA: Harvard University Press.

Roth, Martha. 1995. *Law Collections from Mesopotamia and Asia Minor.* Atlanta: Scholars Press/SBL.

Tacitus. *Annals.* In *Tacitus: The Annals of Imperial Rome.* T. M. Grant. Rev. ed. London: Viking Penguin, 1956.

Thomas, Rosalind. 1992. *Literacy and Orality in Ancient Greece.* Cambridge: Cambridge University Press.

Watts, James W. 1999. *Reading Law: the Rhetorical Shaping of the Pentateuch.* The Biblical Seminar 59. Sheffield: Sheffield Academic Press/London: Continuum.

Wyatt, N. 1998. *Religious Texts from Ugarit: The Words of Ilimilku and his Colleagues.* The Biblical Seminar 53. Sheffield: Sheffield Academic Press/London: Continuum.

Younger, K. Lawson. 1998. "The Phoenician Inscription of Azatiwada: An Integrated Reading," *Journal of Semitic Studies* 43:11–47.

Song to Speech: The Origins of Early Epitaphia in Ancient Near Eastern Women's Lamentations

C. Jan Swearingen

Two approaches to the study of rhetoric before and outside of Greek rhetoric inform this study. Until recently the most common approach has been to use a classical Greek model and find the closest counterpart in a nonwestern or pre-Greek western culture. George Kennedy's recent *Comparative Rhetoric* continues his preeminent work as a pioneer in the field. Using classical models, he finds epideictic, judicial, and deliberative genres in Ancient Near Eastern, Chinese, and Native American cultures—among others. Kennedy's *New Testament Interpretation Through Rhetorical Criticism* uses a similar methodology to define different rhetorical genres as well as uses of ethos, pathos, and logos in a variety of New Testament passages. The strength of this method is that it builds on the familiar and brings into the domain of an already defined rhetoric a group of cultures and languages that had heretofore been excluded from rhetorical analysis.

An alternative approach to nontraditional, excluded, or pre-Greek or nonwestern rhetorics has been developed among ethno-rhetoricians who adopt an emic rather than an etic approach, and prefer to study the "rhetoric" of the Other in its own terms rather than in ours. This approach has the advantage of looking for subtle differences in names for rhetorical genres, purposes, and "proofs": ethos, pathos, and logos. An examination of what we think of as rhetoric in the terms given it within another culture can also reveal the limits of our definitions, and enrich them with alternative understandings. In a chronological sequence, a combined emic and etic approach can look for ancestors to what later became Greek rhetoric and its subdivisions.

The following analysis of women's songs and lamentations in the ancient Near East combines both approaches. Long before male epitaphiasts spoke orations honoring the war dead, women composed and performed songs of celebration and lamentation. It is Miriam, along with Moses, who sings the song of victory at the Red Sea.

Deborah was a judge in premonarchal Israel and leads her people in singing the great songs of victory and lament that are precursors to the Psalms. The Sumerian Enheduanna sings the song of her own downfall and restoration as a priestess. In seventh century B.C.E. Lesbos, near Asia Minor, Sappho composed and taught the composition of songs of love, birth, marriage, and death. In most ancient Near Eastern cultures the task of mourning and lamentation was especially assigned to women who, in choruses, would commemorate the passage from life to death. Mary Douglas's *Purity and Danger,* and Margaret Alexiou's *The Ritual Lament in Greek Tradition* are two among many studies that explain why women, who attend and give birth, in many cultures also perform the rituals surrounding death. Cultural anthropologists of boundaries, such as Douglas and Alexiou, explain that women are liminal, betwixt and between, close to death in giving birth, and unafraid of death in escorting souls through the transition out of life. In a study that includes present day Greece, Alexiou examines the roles of women mourners in both family and professional settings in a continuum with the traditions of the past.

When and how did the women singers and mourners of the ancient Near East become sequestered by laws, such as Solon's, stipulating that women could no longer appear in public ceremonies of mourning, and only in private ceremonies in family homes? At what point did the public political ceremony of the funeral oration come to replace the earlier religious rituals of lamentation and song at the burial? What elements of the funeral oration as we have it in the earliest Athenian models, might have been borrowed or adapted from the songs of lamentations sung by women to commemorate the dead?

Women's rhetorical teaching and practice is emblematized in Plato's *Menexenos,* where Aspasia is depicted teaching Socrates a model for an epitaphios, the funeral oration that was one of the first genres taught in rhetorical schools. Some scholars consider this depiction of Aspasia a joke, on rhetoric and on women, that Plato is using to demean rhetoric and women (Waithe). Yet there is an historical backdrop preserved in this account which, unravelled, allows us to see Aspasia as a trace of the women who taught and led religious ceremonies in Milesia, her home. Near Milesia, Sappho's Lesbos was a similar center of women's learning, teaching, and practice of ritual songs. Asia Minor, then, seems to have been the home of more women's schools than the area around Athens, especially after Athenian annexations of nearby cities such as Mantinea effectively dispersed and exiled groups of Pythagorean women teachers (Waithe). Plato's portrait of Aspasia—via Socrates—in the *Menexenos* may reflect the growing dislike for Pericles' imports after the Persian campaign: including Aspasia and rhetoric. Her teaching of rhetoric along with other sophists came to be associated with foreign influences that Athenians increasingly associated with economic and cultural ruin.

If we go before and beyond the Athenian Greeks of the fifth and fourth centuries B.C.E., we can observe throughout the ancient Near East a number of roles played by women as teachers and composers of ceremonial songs of celebration, worship, and lamentation. Biblical women such as Deborah and Miriam are in the premonarchal period depicted as leaders and singers of songs of victory in war (Meyers, Frymer-Kensky). The patterns and genres of ceremonial song taught and practiced by women parallel the patterns later adopted by the male epitaphiasts in Athens. Although they were spoken rather than sung—an additional gender difference of interest— the first rhetorical epitaphia in Athens bear traces of earlier song traditions, some of them composed and performed by women, as it was traditional for women to perform the lamentations at burials (Ochs, Alexiou). Among the earliest "praise singers," women in early Greek and ancient Near Eastern traditions have too often been demoted to "keening" women, wailing without words, art, or language (Alexiou). It is time to correct this portrait.

Contemporary interpreters of Homeric and biblical representations of women's songs and prophecies are reinstating intellectual content and political agency to genres practiced by women in ancient texts. Antigone, Hecuba, Cassandra, and Clytemnestra in Greek Homeric sagas and plays are being reexamined alongside Miriam, Deborah, and Mary in the Hebrew Scriptures and New Testament. Readings of the roles and voices of women in ancient texts are actively directed at reclaiming meaning and agency for these voices. In a novel refiguring the character of Cassandra that we have viewed through Athenian drama, German novelist Christa Wolf recreates Cassandra's reflections on her role as a seer and prophetess, priestess and princess of Troy, in ancient Asia Minor.

> Words. Everything I tried to convey about that experience was, is paraphrase. We have no name for what spoke out of me. I was its mouth and not of my own free will. It was the enemy who spread that tale that I spoke the "truth" and that you all would not listen to me. For the Greeks there is no alternative but either truth or lies. . . . It is the other alternative that they crush between their clear-cut distinctions, the third alternative which in their view does not exist, the smiling vital force that is able to generate itself from itself over and over: the undivided, spirit in life, life in spirit. (107)

She comes to take refuge in her ceremonial role even after despair about the Greek presence and ways of thinking has eroded her beliefs. "I taught the young priestesses the difficult skill of speaking in choruses, enjoyed the solemn atmosphere on the high feast days" (98). From the perspective of the Trojans, the gods of the Greeks are self proclaimed lies, fictions in the theatre of Dionysus, mastheads for war and excuses for murder. The great horse the Greeks have brought, the gift of an "Athena" totally unlike the Athena Cassandra reveres, is accepted in a frenzy by the Trojans. Cassandra's voice is no longer heard at all.

> The Trojans laughed at my screeches. I shrieked, pleaded, adjured, and spoke in tongues. Eumeolos [her fellow priest]. I saw the face which you forget from time to time and which for that reason is permanent. Expressionless. Pitiless. Unteachable. Even if he believed me he would not oppose the Trojans, and maybe get himself killed. He, for one, intended to survive he said.
>
> Now I understood what the God had ordained. "You will speak the truth but no one will believe you." Here stood the No One who had to believe me, but he could not because he believed nothing. A No One incapable of belief.
>
> I cursed the god Apollo. (136)

Cassandra's role is to speak as a vehicle for a common voice, view, and sensibility. What she speaks enunciates the people as a whole, a vox populi, a common voice that is the undivided spirit in life and life in spirit of the community. Cassandra is also responsible for teaching apt students to speak in the ceremonial way, in chorus, in harmony. Remnants of this tradition, fragmentary remains, but thereby evidence of its existence, survive in the chorus of Athenian drama.

Wolf's depiction of Cassandra's speech, and of her understanding of its powers, exemplifies but also questions views of priestly, prophetic, and ritual speech in primary oral cultures. Performers of rituals past and present are today often depicted as invoking or evoking superstition rather than as promoting persuasive discourses of appeals to volitional belief and affirmation (Kinneavy). The line between religious and secular discourse, primitive and advanced cultures, religious and rhetorical discourse, has often been drawn on just this basis. Questioning the late nineteenth century enthusiasm for Dionysian and Bacchic rites as ecstatic abandon and even sanctioned violence, Jane Ellen Harrison's *Themis* (1927) emphasizes the judiciousness, balance, and beauty in what have come down to us as the early Greek "mysteries"—rituals that were inculcated and practiced in a range of different modes of consciousness and discourse. A line of inquiry that parallels Harrison's and Wolf's has also been advanced in recent studies of premonarchic Israel, revised accounts not only of its social structure—no centralized government, no structured politics, no sense of public as distinct from private or domestic domain—but also of the roles of women in the "primitive" political and economic social structures of Exodus, and Judges (Meyers, Murphy 50–55). In these studies the songs of Miriam, Deborah, and Mary the mother of Jesus are receiving special attention as preserved remnants of traditions that were almost undoubtedly more widespread than the canonical records indicate. And in all cases, birth, death, celebration of victory, and prophecy are included in the genres spoken by women, enunciating the voice of the people, in song. Not keening without meaning; but song with full-throttle meaning.

Biblical representations of women as speakers and leaders are obscured by fragmentary preservation—only traces are left. The same handmaid Miriam who "finds" Moses in the bulrushes, and persuades Pharaoh's daughter to raise him as her own later sings the song of victory at the Red Sea; a second introduction to the song (Numbers 12.15 and 20.1) describes it as "sung by the prophet Miriam, Aaron's sister." Later, Miriam is afflicted with leprosy, exiled, and dies in the wilderness of Zin: a warning? Texts from the ancient Near East preserve timeline after timeline in which women are removed from earlier positions of power, leadership, and religious status, a transition which in many cases accompanies the onset of literacy and with it canonical texts. In the emergence of kingdoms and city states based on land ownership, older virtues of collective shared value, property, and meaning were gradually replaced by higher emphasis upon individualism, individual family ownership of land and wealth, patriarchal family and government structures, and, in the case of Athens, the emergence of secular prose rhetoric.

Earlier Greek concepts of persuasion (*peitho*) had been positive and closely tied to religious inspiration and belief. By the time of the pre-Socratics, beginning in the fifth century, belief (*pistis*) and *pisteuein* (*to persuade*) began to acquire negative meanings related to deception. The double meaning accorded *pistis* in early Greek thinking is treated with illuminating detail in James Kinneavy's study, *Greek Rhetorical Origins of Christian Faith*. He shows that the occurrence and meaning of the words *pistis* (belief) and *pisteuein* (to persuade) show two things: that early Christians were familiar with these rhetorical terms, and that they appropriated them to more positive meanings than they held in the first century B.C. By that time the earlier positive meanings of Peitho, Aphrodite's daughter, had degenerated into the sophistical performances of the Greek and Roman rhetorical schools. The revival of the positive meanings of *peitho* and *pisteuein* by Christians included the adoption of *pistis* to denote not just "mere" belief or opinion, but faith. Similarly, *pisteuein* came to denote the process of volitional assent to change in faith, or, conversion. Recent studies of the Corinthian women prophets, at whom Paul directed his infamous "women shall be silent in church" trace the women's traditions in Asia Minor as priestesses of Cybele (Aphrodite), and their special prominence as leaders and acclaimed speakers in the church community at Corinth (Wire).

Both the process of persuasion by speech, and the relationship of such persuasion to "belief" and "faith" are widely discussed among the early Greek rhetors: Gorgias and Pericles, Isocrates and Demosthenes.

What we need to recover are the self-conscious reflections of women singers of songs, and composers of ceremonial verse whose practices, and whose beliefs about their practices, shaped the common language of the culture before the emergence of city-states and male prose rhetoric. Among other recent recoveries are Pythagorean teachings preserved among Presocratic fragments, particularly Empedocles' renderings of love and discourse as unifying principles of the psyche and of the universe. Like the Mantineans, the Pythagoreans were dispersed during and after the time of the Peloponnesian Wars. Pythagorean communities throughout Magna Graeca were scattered; many of their teachers were forced into hiding (Waithe 11, 59–74). Among the Pythagoreans were a group of women healers, flourishing in the seventh century B.C.E., contemporary to Sappho. Plato's mother is reported to have been a part of this tradition, suggesting that his frequent likening of himself and his philosophy to midwifery may be more than jest, irony, or appropriation of feminine images. His depiction of discourse and love, and his characterization of Diotima bear a strong resemblance to Pythagorean teachings that would have been well known to his auditors. At the center of Pythagorean teaching was the notion of Harmony, a whole in nature, society, and the psyche that could be brought about by teaching new principles of natural and social union. Many elements in Pythagorean teaching, and parallel themes in Empedocles, can be aligned without great difficulty with the notions of divine-human complementarity and of ever-changing qualities and elements that are represented in Diotima's teaching. The theme of the unity of discourse, lovers, and wisdom is sustained throughout the *Symposium* and elsewhere in Plato's dialogues (Waithe 69–71).

Jane Ellen Harrison's analyses of the fragmentation of earlier Greek religion and social beliefs as Olympian religion supplanted the earlier veneration of Demeter, or Ge. She postulates that the earlier religion had

> in it two elements, social custon, [*nomos*], the collective conscience, and the emphasis and representation of that collective conscience. . . . Two factors indissolubly linked: ritual, that is custom, collective action, and myth or theology, the representation of the collective emotion, the collective conscience. And—a point of supreme importance—both are incumbent, binding, and interdependent. Morality is the social conscience made imperative upon our actions, but morality unlike religion save on questions involving conduct, leaves our

thoughts free. Art, which is also, like religion, a representation of the social conscience, has no incumbencies. She imposes no obligation on either action or thought. Her goddess is Peitho, not Themis. (Harrison, *Themis* 249n.4, 513–14)

It is Peitho, "Aphrodite's daughter" according to Sappho, who beguiles mortal hearts with her arts of persuasion. The Peitho of Sappho's description is far gentler and more beautiful than the later characterizations of Peitho as rhetorical seduction in the world of men.

In the *Symposium,* Diotima's speech depicts Love as a daimon, an intermediate spirit that moves, through discourse, between divine and human. Harrison's work allows us to observe the parallelism between Diotima's depiction of Love and slightly earlier understandings of Daimon in Greek religion. Her study integrates phenomena seldom considered in relation to one another: magic, manna, tabu, Olympic games, the Drama, Sacramentalism, Carnivals, Hero-worship, Initiation, Ceremonies, and the Platonic doctrine of Anamnesis (544). The death cult represented by the Olympic games in celebration of the war dead celebrates blood and life through a symbolic algebra strikingly different from the cult in which Herakles, for example must spend time beneath the earth, with Omphale, dressed as a woman, in order to reemerge stronger into the world of men (Kintz 116–118; Wolf 269).

Harrison reminds us, via Cornford, that it is not until the late fifth century, the time of Socrates and Antiphon, that the contrast between the law of Nature *(Phusis)* and human law *(Nomos)* appears, marking one of the earliest explicit recognitions in Greek tradition that social laws are not divine institutions (42). Reflecting the high premium placed on individuality and upon intellectual and moral autonomy that was developed in late nineteenth-century scholarship, though not adhered to by Harrison, Cornford asserts as an axiom:

In the last resort, every individual must see and judge for himself what it is good for him to do. The individual, if he is to be a complete man, must become morally autonomous, and take his own life into his own control" (46).

Individualism and distance from emotion, love, the body, and women were intricately interconnected in this shifting of symbols and rituals.

Dionysus, Harrison emphasizes, first emerged as a symbol of social and political collectivity supplanting the muses and the ineffable Themis. The narration of the mysteries provided in Diotima's speech has been interpreted as an appropriation of earlier ritual traditions (Harrison) and as asceticizing physical love, as a ladder of ascent out of and transcending "brute" physical desire, passion, and reproduction. Her narration may also be seen as doubling the ritual birth narrative employed in the mysteries and taught by women teachers and priestesses, represented by Diotima. In this teaching, love and discourse are seen as mutually intersubjective, consubstantial, and harmonic; Diotima's ladder takes Socrates toward and not away from participation, substance, and the production of discourse as a medium of love, birth, and life. Her speech, like Aspasia's, provides many hints of an earlier group of teachings widely associated with women as teachers and celebrants of the rites governing birth, love, procreation, and death.

The Athenian topos (Loraux) developed in Aspasia's epitaphios is a topos of origin and identity, a complex of metaphors and imagery that effected a rewriting of history, citizenship, and pan-Hellenic nationalism. As self-imaging, the Athenian topos was as important as Phidias' statue of Athena in consolidating Pericles's Athenian empire. Aspasia's speech in the *Menexenos* brings together and exaggerates with chiaroscuro brushstrokes the elements in the Athenian topos that can be found in parallel epitaphia: Pericles, of course, but also Demosthenes, Lysias, Lycurgus, and Isocrates (Loraux 65–69).

Isocrates and Demosthenes give special emphasis to Athenian purity, derived from pureness of birth and loyalty to fatherland over family. The Eleusinian trait of *andreia*—a feminine word meaning "reborn"—is enlisted in the service of the state to become *Andres*—the citizen-man who is twice born and purified in his patronymic and patrilineal definitions and allegiances. Athenians are enjoined to leave their birth parents and be cleansed—born again—in uniting with the polis as both father and mother. The citizenship conferred by the polis on select males is to be further purified and preserved by restricting citizenship to those born of a citizen father and a mother whose father was a citizen. Ironically, this Periclean law rendered the son of Pericles and Aspasia a noncitizen. And is that part of the irony of Plato's rendition of Aspasia's speech, emphasizing again and again that Athenians are not born of immigrants, are not like the strangers in the land born of foreigners?

Several elements in the Athenian topos of identity (Loraux 8) and origin answer the question, are Athenian men born from earth or from women? Repeating the claim that Athenian *Andres*—males that were also citizens—sprung from the earth of the Athenian polis, evokes an image of collective autochthony, fatherless self-birth from mother earth—Ge. However, the metaphors of the polis and fatherland don't work out that way. Like Athena, Athenians are motherless children. The earth from which they are born is the desacralised public space of the polis's burial ground.

The funeral oration delivered in the Kerameikos, the official public burial ground, recites and reenacts the war hero-citizen's birth, as it returns the war dead to the *chora* (Loraux 94:42), the soil of the polis that—each epitaphia asserts—is their true, pure birthplace. The gender elements in the Athenian topos eclipse Ge (Loraux 66)—Demeter and the Demeter cult—through idealizing the polis as the sacred earth (chora) of the burial ground, the polis-pater, in whose public space is delivered the obligatory ritual of the funeral oration. The words of the funeral oration themselves become a subject of the Athenian topos—they are sharply and explicitly distinguished from the lamentations of women, hymns, and the poets' lies. These are official, rational words in the public space, of males, by males, and for males. The official story alludes only indirectly to "the poets' tales" of origin, and by so designating them renders myth pure fiction.

Aspasia's speech in the *Menexenos* begins:

> In respect of deeds, these men have received at our hands what is due unto them; they have been escorted forth in solemn procession publically by the city and privately by their kinfolk. But in respect of words, the honor that remains still due to these heroes the law enjoins us, and it is right, to pay in full. For it is by means of speech finely spoken that deeds nobly done gain memory and renown (Jowett 341).

Providing an account of the exploits of the heroes provides a second point of self-reflexive commentary.

> Those exploits for which as yet no poet has received worthy renown for worthy cause, and which lie still buried in oblivion, I ought, I think, to celebrate, not only in praising them myself but providing material for others to build up into odes and other forms of poetry in a manner worthy of those deeds (Jowett 349).

An important part of the Athenian topos is that "the poets' praises" are not needed by rational Athens and her cerebral, martial goddess. Thus, Pericles asserts,

> We have not left our power without witness, but have shown it by mighty proofs; and far from needing a Homer for our panegyrist, or other of his craft whose verses might charm for the moment only for the impression which they gave to melt at the touch of fact, we have forced every sea and land to be the highway of our daring (II.41).

In the "poets'" story of the birth of Erichthonios—the autochthonic forbear of the Athenian people—the older Demeter myth of origins from life-giving earth are supplanted by Ge handing over the newborn to Athena, who receives him, legitimizes him, and recognizes him as her own. Erichthonios is no longer an offspring of the earth—a citizen of the world—he is now the "son of Athena" with Athena assuming the paternal role of name-giver. In the secular, and prose, discourse of the funeral oration in the Kerameikos—the burial ground where the orations are delivered—"there is no reference to Athena; there is no Ge and no Erichthonios. The myth has been displaced and rationalized. Demosthenes' funeral oration distinguishes first birth from father and mother from the second and more important identity assumed when 'each man attaches himself to a father, and everyone attached collectively to the fatherland'" (quoted in Loraux 65). The secular state prose of the funeral oration establishes the abstraction of the city in a formula of metaphors whose gender is central. The hyperbole with which Plato emphasizes the epitaphiasts' metaphors of identity and birth in the *Menexenos* merit much further scrutiny; the import, or irony, of the emphasis remains ambiguous.

Aspasia's epitaphios as recounted by Socrates and represented by Plato is doubtless meant to say something. But what, and what about? About Pericles and the circle of Sophists that had come under increasing censure as the Peloponnesian War drained Athenian coffers? Very probably. Mock Pericles by mocking his consort's speech, and by alleging that she, not he, composed his well known oration? About rhetoric, and its capacity to make people believe that their history and their identity are other than they are? Very likely, with Socrates saying as much just before he delivers Aspasia's speech, and by stating, with indeterminate humor, that he and Pericles were both taught rhetoric by Aspasia. This series of indictments is an important backdrop for the metaphors of purity of birth, identity and citizenship that pervade the first sections of the *Menexenos*. Yet because these elements in the Athenian topos represented in Aspasia's speech occur in other orations as well, her speech cannot be entirely dismissed as a joke (Waithe), despite the fact that the classical philologists of the eighteenth and nineteenth centuries held that it was patently ludicrous for Plato to depict a woman speaking and to have Socrates refer to her as his teacher and as Pericles' ghostwriter. More recent readers have observed the preservation in the *Menexenos* of what by then had become stock juxtapositions: public praise vs. private family lamentations; the wailing womenfolk contrasted to the sober prose rationality of the epitaphiast. At the very least, Aspasia's rendition of these commonplaces presents us with a complex irony (Loraux) operating on several levels, for she was a woman, a foreigner, and the mother of Pericles' son, for whom Pericles sought to reverse his own laws regarding citizenship and purity of parenthood.

What does the Athenian topos of identity—whose themes are gathered together and highlighted in Aspasia's speech—displace or replace? We are indebted to the work that his been done on this question—and especially on the encoding of gender in Greek antiquity—by Page duBois, Mary Ellen Waithe, Martha Nussbaum, Jacqueline de Romilly, Nicole Loraux, Cheryl Glenn, Susan Biesecker, and Susan Jarratt. Extending their analysis, I emphasize very pointedly that the *Menexenus* portrays a speech **by** a woman and **about** rhetoric, that Aspasia's speech as spoken by Socrates is simultaneously a rhetorical oration, and, like Isocrates' speeches, a handbook of composition:

> How could we praise these valiant men, who in their lifetime delighted their friends by their virtue, and purchased the safety of the living by their deaths? We ought, in my judgment, to adopt the natural order in our praise, even as the men themselves were natural in their virtue. First, then, let us eulogize their nobility of birth, and second their nurture and training: then we shall exhibit the character of their exploits, how nobly and worthily they wrought them (Jowett 341).

Like Sappho, Aspasia is both a practitioner of rhetoric and a teacher of rhetoric. In this speech she is both simultaneously. She not only practices what she preaches; she teaches as she preaches. Aspasia's voice and others like hers were soundly silenced by the later rhetorical tradition.

Antigone cannot bury her brother and is forbidden to speak of him in public. Finally, Creon rebukes her for speaking in public at all. She puns that her bridal bed, her hearth, her home, will be her tomb. In whose *chora* do she and her brother rest? Pericles applauds the virtuous Athenian widow: "Greatest will be her glory who is least talked about among the men, whether for good or for bad" (II.45). To speculate about what speeches might have been spoken by women as composers of funeral "orations"—but then they were songs— before the Athenian Greek consolidation of a rhetorical canon, we must look at the traces we have of those earlier practices in the better documented epitaphia. For the "Greek enlightenment" was also an endarkenment of those who had for centuries been stage center, in culture and religion, the women who sang the lullabies not only for the newborn, but for the dead as well.

Works Cited

Alexiou, Margaret. The Ritual Lament in Greek Tradition. Cambridge: Cambridge University Press, 1974.

Bloedow, Edmund F. "Aspasia and the Mystery of the *Menexenos." Weiner Studien. (Zeitschrift fur Klassiche Philologie und Patristic) Neu Folge* 9 (1975): 32–48.

Calame, Claude. *The Craft of Poetic Speech in Ancient Greece*. Ithaca, NY: Cornell University Press, 1995.

_____. *Choruses of Young Women in Ancient Greece: Their Morphology, Religious Role, and Social Function*. Trans. Derek Collins and Jane Orion. Lanham, MD: Rowman and Littlefield, 1997.

Douglas, Mary. *Purity and Danger: An Analysis of the Concepts of Pollution and Taboo*. Chicago and London: Routledge, 1984.

Eriksson, Anders. "'Women Tongue Speakers Be Silent': A Reconstruction Through Paul's Rhetoric." *Biblical Interpretation* 6:1 (1998) 80–104.

Fornara, Charles W. and Loren J. Samons. *Athens from Cleisthenes to Pericles*. Berkeley: University of California Press, 1991.

Foley, Helene P. *The Homeric Hymn to Demeter: Translation, Commentary, Interpretive Essays*. Princeton, NJ: Princeton University Press, 1994.

Frymer-Kensky, Tikva. *In the Wake of the Goddesses: Women, Culture, and the Biblical Transformation of Ancient Myth*. New York: Free Press, 1992.

Glenn, Cheryl. "Refiguring Aspasia in the History of Rhetoric." *College Composition and Communication* 45:2 (May 1994): 180–200.

Harrison, Jane Ellen. *Themis, A Study of the Social Origins of Greek Religion* (2nd edition, 1927). New Hyde Park, NY: University Books, 1966.

Henry, Madeleine. *Prisoner of History: Aspasia of Miletus and Her Biographical Tradition*. New York: Oxford University Press, 1995.

Hobbs, Thomas. Trans. Thucydides. *History of the Peloponnesian Wars*. Chicago: University of Chicago Press, 1989.

Jarratt, Susan, and Rory Ong. "Aspasia: Rhetoric, Gender, and Colonial Ideology." *Reclaiming Rhetorica*. Andrea Lunsford, ed. Pittsburgh, PA: University of Pittsburgh Press, 1995; 25–52.

Jowett, Benjamin, trans. *The Dialogues of Plato*. New York: Random House, 1937.

Kagan, Donald. *Pericles of Athens and the Birth of Democracy*. New York: Free Press, 1991.

Kennedy, George. *Comparative Rhetoric*. New York: Oxford University Press, 2000.

Kennedy, George. *New Testament Interpretation Through Rhetorical Criticism*. Chapel Hill: University of North Carolina Press, 1984.

Kinneavy, James. *Greek Rhetorical Origins of Christian Faith*. New York: Oxford University Press, 1987.

Kintz, Linda. *The Subject's Tragedy. Political Poetics, Feminist Theory, and Drama*. Ann Arbor: University of Michigan Press, 1992.

Lewis, D. M., John Boardman, J. K. Davies, and M. Ostwald. *The Cambridge Ancient History.* Second Edition. Volume 5. The Fifth Century. New York and Cambridge: Cambridge University Press, 1992.

Loraux, Nicole. *The Children of Athena: Athenian Ideas About Citizenship and the Division Between the Sexes.* Trans. Caroline Levine. Princeton, NJ: Princeton University Press, 1993.

Meyers, Carol. *Discovering Eve: Ancient Israelite Women in Context.* New York: Oxford University Press, 1988.

Murphy, Cullen. "Women and the Bible." *Atlantic Monthly* 272:2 (August 1993): 39–64.

Ochs, Donovan. *Consolatory Rhetoric.* Chapel Hill: University of North Carolina Press, 1983.

Romilly, Jacqueline de. *The Great Sophists in Periclean Athens.* Trans. Janet Lloyd. Oxford: Clarendon Press, 1992.

Trible, Phyllis. *God and the Rhetoric of Sexuality.* Philadelphia: Fortress Press, 1978.

Waithe, Mary Ellen. *A History of Women Philosophers,* Vol. I, 600 B.C.–500 A.D. Boston: Martinus Nijhoff, 1987.

Wire, Antoinette C. *The Corinthian Women Prophets, A Reconstruction Through Paul's Letters.* Philadelphia: Fortress, 1991.

Wolf, Christa. *Cassandra.* Trans. Jean Van Huerck. New York: Farrar Strauss Giroux, 1984.

Suggestions for Teaching Ancient Rhetorics

Mesopotamia

Roberta Binkley

Problems of Origins and Reading Enheduanna

Working with the texts of Enheduanna presents several problems. First, there's the distance of more than four thousand years that seems to make her works and their themes difficult for students to comprehend. Then there's the structure of her hymn, her use of repetition and metonomy, as she ritually addresses the goddess Inanna, that is often puzzling to modern students. Then there's the problem of her context that raises questions such as: What was the civilization like from which she wrote and composed, and how much must be guessed and inferred about that ancient time and place? How much must be inferred about gender and the status of women, even elite women such as Enheduanna? Is the rhetoric of *The Exaltation* one of political expediency, that forefronts the agenda of her father, Sargon? Does Enheduanna's discussion of her own writing present a process theory of rhetoric? How could that rhetoric be characterized? Does the rhetoric of her representation of the goddess Inanna represent a theological argument? And finally, how does her position as Other in terms of gender, period, place, and spiritual tradition color our view of her and her works?

ENHEDUANNA

Working with the hymn, *The Exaltation of Inanna,* provides an excellent introduction to the works of Enheduanna. At only 153 lines long, it in-

227

vites close reading. There are several translations available, and it can be instructive to compare them. There's the first translation of William W. Hallo and J. J. A. van Dijk that was done in 1968 with an excellent explanation that remains the basic scholarly work in English. A popular treatment as well as extensive discussion from a Jungian point of view of this and two other hymns is available in Betty De Shong Meador's book, *Inanna, Lady of Largest Heart: Poems of the Sumerian High Priestess Enheduanna*. Also there's the accessible version in Willis and Aliki Barnstone's book, *A Book of Women Poets from Antiquity to Now*. Michelle Hart's web site at: <http://www.angelfire.com/mi/enheduanna/> helps Enheduanna to come alive for undergraduates on a visual as well as textual level. On that web site Hart offers a recent translation of "The Exaltation of Inanna" from the German Sumeriologist, Annette Zgoll.

CONTEXT

An excellent starting place is the general four-volume reference collection edited by Jack M. Sasson et. al., *Civilizations of the Ancient Near East*. New York: Charles Scribner's Sons, 1995. Two books that deal with questions of the Greeks and their context within the larger Near Eastern world are by Walter Burkert and M. L. West. In *The Orientalizing Revolution,* Burkert focuses on what he calls the "orientalizing period" during the early archaic age (750 to 650 B.C.E.), or roughly the Homeric epoch. M. L.West takes a larger view from the third millennium to the first century. Of course, there is the work of Martin Bernal and Edward Said who certainly bring into question many of the assumptions of contemporary scholarly disciplinary methodology. Extensive feminist criticism of historical writing also helps to raise interesting questions for students to consider. For example, Gerda Lerner's book, *The Creation of the Patriarchy,* an outsider's view of the rise of ancient civilizations such as Mesopotamia has been widely read and used in women's studies courses. Although many specialists have critiqued her details, her thesis still has yet to be refuted.

The larger cultural context of Mesopotamia and Egypt are well described in William Hallo's excellent book with William Simpson, *The Ancient Near East: A History*. There's also the excellent general reference source of Marc Van de Mieroop's, *Cuneiform Texts and the Writing of History* also offers a good background to the cuneiform tradition. Zainab Barhani in her book *Women of Babylon* gives the first extensive postmodern treatment of women. A popular version of the mythic hymnic cycle of Inanna is translated by Samuel Noah Kramer and edited with a controversial commentary by Diane Wolkstein. For overviews of Sumerian literature, see also Jeremy Black's book, *Reading Sumerian Poetry,* which takes a literary criticism approach. There's also the treatment of Thorkild Jacobsen, *The Harps that Once* . . . : *Sumerian Poetry in Translation.*

Paul V. Hoskisson and Grant M. Boswell

Neo-Assyrian Rhetoric

The pompous and grandiose language employed by Sennacherib's scribes is at home in ancient Near Eastern rhetoric. Perhaps in some instances little has changed in the more than two and a half intervening millennia. After reading the annalistic account of Sennacherib's third campaign provided in the text above, selections of other royal inscriptions (see Hallo and Younger, vol. 2, listed below) would provide additional examples of ancient Near Eastern rhetoric. A contrast and a comparison between the contemporary rhetoric of western democracies and the rhetoric of other states and organizations with political agendas illustrate how political leaders use rhetoric to justify and further their aims. Perceptions of the nature of a king or dictator and of the nature of democracy inform the rhetorical structure and guide the rhetorical propaganda of contemporary states.

The Assyrian Empire at its height controlled the territory from modern-day western Iran and southeastern Turkey to the southern border of modern Egypt. A civilization as vast as the Assyrian Empire required the development of a sophisticated system of administration. Their rhetoric formed an integral part of the Assyrian imperial political aims in managing the many peoples and cultures that they had conquered and to some extent assimilated.

A brief history of the Iron Age would place the Assyrian Empire into its ancient Near Eastern context. The Assyrians were heirs to a 2,500 year heritage of Mesopotamian culture, learning, empire building, and literature. The Assyrian kings were very much aware of this heritage and made attempts to collect an exhaustive library of previous laws, scientific texts, royal inscriptions, literary works, etc. Are contemporary states immune to or capable of ignoring their cultural and historical heritage?

A few students may be familiar with the biblical account (2 Kings 18:13–19:37; see also the nearly word-for-word identical account in Isaiah 36–37) of the Assyrian destruction of the Jewish kingdom, including the siege of Jerusalem. The rhetorical exchange contained in the biblical account between the representatives of the Assyrian king, Sennacherib, and the Jewish king, Hezekiah, illustrates the sophistication the Assyrians brought to the exchange. The Bible, in contrast to the annals of Sennacherib above, records the rhetorical conclusion drawn by the Assyrians. What is different about the use of rhetoric on the battlefield and the use of rhetoric in a palace inscription?

Further Readings

The archaeological context:

Mogens Trolle Larsen, *The Conquest of Assyria: Excavations in an Antique Land 1840–1860* (London and New York: Routledge, 1996). Larsen gives a history of archaeological excavations in the land that was Assyria, currently Iraq.

Seton Lloyd, *Foundations in the Dust: The Story of Mesopotamian Exploration,* revised and enlarged edition (London: Thames and Hudson, 1980). Lloyd gives a broader picture of archaeological work than the previous work, in that it covers all of Mesopotamia.

Additional ancient Near Eastern texts:

William W. Hallo and K. Lawson Younger, eds., *The Context of Scripture,* vol. 1, *Canonical Compositions from the Biblical World* (New York: Brill, 1997); vol. 2, *Monumental Inscriptions from the Biblical World* (New York: Brill, 2000); and vol. 3, *Archival Documents from the Biblical World* (New York: Brill 2002). Hallo and Younger have provided up-to-date translations of many of the more important writings to come out of the ancient Near East.

Historical readings:

A. Bernard Knapp, *The History and Culture of Ancient Western Asia and Egypt* (Chicago: The Dorsey Press, 1988). Knapp has written a general history of the ancient Near East, including the Assyrians.

Henry W. F. Saggs, *The Might That Was Assyria* (London: Sidgwick & Jackson, 1984). Saggs, a noted expert on Assyria, provides a fairly detailed history of the Assyrian world.

Cultural studies:

J. E. Curtis and J. E. Reade, eds., *Art and Empire: Treasures from Assyria in the British Museum.* London: British Museum Press, 1995. This work with many illustrations is a readable summary of the range of Assyrian royal and not so royal artifacts.

A. Leo Oppenheim, *Ancient Meospotamia: Portrait of a Dead Civilization,* revised edition completed by Erica Reiner (Chicago: University of Chicago Press, 1977). Oppenheim, with Reiner's revision, presents a topical synthesis of many aspects of ancient Mesopotamian cultural life.

William W. Hallo

The Birth of Rhetoric in the Ancient Near East

I. Introduction: Biblical rhetoric and rhetorical criticism of the Bible
II. Sumerian rhetoric and rhetorical analysis of Sumerian literature in general
III. Sumerian dialogues, diatribes,and debates in particular
IV. Akkadian rhetoric and rhetorical techniques in Akkadian literature and letters generally
   A. Monologues (Edzard)
   B. Auctorial intention (Pearce)
   C. Presumed audience (Porter)
   D. Epic incipits (Wilcke)
   E. High style (Groneberg)
V. The Gilgamesh Epic in particular
VI. Colloquial Language
   A. Plain style (Moran)
   B. Colloquial Sumerian (Hallo)
   C. Colloquial Hebrew (Steiner)
VII. Humanity and the humanities
VIII. Appendix: Rhetoric in the rest of the ancient Near East

Bibliography

I. BIBLICAL RHETORIC AND RHETORICAL CRITICISM OF THE BIBLE

Adele Berlin, "Narrative poetics in the Bible," *Prooftexts* 6 (1986) 273–284; eadem, *Poetics and Interpretation of Biblical Narrative* (Winona Lake, Eisenbrauns, reprint 1994).

Thomas B. Dozeman and Benjamin Fiore in *Anchor Bible Dictionary* 5 (1992) 712–719. Add especially Jared J. Jackson and Martin Kessler, eds. *Rhetorical Criticism: Essays in Honor of James Muilenburg* (Pittsburgh Theological Monograph Series).

Yehoshua Gitay, *Prophecy and Persuasion: a Study of Isaiah 40–48* (Forum Theologiae Linguisticae 14) (Bonn: Linguistica Biblica, 1981); *idem, Isaiah and his Audience: the Structure and Meaning of Isaiah 1–12* (Studia Semitica Neerlandica 30) (Assen/Maastricht: Van Gorcum, 1991).

Edward L. Greenstein, "A Forensic Understanding of the Speech from the Whirlwind," *Studies Haran* (1996) 241–258; idem, review article on "Biblical narratology" in *Prooftexts* 1 (1981) 201–16; idem, "An equivocal reading of the sale of Joseph." In *Literary Interpretations of Biblical Narratives* vol. II, ed. by Kenneth R. R. Gros Louis (Nashville, TN: Abingdon, 1982) 114–25 and 306–10.

Isaac Rabinowitz, *A Witness Forever: Ancient Israel's Perception of Literature and the Resultant Hebrew Bible* (Bethesda, MD: CDL Press, 1993).

Mary Savage, "Literary Criticism and Biblical Studies: A Rhetorical Analysis of the Joseph Narrative," *SIC* 1 (1980) 79–100.

Meir Sternberg, "Delicate Balance in the Rape of Dinah: Biblical Narrative and the Rhetoric of the Narrative Text," *Hasifrut* (1973) 193–231 (in Hebrew; English summary); *idem,* "The Bible's Art of Persuasion: Ideology, Rhetoric, and Poetics in Saul's Fall," *Hebrew Union College Annual* 54 (1983) 45–82; *idem, The Poetics of Biblical Narrative* (Bloomington: Indiana University Press, 1984).

Duane F. Watson and Alan J. Hauser, *Rhetorical Criticism of the Bible: a Comprehensive Bibliography with Notes on History and Method* (Biblical Interpretation Series 4) (Leiden: E. J. Brill, 1993).

II. SUMERIAN RHETORIC AND RHETORICAL ANALYSIS OF SUMERIAN LITERATURE IN GENERAL

Adele Berlin, "Shared Rhetorical Features in Biblical and Sumerian Literature," *The Journal of the Ancient Near Eastern Society of Columbia University* 10 (1978): 35–42.

Robert Seth Falkowitz, *The Sumerian Rhetoric Collections* (Thesis, Philadelphia: University of Pennsylvania, 1980) (Ann Arbor, University Microfilms, 1982).

Joan Goodnick Westenholz, "Enheduanna, En-priestess, Hen of Nanna, Spouse of Nanna," *Studies . . . Sjöberg* (1989) 539–556.

William W. Hallo, "Lugalbanda Excavated," *Journal of the American Oriental Society* 103 (1983): 165–180; reprinted in Jack M. Sasson, ed., *Studies in Literature from the Ancient Near East . . . dedicated to Samuel Noah Kramer* (American Oriental Series 65, 1984) same pagination; idem, "On the antiquity of Sumerian literature," *Journal of the American Oriental Society* 83 (1963): 167–176, esp. pp. 175f.

William W. Hallo and J. J. A. van Dijk, *The Exaltation of Inanna* (Yale Near Eastern Researches 3) (New Haven and London: Yale University Press, 1968).

Thorkild Jacobsen, *The Harps That Once: Sumerian Poetry in Translation* (New Haven and London: Yale University Press 1987).

Samuel Noah Kramer, "Hymnal Prayer of Enheduanna: The Adoration of Inanna in Ur," *apud* ANET (3rd ed., 1969) 579–82.

Piotr Michalowski, "Negation as Description: The Metaphor of Everyday Life in Early Mesopotamian Literature," *Aula Orientalis* 9 (1991): 131–136, esp. p. 134.

Irene J. Winter, "Women in Public: The Disk of Enheduanna, The Beginning of the Office of En-priestess, and the Weight of the Visual Evidence," RAI 33 (1987): 189–201.

III. SUMERIAN DIALOGUES, DIATRIBES, AND DEBATES IN PARTICULAR

Bendt Alster, "Sumerian Literary Dialogues and Debates and Their Place in Ancient Near Eastern Literature." In Egon Keck et al., eds. *Living Waters: Scandinavian Oriental Studies Presented to Professor Dr. Frede Løkkegaard* (Copenhagen, Museum Tusculum, 1990): 1–16.

Åke W. Sjöberg, "Der Vater und sein missratener Sohn," *Journal of Cuneiform Studies* 25 (1973): 105–169; idem, "'He Is a Good Seed of a Dog' and 'Engardu, the Fool'," *Journal of Cuneiform Studies* 24 (1971–72): 107–119.

Herman L. J. Vanstiphout, "Lore, Learning and Levity in the Sumerian Disputations: A Matter of Form, or Substance?" In G. J. Reinink and H. L. J. Vanstiphout, eds., *Dispute Poems and Dialogues in the Ancient and Mediaeval Near East* (Orientalia Lovaniensia Analecta 42, 1991) 23–46; idem, "The Mesopotamian Debate Poems: A General Presentation," *Acta Sumerologica* 12 (1990): 271–318; 14 (1992) 339–367.

IV. AKKADIAN RHETORIC AND RHETORICAL TECHNIQUES IN AKKADIAN LITERATURE AND LETTERS GENERALLY

Dietz Otto Edzard, "Selbstgespräch und Monolog in der akkadischen Literatur." In Tzvi Abusch et al., eds., *Lingering Over Words: Studies in Ancient Near Eastern Literature in Honor of William L. Moran* (Harvard Semitic Studies 37, 1990): 149–62.

Benjamin R. Foster, *Before the Muses: an Anthology of Akkadian Literature* (Bethesda, MD: CDL Press, 1993).

Stanley Gevirtz, "On Canaanite Rhetoric: The Evidence of the Amarna Letters from Tyre," *Orientalia 42* (1973): 162–177.

B. R. M. Groneberg, *Untersuchungen zum hymnisch-epischen Dialekt der altbabylonischen literarischen Texten* (Ph.D. Thesis, Wilhelm's-Universität, Münster, 1971).

Richard S. Hess, "Rhetorical Forms in EA 162," *Ugarit-Forschungen* 22 (1990): 137–148; idem, "Smitten Ant Bites Back: Rhetorical Forms in the Amarna Correspondence from Shechem," In J. C. de Moor and W. G. E. Watson, eds., *Verse in Amcient Near Eastern Prose.* AOAT 42 (1993):95–111.

Laurie B. Pearce, "Statements of Purpose: Why the Scribes Wrote." In Mark E. Cohen et al., eds., *The Tablet and the Scroll: Near Eastern Studies in Honor of William W. Hallo* (Bethesda, MD: CDL Press, 1993): 185–193.

Barbara N. Porter, "Language, Audience and Impact in Imperial Assyria." In S. Izre'el and R. Drory, eds., *Language and Culture in the Near East* (Israel Oriental Studies 15) (Leiden: Brill, 1995: 51–72).

W. Sallaberger, *"When Du Mein Bruder Bist, . . .": Interaktion und Text-gestaltung in altbabylonischen Alltagsbriefen.* (Groningen: Styx, 1999).

Wolfram von Soden, "Der hymnisch-epische Dialekt des Akkadischen," *Zeitschrift für Assyriologie* 40 (1932): 163–227; 41 (1933) 90–183, 236.

C. Wilcke, "Die Anfänge der akkadischen Epen," *Zeitschrift für Assyriologie* 67 (1977): 153–216.

Irene Winter, "Royal Rhetoric and the Development of Historical Narrative in Neo-Assyrian Reliefs," *Studies in Visual Communication* 7 (1981): 2–38.

V. The Gilgamesh Epic in particular

Tzvi Abusch, "Ishtar's Proposal and Gilgamesh's Refusal: An Interpretation of *The Gilgamesh Epic,* Tablet 6, lines 1–79," *History of Religions* 26 (1986): 143–197; reprinted in J. Krstovic et al., eds, *Classical and Medieval Literature Criticism* 3 (Detroit, 1989): 365–374.

Jerrold S. Cooper, "Gilgamesh Dreams of Enkidu: The Evolution and Dilution of Narrative," *Essays . . . Finkelstein* (1977): 39–44.

C. J. Gadd, "Epic of Gilgamesh, Tablet XII," *Revue d'Assyriologie* 30 (1933): 127–143.

Samuel Noah Kramer, "The Epic of Gilgameš and its Sumerian sources: A Study in Literary Evolution," *Journal of the American Oriental Society* 64 (1944): 7–23.

Aaron Shaffer, *Sumerian Sources of Tablet XII of the Epic of Gilgameš* (Ph.D. Dissertation, University of Pennsylvania, 1963).

Jeffrey H. Tigay, *The Evolution of the Gilgamesh Epic* (Philadelphia: University of Pennsylvania, 1982); idem, "Was There an Integrated Gilgamesh Epic in the Old Babylonian Period?" *Essays . . . Finkelstein* (1977): 215–18.

Nicola Vulpe, "Irony and Unity of the Gilgamesh Epic," *Journal of Near Eastern Studies* 53 (1994): 275–283.

D. J. Wiseman, "A Gilgamesh Epic Fragment from Nimrud," *Iraq* 37 (1975): 157–63 and pls. xxxviif.

Hope Nash Wolff, "Gilgamesh, Enkidu and the Heroic Life," *Journal of the American Oriental Society* 89 (1969): 392–398.

VI. COLLOQUIAL LANGUAGE

William W. Hallo, "Notes from the Babylonian Collection, I. Nungal in the Egal: an Introduction to Colloquial Sumerian?" *Journal of Cuneiform Studies* 31 (1979): 161–165; idem, "Back to the Big House: Colloquial Sumerian, Continued," *Orientalia* 54 (1985): 56–64.

William L. Moran, "*UET* 6, 402: Persuasion in the Plain Style," *Journal of the Ancient Near East Society* 22 (1993): 113–120.

Richard C. Steiner, "A Colloquialism in Jer. 5:13 from the Ancestor of Mishnaic Hebrew," *Journal of Jewish Studies* 37 (1992): 11–26.

VII. HUMANITY AND THE HUMANITIES

Samuel Noah Kramer, "A Father and His Perverse Son," *National Probation and Parole Association Journal* 3 (1957): 169–173; idem, *History Begins at Sumer* (Philadelphia: University of Pennsylvania, 1981): 16; cf. Å. Sjöberg, *Journal of Cuneiform Studies* 25 (1973): 116 (lines 70f.).

J. J. A. van Dijk, *La Sagesse Suméro-Akkadienne* (Leiden: E. J. Brill, 1953): 23–25.

Henri Limet, "'Peuple' et 'humanité' chez les Sumériens," *Studies . . . Kraus* (1982): 258–267.

VIII. APPENDIX: RHETORIC IN THE REST OF THE ANCIENT NEAR EAST

John Baines, "Feuds or Vengeance: Rhetoric and Social Forms." In E. Teeter and J. A. Lawson, eds., *Gold of Praise: Studies on Ancient Egypt in Honor of Edward F. Wente* (Studies in Ancient Oriental Civilizations 58) (Chicago: Oriental Institute, 1999): 11–20.

Michael V. Fox, "Ancient Egyptian Rhetoric," *Rhetorica* 1 (1983): 9 22.

Moshe Held, "Rhetorical Questions in Ugaritic and Biblical Hebrew," *Eretz-Israel* 9 (1969) (Albright Volume): 71–79.

J. de Roos, "Rhetoric in the s.c. [so-called] Testament of Hattusilis I." In W. H. van Soldt, ed., *Veenhof Anniversary Volume* (Leiden: Netherlands Institute voor het Nabije Osten, 2001): 401–406.

ABBREVIATIONS

ANET = J. B. Pritchard, ed., *Ancient Near Eastern Texts Relating to the Old Testament* (3rd ed., Princeton, NJ: Princeton University Press, 1969).

AOAT = Alter Orient und Altes Testament. Neukirchen. Vluyr: Neukirchener Verlag.

Essays . . . Finkelstein = Maria de Jong Ellis, ed., *Essays on the Ancient Near East in Memory of Jacob Joel Finkelstein* (Memoirs of the Connecticut Academy of Arts and Sciences 19) (Hamden: Archon Books, 1977).

RAI 33 = Jean-Marie Durand, ed., *La femme dans le Proche-Orient antique: Compte rendu de la XXXIIIe Rencontre Assyriologique Internationale* (Paris: Editions recherche sur les Civilisations, 1987).

RAI 44 = L. Milano et al., eds., *Landscapes . . . Papers Presented to the XLIV Rencontie Assyriologique Internationale* (Padua: Sargon Srl, 2000).

SIC 1 = Carl D. Evans et al., eds. *Scripture in Context: Essays on the Comparative Method* (Pittsburgh: Theological Monograph Series 34) (Pittsburgh, Pickwick Press, 1980).

Studies . . . Haran = M. V. Fox et al., eds., *Texts, Temples, and Traditions: a Tribute to Menahem Haran* (Winona Lake, IN: Eisenbrauns, 1996).

Studies. . . Kraus = G. van Driel et al., eds., zikir šumim: *Assyriological Stud-*

ies Presented to F. R. Kraus . . . (Studia Francisci Scholten Memoriae Dicata 5) (Leiden: E. J. Brill, 1982).

Studies . . . Sjöberg = H. Behrens et al., eds., *DUMU-E₂-DUB-BA-A: Studies in Honor of Åke W. Sjöberg* Philadelphia: University Museum, 1959).

Egypt

Carol Lipson

Ancient Egyptian Rhetoric: It All Comes Down to Maat

A course unit centered on the essay "Ancient Egyptian Rhetoric: It All Comes Down to *Maat*" could be taught from an *emic* perspective; students could examine the texts to address the following questions: What is the desired relation between the individual and society? What are proper modes of behavior and proper modes of communicating and persuading? If *Maat* is used as the central focus of a course unit, attention might well be restricted to the Middle Kingdom period and its texts, revered in later periods as the finest attainments of the culture. Such a course unit could examine *The Instructions of Ptahhotep* in its entirety, and/or *The Instructions for Merikare*. A useful way to visualize the specificity of the Egyptian approach might be to look at the better-known Hebrew Proverbs, to develop a sense of the comparative differences. Such a study could be foregrounded by reading Michael Fox's article outlining the five canons of Egyptian rhetoric (cited in the essay), and by contextual background on the period and the culture. In light of the Fox article, students could then develop their own categories of rhetorical principles and practices in the Egyptian Instruction texts. They could propose what they see as principles for arrangement and for delivery.

Such a unit could also look at narratives—the two most popular being *The Tale of the Eloquent Peasant* and the *Tale of Sinuhe*. The first involves an uneducated peasant who is naturally eloquent, and who is given opportunities to demonstrate his gifts as he seeks to redress a wrong committed against him. The *Tale of Sinuhe* offers opportunities to examine how the ancient Egyptians viewed their own culture in relation to foreign cultures and practices. Both the tales and the instructions afford fruitful material for student inquiry into the Egyptian values and the Egyptian conceptions of persuasion, moral obligation, and communal identity.

An engaging and productive inductive learning unit has been developed by Egyptologist Peter Piccione at the College of Charleston. He has created a unit that invites students to collaboratively stage a performance of an ancient Egyptian sacred drama, "The Victory of Horus." This drama was recorded on the walls at the temple of Horus at Edfu, and was reconstructed by Egyptolo-

Suggestions for Teaching Ancient Rhetorics

gist H. Walter Fairman. Information about this assignment from Piccione's history class is available on the web at *http://www.cofc.edu/~piccione/*. Piccione also provides a substantial list of relevant references. Engagement in this enjoyable activity can enhance students' ability to analyze the rhetorical features of the drama, and thus deepen their learning. The text of the drama is available in H. W. Fairman, trans. and ed., *The Triumph of Horus: An Ancient Egyptian Sacred Drama*. London: B. T. Batsford, Ltd., 1974.

Alternately, students might look at Egyptian art in relation to the textual rhetorical principles. Such a unit could ask students to determine the similarities and differences in rhetorical principles and conventions across media. Mario Perniola, in his 1995 *Enigmas: The Egyptian Moment in Society and Art*, has proposed that a compatible set of principles existed across a wide range of media: art, writing, architecture, pageants, rituals, etc. According to Perniola, the compatibility allowed for these media to easily be combined and interchanged. Students could examine the narratives alongside the rhetorical force of the art.

Finally, another focus of inquiry for a course unit might involve the songs. A large group of Egyptian love songs exists, mainly from the Ramesside Period (1300–1100 B.C.E.), with a wide variety of functions and settings. These might be analyzed in relation to the Hebrew Song of Songs. A comparative study by Michael Fox can offer useful backing for such rhetorical study of the songs as they developed in each of these cultures. (Michael Fox, *The Song of Songs and the Ancient Egyptian Love Songs*. Madison, WI: The University of Wisconsin Press, 1985.)

The following list of citations does not repeat entries from the bibliography to the article discussed. Nor does it repeat entries from the very helpful and extensive list provided by Deborah Sweeney.

SOURCES FOR TRANSLATED EGYPTIAN TEXTS:

Foster, John. *Love Songs of the New Kingdom*. Austin: University of Texas Press, 1992.

Foster, John. *Ancient Egyptian Literature: An Anthology*. Austin: University of Texas Press, 2001.

Lichtheim, Miriam. *Ancient Egyptian Literature*. Berkeley, California: University of California Press. Vol. 1: The Old and Middle Kingdoms, 1973. There are two other volumes, but if only one can be used, the first is the best.

Parkinson, R. B. *The Tale of Sinuhe and Other Ancient Poems*. New York: Oxford University Press, 1997.

Pritchard, James, ed. *The Ancient Near East: Texts Relating to the Old Testa-*

ment. Princeton, NJ: Princeton University Press, 3rd ed., 1969. A 1958 paperback edition exists in two volumes. The first volume would be suitable, giving attention to Mesopotamian, Assyrian, Egyptian, and Palestinian texts.

BACKGROUND ON HISTORY AND CULTURE:

Grimal, N. *History of Ancient Egypt.* Oxford: Blackwell, 1994.

Hornung, Eric. *History of Ancient Egypt.* Ithaca, NY: Cornell University Press, 1999.

Redford, Donald, ed. *The Oxford Encyclopedia of Ancient Egypt.* Vols. 1–3. Oxford University Press, 2000.

Sasson, Jack, ed. *Ancient Civilizations of the Near East.* Vols. 1–4. New York: Charles Scribner's and Sons, 1995.

Shaw, Ian, ed. *The Oxford History of Ancient Egypt.* Oxford University Press, 2001.

BACKGROUND ON EGYPTIAN ART:

Aldred, Cyril. *Egyptian Art.* London: Thames and Hudson, 1980.

Robins, Gay. *The Art of Ancient Egypt.* Boston: Harvard University Press, 1997.

Wilkinson, Richard. *Reading Egyptian Art.* London: Thames and Hudson, 1994.

ADDITIONAL BACKGROUND ON *MAAT:*

Meskell, L. *Archaeologies of Social Life: Age, Sex, Class, etc. in Ancient Egypt.* Oxford: Blackwell, 1999.

Meskell, L. "Intimate Archaeologies: The Case of Kha and Merit." *World Archaeology 29 (3): 363–79.*

Deborah Sweeney

Law, Rhetoric and Gender in Ramsside Egypt

Monarchs and the elite displayed their achievements in monumental inscriptions for the appreciation of their contemporaries, posterity, and the gods. These texts were aimed not only at inspiring admiration, but were also intended to obtain blessings from the gods or offerings to the dead man's spirit from passers-by. In the latter case, various arguments attempt to persuade the addressee that reciting a blessing or making a symbolic offering would be worth their while.

Wisdom texts ("instructions") were used to instruct aspiring scribes in the social norms of their elite. These texts also stress norms for correct speech, which is to be accurate, truthful and appropriate. More creative uses of language for persuasion are less prominent: the plain truth is assumed to prevail unaided.

Literacy was very limited in ancient Egypt—scholars estimate that between 10 percent and 1 percent of adult men in most communities knew how to read and write, and even fewer women. Most of the Egyptian population did not have the skills to appreciate the rhetoric of a written composition at first hand. It is not clear whether and to what extent people beyond the elite had access to literary works and could enjoy them. The implications of limited literacy should be discussed in connection to rhetoric.

The Egyptians themselves imagined that it was nonetheless possible for untutored people to be able to express themselves well. The "Teaching of Ptahhotep" remarks that "Good speech is as rare as emerald, yet it is found with the maids at the grindstone." The story of the Eloquent Peasant relates the tales of an ordinary man, robbed of his goods by a superior, who pleaded his case with such exquisite skill that the officer whom he petitions was ordered to keep the peasant talking, so that he would produce more speeches for the king's delectation. However, the general note of this story is one of astonishment at the paradox of an uneducated man expressing himself so elegantly, and we may assume that it was considered highly unusual.

QUESTIONS FOR STUDY

1. What rhetorical devices are used in royal inscriptions to highlight the heroism and initiative of the king?
2. What rhetorical devices are used in elite biographical inscriptions to demonstrate how a noble or official conformed to the ideals of Egyptian conduct?
3. What rhetorical devices do wisdom texts use to persuade their addressee of the wisdom of undertaking certain courses of action?
4. What do you think are the implications of limited literacy for the function of rhetoric in ancient Egypt?
5. The rhetoric of everyday life in ancient Egypt and its relationship to the literary tradition are still somewhat neglected. How do you think this line of research could be pursued?

6. Do you envisage women using rhetoric in the same way as men in ancient Egypt, or do you envisage any differences in their approach?

ARTICLES ABOUT RHETORIC

Coulon, L. "Veracité et rhétorique dans les autobiographies égyptiennes de la Première Période intermédiare," *Bulletin de l'Institut Français d'Archéologie Orientale* 97 (1997), 109–138.

_____. "La rhétorique et ses fictions: pouvoirs et duplicité du discours à travers la littérature égyptienne du Moyen et du Nouvel Empire," *Bulletin de l'Institut Français d'Archéologie Orientale* 99 (1999), 103–132.

Derchain, P. "Éloquence et politique: L'opinion d'Akhtoy," *Revue d'Égyptologie* 40 (1989), 37–47.

Fischer-Elfert, H. W. "Morphologie, Rhetorik und Genese der Soldatencharakteristik," *Göttinger Miszellen* 66 (1983), 45–65.

Fox, M.V. "Ancient Egyptian Rhetoric," *Rhetorica* 1 (1983), 9–22.

Guglielmi, W. "Der Gebrauch rhetorischer Stilmittel in der ägyptischen Literatur." In A. Loprieno (ed.), *Ancient Egyptian Literature: History and Forms,* London/New York/Cologne, 1996, 465–497.

Junge, F. "Rhetorik." In W. Helck and W. Westendorf (eds.), *Lexikon der Ägyptologie* vol. V, Wiesbaden, 1984, 250–3.

Parkinson, R.B. "Literary Form and the Tale of the Eloquent Peasant," *Journal of Egyptian Archaeology* 78 (1992), 163–178.

THE "PERFORMANCE" DIMENSION OF LITERATURE/RESTRICTED NATURE OF LITERATURE

Eyre, C. J. "The Semna Stelae: Quotation, Genre and Functions of Literature." In S. I. Groll (ed.), *Studies in Egyptology presented to Miriam Lichtheim,* 2 vols., Jerusalem: Magna, 1990, 134–165.

_____. "Why Was Egyptian Literature?" *VI Congresso Internazionale di Egittologia : Atti,* II, Turin, 1993, 115–120.

LITERACY

Baines, J. R., "Literacy and Ancient Egyptian Society," *Man* (n.s.) 18, (1983), 572–599.

Baines, J. R. and C. J. Eyre, "Four Notes on Literacy," *Göttinger Miszellen* 61 (1983), 65–96.

Lesko, L. H., "Literacy." In D.B. Redford (ed.), *The Oxford Encyclopedia of Ancient Egypt,* vol. 2, Oxford, 2001, 297–299.

Tower, Hollis, S. "Oral Tradition." In D. B. Redford (ed.), *The Oxford Encyclopedia of Ancient Egypt,* vol. 2, Oxford, 2001, 612–615.

WOMEN AND RHETORIC

Lesko, B. "Women's Rhetoric from Ancient Egypt." In: M. M. Wertheimer (ed.), *Listening to their Voices: The Rhetorical Activities of Historical Women, Columbia, South Carolina: University of South Carolina Press, 1997, 89–111.*

_____. *"'Listening' to the Ancient Egyptian Woman: Letters, Testimonials and other Expressions of Self." In E. Teeter and J.A. Larson (eds.),* Gold of Praise: Studies on Ancient Egypt in Honor of Edward F. Wente, (Studies in Ancient Oriental Civilization 58), Chicago: University of Chicago Press, 1999, 247–254.

SOURCE MATERIALS

Lichtheim, M. *Ancient Egyptian Literature,* 3 vols., Berkeley: University of California Press, 1975–1980. (Monumental inscriptions and literary texts of all periods).

_____. *Ancient Egyptian Autobiographies Chiefly of the Middle Kingdom (OBO 84),* Fribourg (Switzerland)/Göttingen: Fribourg University Press, 1988. (Note women's texts on pp. 37–38.)

McDowell, A. *Village Life in Ancient Egypt. Laundry Lists and Love Songs,* Oxford: Oxford University Press, 1999. (Texts of all types from the village of Deir el-Medina).

Parkinson, R. B. *Voices from Ancient Egypt: An Anthology of Middle Kingdom Writings,* London: British Museum Press, 1991. (Texts of all types from ca. 2081–1600 B.C.E.)

Parkinson, R. B. *The Tale of Sinuhe and other Ancient Egyptian Poems 1940–1640 B.C.E.,* Oxford: Oxford University Press, 1997. (Literary texts, including the Teaching of Ptahhotep and the Tale of the Eloquent Peasant.)

Simpson, W. K., R. O. Faulkner, and E. F. Wente, *The Literature of Ancient*

Egypt, New Haven/London: Yale University Press, 1973. (Literary texts of all periods).

Vernus, P. "Études de philologie et de linguistique I. No II: Un exemple de rhétorique politique: le discours du vizir *T3* (P. Turin 1880, ro 2, 20–3,4)." *Revue d'Égyptologie* 32 (1980), 121–124. (Speech of the vizier To).

Wente, E. F. *Letters from Ancient Egypt (SBL Writings from the Ancient World Series,* 1), Atlanta, Ga.: Scholars Press, 1990.

Many thanks to Prof. Irene Shirun-Grumach for suggestions of bibliographical items and comments on various points in the lesson outline.

China

George Q. Xu

The Use of Eloquence: The Confucian Perspective

The objective of this chapter is to demonstrate the ancient Chinese Confucians' mistrust of eloquence, the social and philosophical bases of the mistrust, and the politics that motivated the ironic rhetorical maneuvers of employing eloquence in public denunciations of eloquence. As the Confucians' mistrust of eloquence is a derivative of Confucian philosophy, which is itself embedded in the historical context of classical China, it would be helpful for students to gain, from the suggested readings listed below, some basic understanding of the historical period in which Confucianism originated. Roberts (1993, Book II.5 "Ancient China," Book IV.7 "Imperial China"), Fairbank (1994), and Fung (1948) are good sources of succinct information about Chinese history and philosophy. Graham (1989) and Kennedy (1998, "Rhetoric in Ancient China") provide an overview of ancient Chinese rhetoric.

In reading this chapter, students should attend to the following points:

* The Confucians' attitude toward eloquence was closely connected with their perception of the historical circumstances and their role in society.
* The Confucians perceived the practice of eloquence as contradictory to the Confucian doctrines of *li* (the whole system of traditions, customs, ceremonies, and conventions), *ren* (virtue, human-ness), and *yi* (righteousness).
* The Confucians perceived eloquence as an actual subversive political force.

- The Confucian scale of moral valuation of speech acts privileged silence as the ultimate good and devalued eloquence as either an expediency or a detestable act.
- The Confucians had to resort to eloquence to denounce eloquence, thus resulting in a duality between what they did and what they preached while creating a formula for suppressing and silencing opposing voices.
- The Confucians' disparagement of eloquence has a profound and ascertainable influence on Chinese society and Chinese rhetoric up to the present.

Suggested Readings:

Fairbank, John King. *China: A New History.* Cambridge, MA: Belknap Press of Harvard University Press, 1994.

Fung, Yu-lan. *A Short History of Chinese Philosophy.* Ed. Derk Bodde. New York: Free Press, 1948.

Graham, A. C. *Disputers of the Tao: Philosophical Argument in Ancient China.* La Salle, IL: Open Court, 1989.

Kennedy, George A. *Comparative Rhetoric: An Historical and Cross-Cultural Introduction.* New York: Oxford University Press, 1998.

Oliver, Robert T. *Communication and Culture in Ancient India and China.* Syracuse, NY: Syracuse University Press, 1971.

Roberts, J. M. *History of the World.* New York: Oxford University Press, 1993.

Arabella Lyon

Confucian Silence and Remonstration: A Basis for Deliberation

Since the literature on Confucius is extensive, it makes sense to limit the focus of your undertaking and build on what students already know. In my essay, I promote the lens of deliberative rhetoric, but feminist care ethics or a pedagogical methods investigation also would work. In my approach I emphasize how different cultures have different conceptions of persuasion, advising, remonstration, and communication.

Initially one would need to provide lectures that build some cultural context. Topics such as the rise of literacy, the nature of the city-state, and concurrent thinking would set the stage for discussing what is uniquely Confucian. Background readings in Chinese rhetoric would help prepare the students (Lu), and *The Emperor's Shadow,* a film about China's first emperor, is very useful in laying out the place of rites in Chinese politics.

The second part of the unit could be driven by student interactions with Confucianism. *The Analects* and *Mencius* are written in short segments, aphorisms, and brief conversations, and so they invite close readings. I suggest picking key quotations and having the students analyze their meaning. After students are comfortable with Confucian ideas, they can place them in relationship to western rhetoric, other Chinese rhetoricians, and their own discursive strategies.

Annotated Bibliography to facilitate a discussion of Confucian deliberation:

Confucius. 1998. *The Analects of Confucius: A Philosophical Translation.* Trans, Roger T. Ames and Henry Rosemont Jr. New York: Ballentine. This translation utilizes recent archaeological discoveries and scholarship.

DeBary, Wm. Theodore, and Irene Bloom, eds. 1999. *Sources of the Chinese Tradition: From Earliest Times to 1600.* Vol 1. 2nd edition. New York: Columbia University Press. This collection provides the basic context for discussing the culture surrounding the rise and establishment of Confucianism and Neo-Confucianism (arising around 1200 A.D.E.).

Fairbanks, John King, and Merle Goldman. 1998. *China: A New History.* Cambridge: Harvard University Press. Good desk reference for placing discussions of Confucius.

Hall, David L., and Roger T. Ames. 1987. *Thinking Through Confucius.* Albany: State University of New York Press. A great introduction that is sensitive to the issues of translation and cross-cultural blindness.

Lu, Xing. 1998. *Rhetoric in Ancient China: Fifth to Third Century B.C.E.* Columbia: University of South Carolina. This thorough survey of rhetorical activity of the period is wonderful for its ability to read China through western terms.

Mencius. 1970. Trans. D. C. Lau. New York: Penguin. Meng Ke or Mencius followed Confucius by more than a century. This record of his conversations with rulers, disciples, and philosophical adversaries fleshes out the terse comments of *The Analects.*

Rubin, Vitaly A. 1976. *Individual and State in Ancient China.* Trans. Steven Levine. NY: Columbia University Press. This Russian book views Chinese thinkers through the concepts of authority, order, freedom, and tradition. Its orientation to city-states makes it a good text for beginning a comparison between classical Greek and Chinese rhetoric and politics.

Yameng Liu

Rhetoric and the Invention of Classical Chinese Discourse

Any meaningful discussion of "ancient Chinese rhetoric" would necessarily have to engage two sets of contentious issues: the historiographic issues of representing the past and the cross-cultural ones of representing the foreign. If these intertwined general problematics were not challenging enough, the specificity of "classical Chinese rhetoric" as a subject, with its overdetermined, complex, and unsettled character and its ever shifting and expanding evidentiary basis, poses many additional difficulties.

Because of the theoretical prerequisites demanded by the need to meet these formidable challenges, the subject is best taught as a theory-driven graduate seminar in conjunction with classes dealing with hermeneutics, historiography, and cultural representation, etc. Using the model of reconstructing ancient Chinese rhetoric as a particular case for exemplifying relevant theoretical insights, the class should ideally aim at a fourfold end:

1. Raising awareness of the constructive nature of any historical/cross-cultural narrative
2. Sharpening sensitivity to the converging of interests, purposes, assumptions, methodology, and other available resources in the production of the narrative concerned, as well as to the functioning of all these as at once enabling and constraining conditions
3. Fostering ability to make informed evaluation of any such narrative by comparing its underlying presuppositions and modes of justification or argumentation with those of alternative stories
4. Familiarizing the class with the topics, problematics, available evidence, established perspectives, relevant arguments, and notable texts that currently make up the area of inquiry known as classical Chinese rhetoric

On an operational level, one might want to use the comparison of a comprehensive yet conventional account [e.g., Lu (1998) and the current chapters] to anchor the seminar, examining in the process selected authors and texts from the bibliographies concerned or those of other publications. By teasing out, contrasting, and critically evaluating the differing modes of production involved, the end, set above, could be accomplished.

Alternatively, one might want to focus only on a representative case, such as Confucius, finding out, comparing, and assessing whatever has been said about his "rhetoric" or "rhetorical thinking." We could start with a review of the numerous privileged translations of *The Analects,* from James Legge's classical rendition to what Ames & Rosemont Jr. have unabashedly presented as "a philosophical translation" (Ballantine Books, 1998). This is followed by a careful examination of available commentaries on the sage as a rhetorician. And finally, such notable sinological works as Hall & Ames's *Thinking Through Confucius* (1987) and especially L. M. Jensen's *Manufacturing Confucianism* (1997) could be brought to the attention of the class for a broadened, more sophisticated, and more illuminating conceptual framework.

Biblical Rhetoric

David Metzger

Pentateuchal Rhetoric and the Voice of the Aaronides

I. UNDERGRADUATE: "INTRODUCTION TO RHETORICAL STUDIES"

IA. Goals: At the end of a unit of "Voice Analysis," I used my essay as an example of how a more-experienced rhetorician might use the techniques of voice analysis to account for the particularities of a given text. Before assigning my essay, I had modeled the use of voice analysis with several examples from Bazerman's textbook; students had practiced the techniques of voice analysis in groups, and the individual groups had given reports on their findings. The reading from Bazerman had introduced students to the distinction between "direct" and "embedded" voices, and it provided several short texts that lend themselves to the identification of such voices. Bazerman also clearly demonstrates how a "voice" constructs the authority for a given utterance: (1) a "voice" can function as a synecdoche for the experiences, institutions, and research protocols that can support a particular utterance; (2) a "text," understood as the association and/or disassociation of particular voices, can test, demonstrate, and construct the relative authority of one voice over another.

IB. Description of the Class: Before launching into my essay, I asked the students to list the names of the key figures/speakers in the Hebrew Bible. As a class, we generated a list that included the following: Moses, Abraham and the other patriarchs, G/d, The Prophets, Aaron, Kings, The Matriarchs, hostile dignitaries (Pharoah, Abimelech). I then asked, "On what authority does this or that voice (these 'key figures') speak?" For Abraham, some students said, "G/d spoke to him, and he had the good sense to obey." Others pointed out that Abraham tried to convince the deity not to destroy Sodom and Gomorrah. We then moved on to talk about Sarah, Jacob, the prophets, and Moses. Then, I asked on what authority the deity speaks. The deity is the creator, some said. And we talked about what privilege, force, or special knowledge we might associate with the creator or inventor of something. Others said that the deity was "like a king." And we talked about the privilege, force, or special knowledge associated with the position and experiences of a "king." We then paired up several different voices and wrote dialogues using those voices: Sarah and Abraham on the joys of parenting, Aaron and a prophet on expiation, Jacob and Esau on inheritance, King David and a prophet on the responsibilities of a monarch, Joseph and Moses on assimilation. After this discussion, the students were ready to imagine a dialogue between the priests and the *beit avot* (those who speak for the tribes, those who speak with the authority of the patriarchs—their great-great. . ..grandfathers—on the function and responsibilities of the priesthood.

The bulk of my essay might then be understood as a discussion of the "embedded" and "direct" voices utilized in such a dialogue. I then used the final section of my essay, "How the Aaronides Made a Rhetoric," to prompt a discussion where we compared and contrasted how a voice analysis and an appeals analysis account for an individual's acceptance or disaffection with what the Pentateuch has to say. Discussion questions included the following: "What evidentiary difficulties can the 'orchestration of voices' resolve? What does a voice analysis show us that an appeals analysis would not? What does a voice analysis show us that an appeals analysis would not?" Discussion prompts included the following: "Assume that appeals analysis and voice analysis are representative of two different world views. Compare and contrast the assumptions about language, truth, knowledge, ethics, and human psychology that are implicit in these approaches (appeals/voice). If you like, you can simply provide two lists of definitions for these terms, along with arguments and examples supporting your definitions."

IC. Bibliography:

Bazerman, Charles. "Recognizing the Many Voices in a Text." In *The Informed Writer.* 5th edition. Boston: Houghton Mifflin Co., 1995, 162–188.

II. GRADUATE (M.A.): "CLASSICAL RHETORIC"

IIA. Goals: In addition to the general goal of introducing students to the "touchstones" of the western rhetorical tradition, I wanted students to see how a rhetorical theory might be constructed from the ground up: "What does a rhetoric do? What are the essential parts of a rhetoric? How do we know a rhetoric when it walks up to us on the street?" So, I paired biblical texts with the "standards" the students would be asked to read again as doctoral students (Phaedrus, Gorgias, etc) in order to prompt students to generate the key (metarhetorical) concepts necessary for "theory building" in rhetorical studies.

IIB. Description of Class: Plato's *Phaedrus* was paired with the *Shir haShirim* (The Song of Songs); both deal with "love"; both relate a particular vision of how consciousness might be evoked, described, and proscribed by language. Discussion questions included the following: "Is rhetoric nothing more than the imposition of self upon others? How can language create (the sense of) a consciousness? Is 'rhetoric' a way of 'textualizing' consciousness?" Deuteronomy was then paired with Books I and II of Aristotle's *Rhetoric,* since both texts require the elaboration of particular psychological models in order to account for the fact that particular uses of language obligate us to participate in and perform communal forms of action. Discussion questions included: "Why does rhetoric need psychology? What obliges us to be persuaded? Is there a rhetoric of hearing as well as a rhetoric of speaking?"

As the midterm approached, the students were anxious to summarize and chart the similarities and differences between Hellenic and Hebraic rhetoric. At this point, I introduced my essay "The Voice of the Aaronides" and the first section of Boman's *Hebrew Thought Compared to Greek.* Boman's text is organized into sections that readily appeal to the rhetorician: "dynamic and static thinking," "impression and appearance," "time and space." The students contrasted my discussion of the "dialogical" nature of the Pentateuch with Boman's discussion of the how the Pentateuch teaches us to read "dialectically." Discussion prompts included: "Is Boman's own study developed in accordance with Hellenic or Hebraic epistemological and rhetorical models? How does Boman account for the development of Christianity as an intellectual tradition—Hellenic and/or Hebraic? In what ways might Boman's work be understood as Christian?"

In the last half of the course, Augustine's *On Christian Doctrine* was paired with a section from the Mishnah (the written compilation of the "Oral Torah" edited by Judah the Prince in 200 C.E.) called the *Pirkei Avot* (Chapters/Ethics of the Fathers) to show how ethics might be used to chart the "internal landscape" of a rhetoric and to identify human subjects who are "open to persuasion/communication." This discussion nicely moved into an examination of the conceptualization of teaching and learning in early rhetorical thought, focusing on selections from Cicero's *De Oratore* and Quintilian's *Institutes of Oratory.* Discussion questions included: "Is there a rhetoric of teaching? Is there an ethics of teaching? Is education a form of persuasion that obligates and/or an obligation that persuades? Can ethics be taught?" For the final exam, we compared and contrasted the topics Cicero's *De Oratore* identifies with rhetoric to the subjects we covered over the course of the semester: psychology, ethics, reading, communication, teaching.

IIC. Bibliography:

Boman, Thorleif. *Hebrew Thought Compared with Greek.* New York: W. W. Norton & Co., 1960.

Handelman, Susan. *The Slayers of Moses.* Albany: State University of New York Press, 1982.

Rivkin, Ellis. *The Shaping of Jewish History.* New York: Scribner's, 1971.

_____. *A Hidden Revolution: The Pharisees' Search for the Kingdom Within.* Nashville, TN: Abingdon Press, 1978.

Alternative Greek Rhetoric

Richard Leo Enos

The Art of Rhetoric at Rhodes

Unit Purpose and Objective

The purpose of this unit is to use the essay on rhetoric at Rhodes to illustrate not only that Rhodes was a prominent and enduring center for the study of rhetoric, but also that Rhodian rhetoric reveals that our current accounts of classical rhetoric need to be revised. Classical rhetoric traditionally has been characterized as the study of Greek and Roman rhetoric. Greek rhetoric has been equated with Athenian rhetoric and discussed only in terms of how rhetoric operated in that democracy. The characterization of rhetoric in Aristotle's *Rhetoric* reinforces the view that Greek rhetoric was civic, agonistic, and capable of functioning only in an egalitarian climate. Roman rhetoric is portrayed as functioning in two ways. First, during the Republic, rhetoric is seen as a political force with Cicero as the primary example of an effective orator and rhetorician. Second, during the Empire, rhetoric is seen as an academic subject with Quintilian as the primary example of an effective educator and rhetorician. Finally, discussions of classical rhetoric rarely explain the interaction between Greek and Roman rhetoric but rather treat them as complementary but discrete manifestations of the discipline. The discussion of Rhodian rhetoric presented in this volume offers a rival perspective to these established characterizations of classical rhetoric. The objective of this unit is to have students learn that generalized views on classical rhetoric are best understood when they are qualified. These qualifications become evident when students realize that diverse and interactive manifestations of rhetoric occurred not only within Hellenic culture but also within the context of the other versions of non-Greek rhetoric studied in this volume.

UNIT OUTLINE

After understanding the conventional representation of classical rhetoric, students are encouraged to read the essay on Rhodian rhetoric and discuss the following topics listed below in chronological order. Please note that the first of the three topics are discussed in the suggested readings listed below. The last three topics are discussed in the essay itself.

- Pre-disciplinary Notions of Rhetoric;
- Corax-Tisias and the "invention" of Rhetoric in Sicily;
- The Classical Rhetoric of Platonic and Aristotelian Athens;
- Rhodes as a Rival Center for the Study of Rhetoric;
- Rhodes and the Relationship of Greek and Roman Rhetoric;
- The Endurance of Rhodian Rhetoric in the Roman Empire.

SUGGESTED READINGS

The following works are recommended as a complement to this essay by providing general and related background reading.

Bowersock, G. W. *Augustus and the Greek World*. Oxford: Clarendon Press, 1965.

_____. *Greek Sophists in the Roman Empire*. Oxford: Clarendon Press, 1969.

Caplan, Harry. "The Decay of Eloquence at Rome in the First Century." In *Of Eloquence: Studies in Ancient and Medieval Rhetoric*. Eds. Anne King and Helen North. Ithaca, NY, and London: Cornell University Press, 1970: 160–95.

Enos, Richard Leo. *Greek Rhetoric Before Aristotle*. Prospect Heights, IL: Waveland Press, 1993.

_____. *Roman Rhetoric: Revolution and the Greek Influence*. Prospect Heights, IL: Waveland Press, 1995.

Harris, William V. *Ancient Literacy*. Cambridge, MA, and London: Harvard University Press, 1989.

Kennedy, George A. *A New History of Classical Rhetoric*. Princeton, NJ: Princeton University Press, 1994.

Marrou, H. I. *A History of Education in Antiquity*. Trans. George Lamb. Madison, WI: The University of Wisconsin Press, 1956 (reprinted in 1982).

Robb, Kevin. *Literacy & Paideia in Ancient Greece.* New York and Oxford: Oxford University Press, 1994.

Cross-Cultural Rhetorical Studies

James W. Watts

Story–List–Sanction: A Cross-Cultural Strategy of Ancient Persuasion

Teaching comparative ancient rhetoric should build on studies in the history and rhetoric of individual societies, to guard against collapsing various periods and cultures into an undifferentiated mass in the minds of students. But scholarship on the ancient world has tended to perpetuate the opposite mistake by adhering to linguistic boundaries (e.g. between Indo-European languages like Greek and Old Persian, Semitic languages like Akkadian and Hebrew, and Egyptian in all its phases) to such an extent that comparative study of ancient literature remains in its infancy. The exception is biblical studies, which has compiled deep bibliographies comparing biblical and ancient Near Eastern literature. Yet comparative rhetorical criticism that is more than just literary analysis remains underdeveloped for the literature of the Hebrew Bible as well. Only in New Testament studies has rhetorical analysis flourished because of the application of classical rhetorical theory to these Hellenistic texts.

Fortunately, a number of excellent anthologies of primary texts in English translation have been published in the last few decades. They allow students to make literary and rhetorical comparisons among ancient literatures directly. I suggest that, after using the essays in this volume to establish examples of ancient rhetorical forms, assignments should challenge students to scan the anthologies for repeating literary patterns and rhetorical forms. Class discussions of such examples should include the following questions:

- Do different ancient cultures manifest this rhetoric in distinctive ways? What might account for similar rhetoric in different cultures and time periods?
- Is this rhetoric confined to or characteristic of distinctive literary genres? If so, why?
- Given low literacy rates and typical ancient reading practices, how would these texts usually have been experienced?
- Who were the intended readers and hearers of these texts?
- Does persuasion explicitly or implicitly motivate these texts' production and use?

• How do these rhetorical practices compare to Greco-Roman and later western rhetoric? Have they influenced later rhetoric?

Bibliography for Comparative Ancient Near Eastern Rhetoric

Anthologies: The new cross-cultural anthology by Hallo and Younger provides the best starting point for comparing ancient texts:

Hallo, W. W., and K. L. Younger Jr., eds. *The Context of Scripture: Canonical Compositions, Monumental Inscriptions, and Archival Documents from the Biblical World.* 2 vols. Leiden: Brill, 1997, 2000, 2002.

Foster and Lichthiem have provided deeper historical surveys of Akkadian and Egyptian literatures:

Foster, Benjamin R. *Before the Muses: An Anthology of Akkadian Literature.* 2 vols. Bethesda, MD: CDL Press, 1993.

Lichtheim, Miriam. *Ancient Egyptian Literature.* 3 vols. Berkeley: University of California Press, 1973, 1976, 1980.

The following are less complete but also less expensive paperbacks that can be required as textbooks:

Foster, Benjamin R. *From Distant Days: Myths, Tales and Poetry of Ancient Mesopotamia.* Bethesda, MD: CDL Press, 1995.

Foster, John L. *Ancient Egyptian Literature: An Anthology.* Austin: University of Texas Press, 2001.

The Writings From the Ancient World Series from the Society of Biblical Literature/ Scholars Press (Atlanta) provides narrower collections on particular cultures, periods, and genres. These paperbacks include:

Beckman, Gary. *Hittite Diplomatic Texts.* 1996.

Hoffner, Harry A., Jr. *Hittite Myths.* 1990.

Murnane, William J. *Texts from the Amarna Period in Egypt.* 1995.

Pardee, Dennis. *Ritual and Cult at Ugarit.* 2002.

Parker, Simon. *Ugaritic Narrative Poetry.* 1997.

Roth, Martha. *Law Collections from Mesopotamia and Asia Minor.* 1995.

Studies in the Rhetoric of other Ancient Near Eastern texts: Critical studies of the rhetoric of nonbiblical ancient texts are scarce and very diverse in contents and methodology. In addition to the articles in this volume, Hess and Moran have addressed features of some Akkadian texts, while Newsom has analyzed the rhetoric of two of the Dead Sea Scrolls.

Hess, Richard S. "Smitten Ants Bite Back: Rhetorical Forms in the Amarna Correspondence from Shechem." *Verse in Ancient Near Eastern Prose.* Ed. J. C. de Moor and W. G. E. Watson. Neukirchen-Vluyn: Neukirchener Verlag, 1993. 95–111.

Moran, William L. "UET 6, 402: Persuasion in the Plain Style." *Journal of Ancient Near Eastern Studies 22* (1993): 113–120.

Newsom, Carol A. "Kenneth Burke Meets the Teacher of Righteousness: Rhetorical Strategies in the Hodayot and the Serek Ha-Yahad." In H. W. Attridge, J. J. Collins, and T. H. Tobin, S.J. (eds.), *Of Scribes and Scrolls: Studies on the Hebrew Bible, Intertestamental Judaism, and Christian Origins presented to John Strugnell.* College Theology Society Resources in Religion 5. Lanham, MD: University Press of America, 1990. 121–131.

Studies in the Rhetoric of the Hebrew Bible: Useful surveys of rhetorical criticism of the Hebrew Bible (which has included a purely literary analysis as well) have been written by Dozeman and Howard:

Dozeman, Thomas B. "OT Rhetorical Criticism." *Anchor Bible Dictionary.* Ed. D. N. Freedman. New York: Doubleday, 1992. 5:712–15.

Howard, D. M. "Rhetorical Criticism in Biblical Studies." *Bulletin for Biblical Research* 4 (1994): 87–104.

Dale Patrick has pioneered the application of rhetorical models of persuasion to the Hebrew Bible. Other studies have applied rhetorical analysis to one or more books:

Duke, Rodney K. *The Persuasive Appeal of the Chronicler. A Rhetorical Analysis.* Journal for the Study of the Old Testament. Supplement series 88. Sheffield: Almond, 1990.

Gitay, Y. *Prophecy and Persuasion: A Study of Isaiah 40–48.* Bonn: Linguistica Biblica, 1981.

Lenchak, Timothy A. "Choose Life!": *A Rhetorical-Critical Investigation of Deuteronomy 28, 69–30, 20.* Analecta Biblica 129. Rome: Pontificio Instituto Biblico, 1993.

Patrick, Dale. *The Rhetoric of Revelation. Overtures to Biblical Theology.* Minneapolis: Fortress, 1999.

Patrick, Dale, and Allan Scult. *Rhetoric and Biblical Interpretation. Journal for the Study of the Old Testament Supplement 82.* Sheffield: Almond, 1990.

Watts, James W. *Reading Law: The Rhetorical Shaping of the Pentateuch.* The Biblical Seminar 39. Sheffield: Sheffield Academic Press, 1999.

C. Jan Swearingen

Song to Speech: The Origins of Early Epitaphia in Ancient Near Eastern Women's Lamentations

GUIDE TO TEACHING WOMEN'S RHETORICS IN THE ANCIENT NEAR EAST

A growing literature on Ancient Near Eastern women is helping supplement the studies of literature and rhetoric by male authors, or by anon. It is likely that some of the unattributed works of Ancient Near Eastern poetry, religion, and myth, including biblical texts may have been authored by women in the traditions of Sappho, Aspasia, and the Corinthian women prophets. Harold Bloom's *The Book of J,* however tongue in cheek, attributes Ecclesiastes to a woman's pen. The study of women's cultural roles as singers of songs celebrating birth and victory, lamenting death and loss, has just begun to bring together the traditions of the Near East, Greece, Israel, and Egypt.

In studying individual figures such as Enheduanna, Sappho, Cassandra, Miriam, Deborah, Mary the mother of Jesus, the women represented in the Greek dramas, the Pythagorean women philosophers, the girls' choruses studied by Calame, a number of intriguing questions emerge for those interested in rhetoric and speech genres more generally. What distinguished rhetoric from song, from sermon, from the incantations of a priestess, or the ritual lament of a mourner? What can we deduce form the transition from female song to male prose rhetor? Why was early rhetoric not a song, since song and poetry had been so central to earlier cultural ceremonies? Or was it? Was ceremony itself somehow diminished, as Wolf's novel *Cassandra* suggests, when religious poetry became the "the poets' lies." If so, how interesting that the negative aspects of rhetoric came to be equated with seductive women.

Most of the primary texts from the ancient world are fragments and short songs that can easily be read and examined in class discussion. Waithe's *His-*

tory of Women Philosophers provides translations of all the primary texts she discusses and good biographies. The biblical texts discussed by Meyers, Murphy, and Trible, are provided within the discussion. Novels based on these early women figures are illuminating and thought provoking, especially for undergraduate readers.

SUGGESTED READINGS, IN ADDITION TO THE BIBLIOGRAPHY AT THE END OF THE ESSAY:

Willis and Aliki Barnstone. *A Book of Women Poets from Antiquity to Now.* New York: Shocken, 1987. World cultures and traditions including Chinese, Middle Eastern, ancient and modern. Good bases for comparisons. Well selected and translated.

Brindel, June. *Aridane.* New York: St. Martins, 1980. *Phaedra.* New York: St. Martins, 1985. A sequence of two novels on the last priestesses of Knossos, the Minoan culture before it was savagely overtaken by the Greeks, c. 1800 B.C.E.. Compares well with the Troy legend and Cassandra. As in Wolf's *Cassandra,* the women are shown reflecting about their own uses of language.

Contributors

Roberta Binkley received her Ph.D. from the University of Arizona. Her fascination with Enheduanna began more than twenty years ago, when she discovered the translation by William W. Hallo and J. J. A. van Dijk. Just as Enheduanna wove through her dissertation, she continues to weave through her life and interests. She currently teaches as a lecturer at Arizona State University and is working on a book about Enheduanna.

Grant M. Boswell received his Ph.D. from the University of Southern California in Rhetoric, Linguistics, and Literature. He teaches classes in the history of rhetoric, rhetorical theory, and rhetorical criticism. His research focuses primarily on the influences of rhetoric on education and culture in Early Modern Europe.

Richard Leo Enos is the holder of the Lillian Radford Chair of Rhetoric and Composition at Texas Christian University. His area of research is in classical rhetoric with an emphasis on the relationship between thought and expression in Antiquity. He studied at The American School of Classical Studies at Athens and is the recipient of the Karl R. Wallace Award (1976) and the Richard E. Young Award (1992) for research in Hellenic rhetoric.

William W. Hallo taught at Yale from 1962 until his retirement in 2002, since 1975 as the William M. Laffan Professor of Assyriology and Babylonian Literature. He also served as Curator of the Yale Babylonian Collection. Hallo has authored or coauthored ten books, including *The Exaltation of Inanna* (1968), *The Ancient Near East: A History* (1971, 1997), *The Book of the People* (1991), and *Origins* (1996). He has edited or coedited ten other scholarly books, most recently *The Context of Scripture* (3 vols., 1997–2002).

Paul Y. Hoskisson received his Ph.D. from Brandeis University, where his dissertation dealt with religion in the Old Babylonian city-state of Mari. He has taught ancient Near Eastern history, Akkadian (Babylonian and Assyrian), Ugaritic, and Hebrew, both in the United States and in Europe. He was an institutional trustee of the American Schools of Oriental Research and served for a season as epigrapher on a dig in Syria.

Carol S. Lipson is an Associate Professor of Writing and Rhetoric in the Writing Program at Syracuse University. She received her Ph.D. in English at University of California–Los Angeles, where she began the study of Egyptology with Professor J. Callendar. She has published on ancient Egyptian medical rhetoric and has an article forthcoming on the multimedia nature of ancient Egyptian public texts, which will appear in an MIT Press collection entitled *Eloquent Images.* She also publishes on technical communication, with a coedited book under contract for Erlbaum. In 2002, she was elected as a fellow of the Association of Teachers of Technical Writing.

Yameng Liu is Associate Professor of English and Rhetoric in the English Department at Carnegie Mellon. His research focuses on contemporary rhetorical studies, with special interest in the ways that modern rhetoric endeavors to conceptualize nonwestern traditions of oratory in its own terms. He has published on issues in comparative and contrastive rhetoric, with special attention to studies of Chinese rhetoric.

Arabella Lyon, Associate Professor at State University of New York–Buffalo, is currently working on a book on deliberation, building on the work in her *Intentions, Negotiated, Contested, and Ignored* (Penn State, 1998). This volume was awarded the 1999 Ross Winterowd Prize as outstanding book in composition theory. In 1999–2000, she was a Fulbright Lecturer at Sichuan University in China.

David Metzger is an Associate Professor of English at Old Dominion University, where he is the founding Director of Writing Tutorial Services and the Coordinator of Jewish Studies (College of Arts and Letters). His books include the following: *The Lost Cause of Rhetoric* (Southern Illinois, 1995), (co-ed) *Medievalism and Medieval Studies* (Boydell & Brewer, 1999), (ed) *Medievalism and Cultural Studies* (Boydell & Brewer, 2000), (co-ed) *Proving Lacan* (forthcoming), *Transcendent Persuasion: Levinas and the Rhetoric of the Hebrew Bible* (forthcoming).

C. Jan Swearingen is Professor of English at Texas A&M University. She has been a Fellow of the Centre for Rhetoric Studies at the University of Cape Town, and was given the Outstanding Research Achievement Award in 1995 at the University of Texas at Arlington. From 1998 to 2000, she served as President of the Rhetoric Society of America. Her publications include *Rhetoric and Irony: Western Literacy and Western Lies,* published by Oxford

University Press in 1991, as well as *Old Wine in New Wineskins: Classical Rhetoric in Multicultural Classrooms,* to be published by Boynton Cook/Heinneman. In addition, she has published chapters in numerous collections as well as articles in *Rhetoric Society Quarterly, Rhetoric Review, Pre/Text,* and other journals.

Deborah Sweeney received her Ph.D. from the Hebrew University of Jerusalem in 1990 and is now Senior Lecturer in the Department of Archeology and Ancient Near Eastern Cultures at Tel Aviv University. She is the author of *Correspondence and Dialogue: Pragmatic Features in Late Ramesside Letter-writing (Ägypten und Altes Testament 49)* (Harrassowitz: Wiesbaden, 2001), and of several articles about women and language in ancient Egypt.

James W. Watts is Associate Professor in the Department of Religion at Syracuse University. He received his Ph.D. at Yale University in 1990. At Syracuse, he teaches Hebrew Bible and ancient Near Eastern textual traditions. He is the author of *Reading Law: The Rhetorical Shaping of the Pentateuch* (1999) and *Psalm and Story: Inset Hymns in Hebrew Narrative* (1992).

George Q. Xu, Professor of English, teaches Composition Studies and Rhetorical Theory at Clarion University of Pennsylvania. He has published articles in the areas of Composition Studies, Second Language Writing, and Comparative Rhetoric.

Index

261